W9-CIH-295

Foundation is a non-profit organization working to improve
onomic and social well being of U.S. agriculture, the food
and rural communities by serving as a catalyst to assist
- and public-sector decision makers in identifying and
tanding forces that will shape the future.

978-0-615-17375-7

of Congress Control Number: 2007940452

esign by Howard Vitek
ign by Patricia Frey

Foundation
West 22nd Street, Suite 615
Brook, Illinois 60523
ite: *www.farmfoundation.org*

n. Published 2007

SINCE 1933

Farm Foundatio

75 years as a cataly

agriculture and rura

© 2

This
educ

Farm
the e
syste
privat
under

ISBN:

Librar

Cover
Page de

No part
means

Farm
130
Oak
Web

First editi

David P. Ernstes • R.J. Hildreth

Table of Contents

R.J. "Jim" Hildreth: A Tribute

"Education is the process of moving from cocksure ignorance to thoughtful uncertainty."
—R.J. "Jim" Hildreth

From his boyhood on a farm near the "Norwegian Ghetto" of Huxley, Iowa, to his sunset years at the Beacon Hill Retirement Community in Lombard, Illinois, Jim Hildreth touched thousands of lives. I count myself lucky to have been one of them.

I first met Jim in late 1997, at the Farm Foundation offices near Chicago. He introduced himself, refused to shake my hand because he had a cold, tried out a few jokes and puns, and then proceeded to drill me about Texas A&M University and College Station, Texas. A few minutes later, I learned the source of Jim's fascination with Texas A&M. He had once served as assistant director of the Texas Agricultural Experiment Station before coming to Farm Foundation. Jim had found a new friend and so had I.

As I saw Jim more, I was a frequent victim of his dreadful, worn-out jokes and puns. Although I had heard the same stories many times, Jim was shamelessly unrepentant. His enthusiasm was contagious. How could you not laugh?

In subsequent visits, our conversations turned to the history of Farm Foundation. Surprisingly, Jim knew little of the history and lore before his tenure (1962-1991). Walt Armbruster and Steve Halbrook thought writing the history of Farm Foundation would be a good project for a retired managing director and a researcher from Texas A&M.

With cocksure ignorance, we began. Details were very sketchy, evidence was hard to find, and most of the founders had died 50 or more years before. Jim and I worked on it off and on for about three years. During this time, Jim was battling illness, but he dutifully learned word processing, explored archives and worked on drafts. Jim was frequently amused to rediscover some of his accomplishments.

Jim was very reluctant to write about himself or to identify credit. It just was not the Farm Foundation way. To listen to Jim, it was almost as if he had been on vacation from 1962-1991.

I was crushed when Jim died in May 2002. Ron Knutson and I completed the draft of this book. The only consolation we have is that this book includes Jim's lifetime of achievements and the hard work of other staff members.

—David P. Ernstes

Prologue

Numerous individuals in both the public and private sectors owe at least a portion of their success to their involvement with one or more Farm Foundation networks. As a catalyst for change, Farm Foundation has fostered discussion of current and evolving issues for 75 years. It has done this by laying a factual foundation through underwriting research and education projects and programs. By wise investment, expenditure and leveraging of its relatively small endowment, it has had a much greater impact than could have been imagined when it was formed or at any point in its history.

The success of Farm Foundation in fostering adjustment to change is attributable to visionary leaders who served as its founders, as managing directors or presidents, as Trustees and to those who have contributed to the growth of its endowment. These leaders provided the vibrant learning environment that attracted the best minds to assemble facts, to complete objective research, and to present results for study and discussion in words that could be understood by all who were interested. When combined with the values of those who read and listened, those discussions, while sometimes heated, were better reasoned and inevitably led to more informed decisions.

This book traces the history of those visionary leaders who have been responsible for Farm Foundation's success as a catalyst for change from its beginnings as an idea and felt need through 2007. It also looks to the future of the Foundation in an agricultural and rural environment marked by many new and different challenges.

Chapter 1

Legge and Lowden

arm Foundation owes its origin to the work and fortunes of two remarkable individuals: Alexander Legge and Frank O. Lowden. Legge, the son of
an immigrant farmer, and Lowden, the son of a blacksmith, were men with
Midwestern roots and Scottish ancestry who, through hard work and honesty,
rose to assume impressive positions in industry, agriculture and politics. Their
lives could have been models for the Horatio Alger stories which were popular
in their formative years.

Yet, their "rags to riches" tales did not end with the accumulation of wealth
and power. Together they donated significant portions of their fortunes to a
foundation "to be devoted to the general welfare of the farming population of the
United States and improvement of the conditions of rural life."[1] Their legacy
continues eight decades later through Farm Foundation.

Legge and Lowden began working together on the Farm Foundation project
in 1928. This chapter briefly reviews the lives of these two remarkable men until
about 1930. The Legge section that follows is based extensively on *Alexander
Legge: 1866-1933* written by Forrest Crissey in 1936 for the Alexander Legge
Memorial Committee.[2] The section on Lowden is based extensively on the excellent two-volume biography, *Lowden of Illinois* by William T. Hutchinson.[3]

Alexander Legge

*"I have known a lot of men—eminent men, but none have I known that impressed me
as being as outstanding in their own right as Alex Legge. Maybe that does not mean so
much for there are many of the great and near-great I never knew; but it does mean a
lot when men of the widest acquaintance make that same statement."[4]*
—Samuel R. McKelvie, *The Nebraska Farmer*

Alexander Legge was born January 13, 1866, on a farm in Montrose
Township, Dane County, Wisconsin. Legge's father had established himself as
a successful veterinarian and farmer after emigrating from Scotland with his
wife in 1857. In 1874-1875, several crop failures and a poor business decision
financially ruined the senior Legge. In 1876, he accepted a friend's offer to take
a partnership in the new 2,000-acre Fuller Ranch in Colfax County, Nebraska.

1

The move to Nebraska had a profound impact on 10-year-old Alex Legge. He was transplanted from the small farms and tree-lined fields of Wisconsin to a seemingly boundless land. Not only was the landscape vast, but the business enterprise was to be of a grand scale. Planning was paramount as there were fences to make, barns to build and water to provide for the livestock. One of his early memories was watching scores of plows breaking 700 acres of virgin sod on the ranch. Crops were planted on a scale that dwarfed the farms of Wisconsin. Young Alex was with his father as these decisions were made. Although formal educational opportunities were lacking at the ranch, the foundation of Legge's business education was being honed by practical experience.

Legge began to have more and more responsibilities around the ranch. By the age of 15, he assumed the job of foreman of the hired help during his father's temporary absences. He was very adept at purchasing machinery and also traveled throughout the state to pick up feeder cattle his father had previously selected. On one such trip, as Legge was loading up the cattle into railcars at a shipping station, two Iowa farmers offered to buy the lot. Legge sold them at a price $1,500 higher than the price his father had agreed to pay. He added the extra profit to the funds his father had allotted him and purchased a better lot of feeders. By the age of 16, Legge was sent on cattle buying trips with the freedom to use his own judgment.

Legge had a keen mind and during his teens attended school in Schuyler, Nebraska. His success convinced his mother that he may even be on the way to a college education. In February 1883, there was an intense snowstorm while Legge was at school. Fearing he might attempt to walk home rather than stay in town, his mother dispatched his friend, Charlie Wertz, with two horses to pick him up. The snowstorm became one of the worst on record—the historic blizzard of February 1883. Trapped in the open, fighting blinding snow, snowdrifts and temperatures of 30 degrees below zero, Legge and Wertz were forced to trust the instinct of the horses to find their way back to the ranch. Both arrived near death. Legge developed a pulmonary condition. Four years later, the family doctor recommended he move to a drier climate and higher altitude for his health.

A Wyoming Cowboy. On one of his cattle buying expeditions, Alex had visited the V-R Ranch, located 45 miles from Douglas, Wyoming, at the terminus of the Chicago & North Western Railway. The operations there had fascinated him. The ranch was stocked with about 12,000 cattle and more than 1,500 horses being raised for the United States Cavalry. With its higher altitude and drier climate, Legge decided to approach the ranch for a job. In 1887, he and his friend Charlie Wertz were hired as "fence riders," living on the range for $35 a month. The two boys were soon recognized for their dependability and intelligence, and were promoted to the dangerous duty of payroll couriers. The ranch was the supply station for several nearby businesses, and to meet all of the payrolls, the boys sometimes transported as much as $5,000. Every weekend, the two traveled 45 miles to the bank in Douglas at differing times and by using varying routes to confuse the outlaws in the area. It was a job with many perils, but they were never harmed.

Legge enjoyed his ranching experiences tremendously. He probably would have continued as a cowboy had he not received a letter saying his mother was seriously ill and wanted to see him. He returned home to Nebraska in 1891, where he helped nurse his mother back to health. The decision to return to Nebraska was also a good choice because the dusty nature of working with cattle had aggravated his medical condition.

Several years before, in 1884, Legge's father had discontinued his partnership with the Fuller Ranch and purchased a 240-acre farm in nearby Maple Creek Valley. While on the new farm, Alex purchased a power threshing machine, the first implement of its type in Colfax County, Nebraska. Not only did he recognize the superiority of the new machine and the increased productivity it would bring to his father's farm, but he also organized a crew and earned money threshing wheat on neighboring farms.

Recognizing the delicate nature of his health, Legge began looking for a job that would limit his exposure to dust and weather. With his natural mechanical knack, he found a temporary job assembling farm machinery for a local dealer. He also began collecting debts for the McCormick Harvesting Machine Company's agency, based in Omaha. With his success, he was advised to go to Omaha and seek full-time employment.

Starting a Business Career. At 25 years of age, Legge was offered a trial appointment with P.M. Price, the McCormick collection manager in Omaha. The job would not be easy. Many of the farmers in the area had come from Eastern Europe and were thoroughly misinformed about the United States and business practices. To these farmers, the concept of purchasing on credit and making payments was meaningless; once an exchange took place, possession and use of an implement meant ownership.

After the company wrote overdue farmers, it was Legge's responsibility to visit those who had not responded and notify them in person that their payments were overdue. If no collection was possible, he was to repossess the machinery. As a test in his first month, he was given the toughest cases and he settled all the claims. He also sold 20 mowers, earning himself a quick promotion. While repossessing machinery, Legge was sometimes confronted by farmers wielding pitchforks or shotguns, but he always calmly explained the justice of his action. Aware that many farmers did not understand why the machinery was being removed, Legge spent time and effort explaining business practices in the United States.

Legge's collecting abilities became legendary. Some of the toughest cases were those in which no payment had been made in five years or more. Under

Nebraska law at that time, a note with no payment in five years became void. In such cases, Legge would ask the farmer to make a small payment, such as $2, as an act of good faith. If that appeal failed, he would then ask the farmer for $2 to cover his own expense of coming to visit. Once money was received, it was promptly endorsed on the note, resurrecting the claim. Although the practice might be viewed as questionable, Legge believed any farmer who used a machine for five years without payment was in no position to argue.

Once when confronting a farmer who had used a bull as collateral, Legge asked that the bull be presented as he intended to settle the claim. The farmer pointed to a field and said the bull was dead and buried, and there was no money. Legge asked for shovels, remarking that at least the bones would bring some money at a rendering plant. Not wanting his lie exposed and facing possible prosecution, the farmer settled the account.

Legge's early work with the McCormick Company foreshadowed his exceptional business skills, as well as his humanitarian side. Throughout his collection duties, he tried hard to work out agreements so farmers could stay in business and continue to utilize the equipment. Very concerned with the hungry and homeless in towns he visited, he arranged meal tickets with local restaurants which he would hand out to panhandlers. He also had a soft spot for lending money to his friends and soon accumulated a rich assortment of IOUs.

Legge's work and ability at the Omaha branch office soon caught the attention of the general manager of the McCormick Company in Chicago, who went to Omaha to meet him personally. In these few short years, most of the employees at the branch office had come to look to Legge for leadership. He received promotions until he was head of the collections department. One of the problems at the Omaha office was that the local manager believed the sales office should make sales with no regard to the farmers' ability to pay, and leave responsibility for payment on the collections department. Legge had a row with the local manager over this issue, which he eventually settled by going directly to the general manager in Chicago. After Legge's intervention, the local manager was replaced.

Moving Up. The replacement for the local manager was none other than Harold F. McCormick, the recently married, 23-year-old son of the company's founder, Cyrus H. McCormick. Legge was chosen to show young McCormick the ropes and hone his business skills. When McCormick left after several years, Legge assumed the position of local manager.

By 1899, the 33-year-old Legge was leading the Omaha office he had joined as an apprentice in 1891. He was considering resigning his position and going to college to become a lawyer. Before he could act on his plans, Harold McCormick, now first vice president of the McCormick Company, asked him to move to Chicago to head the company's worldwide collection interests.

Like the move from Wisconsin to Nebraska in his youth, the new position would considerably broaden Legge's horizons and demand considerable readjustment. He had rarely left the South Platte area of Nebraska and still retained his cowboy qualities. Now he was being called on to take a desk job and head the collections department of a worldwide organization. Furthermore, he was used to dealing with farmers and local implement dealers. The new position would involve interacting with large distributors in other countries.

His first responsibility was to reorganize the worldwide collection system. Legge evaluated the company's collection operations and proposed new procedures. While the abilities of this former cowboy were viewed skeptically at first, his logic, conviction and talents soon impressed the management and his co-workers. His reorganization plan was viewed favorably and implemented. During this time, the McCormick Harvesting Machine Company was engaged in prolonged negotiations with five other leading farm implement manufacturers to form the International Harvester Company. First Vice President Harold McCormick was leading the organization, while his brother Cyrus H. McCormick, Jr. was in New York negotiating the merger.

Legge's ability was recognized by the management of the McCormick Company and Harold McCormick. He not only survived the turmoil of the 1902 merger, but was promoted to assistant manager of sales in the new company. Legge had the difficult task of arranging the organizational components from the merger and fusing them into an integrated organization. After only a short time in this position, he was promoted to assistant general manager under Manager Clarence Funk. When Funk retired, Legge became general manager. In 1918, when Harold McCormick became president, the company bylaws were rewritten, eliminating the position of general manager. Legge became senior vice president, in charge of the entire company under the president.

Legge's One Romance. Legge did not marry until he was 42 years old. For most of his life up to this point, many of his associates thought he would never get married. "Girl shy" Legge was usually too caught up in his work to notice the attractions of the opposite sex. The woman he would eventually marry was the wife of a close associate, Tom Hall, a lawyer he had worked with in Omaha.

Katherine Hall helped her husband in the legal firm and had studied law while working as a stenographer. The couple joined Legge in Chicago after his promotion, and when Mr. Hall became ill, Mrs. Hall continued to help with the legal matters of collection. After her husband's death, Mrs. Hall and Legge became close friends and began to appear together socially. They soon planned a private wedding ceremony. Only the minister and the family across the street were aware of the secret.

Katherine was a devoted wife and valuable teammate to Legge, a full confidante in his business affairs. She reformed his shortcomings in social etiquette and was an incomparable hostess. One of her strengths was her ability both to impress and put at ease the variety of people Legge brought home at a moment's notice, whether they be equipment demonstrators, engineers, local implement dealers, executives or foreign officials.

In 1908, Legge made his first overseas trip to visit sales offices in England, France, Germany, Belgium, Sweden and Russia. He met with many Harvester Company officials, who were impressed by his knowledge and familiarity with the overseas staff, many of whom he had placed.

In his duties in senior management at the Harvester Company, Legge continued to travel widely. His associates were consistently amazed by his knowledge of the company's international markets. Working hard to develop contacts in agriculture, financial institutions and foreign governments, Legge was intent not only on selling more Harvester Company implements, but was also leading a personal crusade to advance and improve agricultural productivity overseas.

Public Service. In July 1917, four months after the United States entered World War I, the War Industries Board was established to mobilize U.S. industry for the conflict.[5] The Board was seen as a clearinghouse for ideas and methods to increase military production and allocate strategic resources. Wall Street financier Bernard M. Baruch, head of the Board's Raw Materials Division, was looking for an industrialist to act as his "right hand man." Questionnaires were sent to hundreds of industry leaders asking for suggestions of candidates. Baruch was reviewing the suggestions with Leland Summers, a technical advisor to the War Industries Board, when Legge's name was noted on literally dozens of the returned questionnaires. According to Baruch, "Suddenly he [Summers] pointed to the name of Alex Legge on a dozen of the cards and exclaimed: 'There's your man! He knows Europe, knows human nature, is a shrewd trader, as straight as a die and an unbeatable fighter. His is the best mind in the International Harvester Company—but I don't think you can get him.'"[6]

Baruch's first response to Summers was that he had never heard of Alex Legge. However, he summoned Cyrus H. McCormick, president of International Harvester, for a meeting and after talking with McCormick was satisfied with Legge's abilities. McCormick agreed Legge was the best man for the job and helped persuade him to become Baruch's chief of staff. When President Wilson appointed Baruch chairman of the 12-member War Industries Board, Baruch drafted Legge as vice chairman and, as an indication of his confidence, conferred on Legge all of the authority Wilson had delegated to him.

The Board's responsibilities were revolutionary and far sweeping—to suspend free enterprise and initiate a new relationship among industries and between industry and government. Business institutions that were previously punished under the Sherman Antitrust Act were now encouraged to coordinate their activities. The Board determined resource allocation and was also allowed to fix prices. It was an extraordinary accumulation of power, as noted by Robert D. Cuff in *The War Industries Board*: "Baruch and the WIB [War Industries

Board] have since come to represent the greatest concentration of delegated authority in American history..."[7]

Legge exhibited the same leadership skills in his War Industries Board service as he demonstrated at International Harvester. Howard P. Ingels, secretary of the War Industries Board, noted: "He was always for direct action without pussy-footing or evasion. All personalities looked alike to him. He treated every problem with only one idea in mind: how to get supplies and equipment across to our soldiers and our Allies with the utmost promptness."[8]

General Hugh S. Johnson,[9] who represented the U.S. Army on the War Industries Board, commented: "Despite the fact that his formal education was very meager, he had as complete a knowledge of world economics as any man who helped to solve the big problems that came with the World War. I speak carefully when I say that he was one of the greatest practical economists that this country has ever produced."[10]

Board member George N. Peek noted: "One conspicuous factor of Alex Legge's equipment for his great responsibilities on the War Industries Board was his intimate and comprehensive knowledge of conditions in all the different countries involved. This had been gained by years of first-hand observation and experience. He had been over the ground until he was as familiar with it as with his own Nebraska country. It is my conviction that in this feature of equipment for his job, he was unapproached by any of his colleagues."[11]

Vice chairmanship of the War Industries Board was a thankless job in which Legge excelled. Postwar accounts wrote glowingly about the cooperation and cohesiveness of the Board and industry, but revisionist analysis has not been so kind, painting the picture of "an organizational maze over which they never had sufficient control."[12] Much of the image projected at the time has since been attributed to Baruch, who gave the Board "an image of unity and form to what in retrospect was an extraordinarily chaotic, disjointed process."[13]

Regardless of the controversy, Legge's contribution and service to the War Industries Board can best be summed up from this passage in Benedict Crowell and Robert Forrest Wilson's *The Giant Hand*, a contemporary history of the industrial mobilization effort in World War I:

> "Consider Alexander Legge as an example. He filled the position next in importance to the chairmanship itself. Yet Legge, who was an active officer of the International Harvester Company, had no more than a local reputation outside his own branch of industry. Baruch knew him, and all American industry came to know him; and the statement is ventured here that if the Board's chairman had raked the country from Maine to California, he could not have made a happier choice. Legge possessed evenness of mind in combination with a tremendous store of energy and initiative. He could plan or execute his

chief's plans equally well. A tower of strength in the War Industries Board—that was Legge."[14]

Members of the War Industries Board were sent to Europe in October 1918, a month before the armistice. The first U.S. diplomatic mission to Europe, they were dispatched over a disagreement with Great Britain over the price of war supplies. When the armistice was signed, the mission from the War Industries Board was given the task of determining industrial capacity in the countries touched by the war. After President Wilson's arrival in Europe, the War Industries Board disbanded, and its members returned to the United States.

Legge returned to his duties with the International Harvester Company, but his stay would be short-lived. Baruch asked Legge to serve his country again as part of a mission to develop the economic section of the Treaty of Peace at Versailles. Legge agreed and returned to Europe. Baruch remarked:

> "Alex Legge's contribution to this task was of high value. His gift of hard common sense was nothing short of genius. Most of his colleagues on this work were highly educated men. His own academic education had stopped about midway in a country high school course, but he knew the meaning of figures to an extent that was almost uncanny.
>
> "The treaty-makers on the other side were wizards in diplomacy and economics but Alex was fully capable of meeting them. His mental shortcuts were amazing and his European business experience had given him a specific and comprehensive knowledge of the value of things over there. This was invaluable in connection with reparations estimates."[15]

Forrest Crissey noted: "It became known at once throughout the highest circles that this tall, awkward, unpretentious man was strikingly 'different'—a most interesting novelty. The fact that he had been a cowboy greatly increased his popularity with the sophisticated Europeans. An American cowboy helping to divide the war debts and the economic responsibilities of the great powers of Europe—here was a real spectacle!"[16] For his efforts during and after the war, Legge was awarded the Distinguished Service Medal in 1923. He also received the decorations of Commander of the Crown of Belgium, Officer of the Legion of Honor of France, and Officer Knight of the Crown of Italy.

President of International Harvester. In 1919, Alex Legge returned from the peace negotiations to International Harvester. World War I had changed the company in many profound ways. Harvester's German and French factories had been casualties of war, and the company lost all of its assets in Russia, including financial investments, when the Communists took control. Harvester only survived due to a rainy day fund set up years before by Legge.

The war had also changed the industry. High commodity prices during the war encouraged farmers to purchase labor-saving machinery, and tractors became Harvester's main seller. Harvester had been the preeminent manufacturer of tractors but, by 1918, was supplanted by Henry Ford's Fordson. The new Ford tractor utilized the same manufacturing techniques and engineering know-how that had revolutionized the automobile industry. By 1920, Ford controlled two-thirds of the tractor market.

At the same time, U.S. agriculture suffered a severe economic downturn. The high commodity prices of the war years, wistfully known to this day as "the golden years of agriculture," collapsed. Farmer income fell to $3.9 billion in 1921 from $9.6 billion in 1919.

When tractor sales dropped, Ford responded by slashing its prices until they were below the cost of production. The cost of a new Fordson tractor dropped some $230 over the period to $395. Historian Barbara Marsh notes:

> "Ford's action infuriated Legge, who was inspecting new company facilities in Springfield, Ohio, when he received a call from Chicago headquarters. 'What's that? How much? Two hundred and thirty dollars? Well, I'll be,' he exclaimed, realizing that Harvester's future in tractors, indeed its traditional leadership in farm machinery, was now at stake. He reckoned Harvester had no choice but to sell below cost too.
>
> "'What'll we do about it? Do? Why, damn it all—meet him, of course! We're going to stay in the tractor business. Yes, cut two hundred and thirty dollars. Both [Harvester] models—yes, both.'
>
> "Then Legge brilliantly upped the ante. Ford was so low, the Harvester tractor still left a price gap of $275. Yet Legge knew the American farmer better than Henry Ford and could offer more than tractors. 'Say, listen,' Legge told the caller. 'Make it good! We'll throw in a plow as well!'
>
> "He then took the contest to farmlands, where he employed tactics he'd learned in the Harvester Wars. Whenever a Harvester salesman learned of a Fordson sale, it became his duty to challenge his competition to a tractor contest. Harvester salesmen argued that, unlike existing Harvester tractors on the market, the Fordson was too light to gain the traction needed to pull fourteen-inch plows and failed in uneven soil conditions. After thousands of contests, Legge's men started to win back customers."[17]

Ford's near takeover of the tractor market forced Harvester to revisit experimental engineering ideas. One concept, which had been undeveloped for more than 10 years, was a new all-purpose tractor, the Farmall.

"Unlike competing machines, the Farmall could do all sorts of light farm work and, for the first time, made possible the horseless farm. It could push a cultivator through the soil, pull a plow, transmit power to an implement through a power takeoff, and supply belt power to a stationary silo or threshing machine. In contrast to the Fordson, which was ill suited for cultivating row crops, the Farmall was specially designed for row-crop work. Its high rear-wheel drive provided maximum clearance over crops and its narrow front wheels were designed to run between the rows. Farmall's versatility not only spelled the end of the era of the farm horse, but also promised the farmer huge savings on his equipment investment by reducing the need for more than one tractor."[18]

The Farmall entered full-scale development in 1921. Legge insisted that the new tractor accommodate present Harvester implements and be fully developed before it was marketed to farmers. Harvester sold its first Farmall in 1924. By 1925, four-row attachments were available. Sales were so brisk that by 1926 advertising was not necessary, and a plant was purchased specifically for manufacturing the tractors. By 1928, Harvester was producing 24,000 Farmalls a year and Ford had quit manufacturing tractors in the United States. Legge had beat Henry Ford at his own game.

Legge was named president of International Harvester in 1922. In July 1923, the government brought an antitrust suit against the company, alleging that Harvester had not lived up to the terms of a 1918 consent decree from a 1912 antitrust suit.

Legge took the reins defending the company. All of the knowledge and expertise he had accumulated was put to work organizing an effective defense. Ultimately, International Harvester was acquitted by a decision of the United States Supreme Court. An attorney who took part in both cases noted, "It is my personal opinion that Alex Legge would have lived years longer if he could have been spared the anxiety and labor involved in meeting these two Government attacks on the company's right to exist. In large part it was his work in assembling and presenting the facts in the case that brought ultimate victory for the company. I have never heard of a case of such magnitude where counsel received more discriminating help from a layman than Mr. Legge gave the company's lawyers in the Harvester anti-trust litigation."[19]

The stress of the antitrust case weakened Legge considerably. After the trial, he became seriously ill. When his condition did not improve in Chicago, he decided to travel to the warmer Imperial Valley of California, where International Harvester had a field station. He intended to view demonstrations there, but his condition did not improve and he was admitted to a hospital, where he was attended by doctors and specialists from across the country. Legge recovered, but the illness took its toll: he had walked into the hospital weighing 218 pounds. He walked out weighing 143 pounds.

During his recovery, Alex and Katherine Legge spent time visiting friends and relatives in the area. Late that summer, they decided to return to Chicago, but Katherine became seriously ill. She was admitted to a hospital and diagnosed with typhoid. She declined steadily and died on August 21, 1924.[20]

Legge returned to his duties as president of International Harvester and, by the end of the 1920s, restored the company to its preeminence in the agricultural equipment industry. Harvester's domestic farm equipment sales were "... $150 million in 1929...nearly triple those of its nearest competitor, Deere & Co., of Moline, Illinois."[21] Legge also established Harvester as a leader in the manufacture of medium and heavy-duty trucks.

"Alexander Legge's clear vision for Harvester in a rapidly changing marketplace drove the company to a new pinnacle of success by 1929. Its U.S. sales reached a record $262 million, its worldwide profits a record $37 million, and the value of its common stock peaked during the market's speculative soar that year at $142 a share. With Harvester's accomplishments came the respect of the financial community. A *Fortune* magazine profile of the company blithely noted several years later: 'Harvester is, of course, the greatest single agricultural enterprise in the world.'"[22]

In 1985, historian Barbara Marsh related, "Nearly half a century following Legge's death in 1933, a retired Harvester executive confides: 'Alexander Legge was probably the greatest president Harvester ever had. He was a common-sense, hard-nosed guy who could relate to customers. A farmer, a Scotsman, and smarter than hell.'"[23]

The Federal Farm Board. Although International Harvester was experiencing unprecedented success, the U.S. farmer was not as well off. Agricultural prices continued to be depressed, and surpluses mounted. Farm interests lobbied the government to intervene directly in agricultural markets. The newly elected President Herbert Hoover opposed direct intervention and looked instead for indirect means to stabilize prices. He believed that by encouraging farmers to organize, some of the inequalities between the agricultural and industrial sectors could be resolved. The Federal Farm Board, created by the Agricultural Marketing Act of 1929, was designed to assist in the formation of cooperatives and to stabilize commodity prices in times of emergencies. In July 1929, Hoover appointed Legge chairman of the Federal Farm Board.

Legge's association with Hoover went back to World War I when Legge was vice chairman of the War Industries Board and Hoover was United States Food Administrator. Some agricultural commodities fell within the jurisdiction of both agencies, and Legge and Hoover were well acquainted. Also, Hoover had represented the United States government in the armistice negotiations in France and conferred with Legge during the Treaty of Paris negotiations. When Hoover became Secretary of Commerce in 1921, he asked Legge's assistance in helping to reorganize the Department of Commerce. Throughout Hoover's term, 1921 to 1928, he continued to rely on Legge for advice. In 1928, after being elected President, he asked Legge to be Secretary of Commerce, but Legge refused. When Hoover floated Legge's name as a candidate for chairman of the Federal Farm Board to the leaders of U.S. farm cooperatives, he received an almost unanimously favorable response. Legge accepted the position on the condition that it would only be for one year.

The Federal Farm Board was the government's first response to the problems in agriculture. Legge accepted the position because he saw it as a way to help farmers organize and help themselves. Carl Williams, the cotton expert on the Board, recounted Legge's decision to join the Board: "I went to Chicago to talk

---

Legge in Washington

Sam R. McKelvie, a member of the Federal Farm Board, recalled Alex Legge's experiences with Washington, D.C., society during the Hoover administration:

"The anecdotes illustrating Alex Legge's indifference to social customs are so many that one scarcely knows where to begin or end in telling them. Not infrequently I find myself laughing out loud at the outlandish things he said and did. No sooner had he been appointed a member of the Farm Board than the newspapers flared forth with his answer to the reporter who wanted to know where he would be seated at the White House dinners. That was when the Dolly Gann-Alice Roosevelt Longworth contest was hot news. 'In the kitchen with the cooks will be all right with me,' he blurted out.

"And had that been his portion he would have been perfectly happy. He liked company but loathed so-called society. It seemed to him such a waste of time. At some of the early White House functions he violated the customs that the mentor of social proprieties – a lady – felt called upon to remind him, for instance, that it was not proper to leave the party until the President withdrew. This came to Martha [McKelvie]'s attention when I committed the same faux pas one evening, and the next time she got us together she proceeded to propound the law. He drawled, 'Ah gosh, the Chief [President Hoover] likes it. It gives him an excuse to break away.'

"When [British] Premier Ramsay MacDonald visited the President, Washington society was on its ears. A bid to the dinner that was given him at the White House was prized above all else. Alex received one. That day as we were returning from Chicago he bewailed the invitation. To go would knock him out of a 'whole evening's work.' I expressed my regret that the invitation was not transferable. I would go, and gladly. When I went to the office that evening, lo, here was the chairman. 'Not going to the party for the Premier?' queried I.

'No, those darned things bore me to tears. I called the Chief up and he let me off.'"[56]

with Alex about the Farm Board. We were familiar with the farm problem and had studied the new Agricultural Marketing Act. After discussing its virtues, defeats and possibilities for two days, Alex said, 'Any man would be a damned fool to take a job on that Board!' 'I know it,' I said. 'But there have to be a few damned fools in the world in order that the work of the world may get done.' Alex's heels swung off the table, his feet came down flat on the floor, and he said: 'Well, I suppose you and I might as well be two of 'em!' He turned to the telephone, called Washington, and talked to the President. The die was then cast for both of us."[24] Legge took a leave of absence from International Harvester and moved to Washington.

The Federal Farm Board had the misfortune of being the government's first real intervention into the agricultural sector during one of the agricultural sector's most trying eras: the Great Depression and the Dust Bowl droughts. At first, the Farm Board's efforts were primarily directed toward assisting farmers to organize farmer cooperatives. With the collapse in commodity prices after the onset of the Depression, the Farm Board worked toward commodity stabilization through loans and purchases.

Desperate times breed desperate measures, and the Farm Board was perceived as being ineffectual. Forrest Crissey noted: "As chairman of the Farm Board, Alex Legge bore the brunt of the widespread and skillfully propagandized criticism of this venture. Abnormal conditions forced the Board into market operations of a kind that normally would not have been attempted. The measures were designed to meet an emergency...If he was sometimes hurt by this criticism, he gave no indication of it. He was interested solely in the thing to be done and in the result of his efforts, without thought of himself or what people were going to say or think about it. If he was convinced that he was doing the right thing, he would go ahead and do it."[25] Sam R. McKelvie, a grain member of the Board, noted: "It was with the utmost reluctance that Mr. Legge accepted a place on the Farm Board, but having once undertaken the task, no work was too great. Night after night he left the office carrying a portfolio filled with mail he had not had time to read during the day."[26]

Although Legge had promised only to stay as chairman for one year, under Hoover's encouragement he remained for 20 months until the Board was fully organized. He resigned on March 5, 1931. The work had broken him physically. According to his niece, Ina Sharman: "When he came back, I noticed that Uncle Alex had become bent. He said he thought he had worked for the International Harvester Company, but he never knew what work was till he went to Washington on the Farm Board. When I remarked that he had at least got back alive, he said, 'Oh, they really used me very nicely. I have no complaints whatever. It was hard work, of course!'"[27]

Return to Private Life. Once again, Legge returned to International Harvester. He confided to his associate Henry Cowan, "Henry, I don't give a damn for money. Since Mrs. Legge passed away this business has become everything to me. It is my chief interest in life. It keeps me going."[28]

The 4-H Club movement also attracted Legges's attention. 4-H Clubs had been founded around the country since 1899, and the National Committee was formally organized in December 1921. Legge had served as a director since 1923. Guy L. Noble, managing director of the organization, recalled the first board meeting Legge attended: "At a point in the proceedings where it seemed that nothing was going to be done, Alex Legge suddenly said, 'Well, men, we haven't done anything for Noble and his farm boys and girls yet. Let's decide to help them out.' He saved the situation so far as I was concerned. A program was adopted, and he helped put it over."[29] Crissey noted: "Mr. Legge attended every Directors' meeting that was called and even urged that additional meetings be held to determine how the National Committee might further assist in the development of the 4-H program for farm boys and girls. He was a generous annual contributor to the work and very influential in securing support from other quarters. He originated the plan of entertaining the 4-H Club members in attendance at the annual International Live Stock Show and the National 4-H Congress."[30]

The catastrophe gripping the agricultural sector greatly troubled Legge. Farmers in need of funds were being denied loans due to the Depression. He sent a check for $10,000 to the local bank in Schuyler, Nebraska, and a check for $100,000 to a bank in Omaha, Nebraska, to provide loans to smaller farmers.

He began to receive some of the recognition he rightfully deserved. In 1930, he was featured on the cover of *Time* magazine.[31] In 1932, the University of Wisconsin's College of Agriculture recognized him for his service to agriculture and rural life. That same year, he served as a member of the National Transportation Committee, whose membership included Calvin Coolidge, Bernard Baruch and Alfred E. Smith.

Legge's home and estate was in Hinsdale, Illinois, near Chicago. After Katherine's death, he took a keen interest in the children of that village. Herbert Hoover, a frequent visitor remarked: "Alex Legge was greatly interested in the children of the village and did not fail to bring around a horde of them to get autographs each time I appeared. He seemed to have incurred obligations in this direction prior to my arrival. What was more, he appeared to have relations to the automobile of every boy who drove into the place. There was a procession of these youngsters coming to the steps and receiving mystic signs from Mr. Legge which entitled them to go to the garage and fill up with gas and oil."[32] Legge also provided assistance to many of the under-privileged in the Hinsdale area.

Legge also took great care to show off his physical abilities and endurance. He had a 53-acre farm near his Hinsdale estate, where visitors were frequently invited to work with him. Those who politely tried to avoid field work by pointing out their lack of suitable clothes were shown to a closet stocked with work clothes. Visitors of every rank and social status left the Legge farm tired, sore and appreciative of the work of the farm laborer.

There is much documentary evidence of what Alexander Legge's contemporaries thought of him. Forrest Crissey, his biographer, wrote: "Very few men who worked with Alex Legge can discuss him without spontaneously comparing his individuality to that of Abraham Lincoln. This similarity is remarked by nearly every one of his surviving associates. It persists almost to the point of monotony, but it cannot be ignored. The volume, character and source of the testimony supporting it forbid. Alex Legge was strikingly Lincolnesque in mind, soul and body. Perhaps no other American has lived since Lincoln who was more so."[33]

Harold McCormick, of the International Harvester Company observed: "One of the main elements in the confidence which Alex Legge inspired in those who had personal contact with him was the fact that his reasonings and his decisions were based upon practical experience and close personal observation. He was not a theorist. Experience had been practically his only school and his loyalty to his alma mater was unswerving. He was gifted with a combination of great determination and tenacity. This was not, to my mind, stubbornness, but something very much above it. He could and did yield to the opinions of others when convinced that he was in error and when this occurred—which was not often—his yielding was wholehearted and gracious. He was too big and too honest to stick stubbornly to an opinion when his good sense told him that he was mistaken."[34]

Donald R. McLennan, who served on the War Industries Board with Legge, noted: "Those who knew Alex only as a dynamo of executive energy missed acquaintance with his most charming side. He had as great a capacity for sentiment as he had for business. He would do almost anything for a friend—but he suffered keen embarrassment in being thanked for a kind deed. Repeatedly I have seen him walk away under such an ordeal, usually with the remark: 'Oh, go to hell!'"[35]

General Hugh S. Johnson of the War Industries Board commented: "In a fight of any sort he was one of the toughest, and had a tongue like a mule-skinner's lash when he felt he had to use it. Probably some people think that my language is rough; I'm just an amateur compared with Alex Legge when he let loose, but his sympathies were with all toilers, especially with tillers of the soil. This was his strongest complex—which is proved by the fact that he gave about a million dollars of his fortune, after providing generously for the surviving members of his family, to the Farm Foundation for the continued and systematic study of farm problems. He was a farmer and the friend of all farmers to the end of his days."[36]

From his record of accomplishments and the accounts of his contemporaries, it is clear that Alexander Legge was a remarkable individual. A self-made man, a self-taught industrialist and a fine public servant, he earned the respect and loyalty of his peers and colleagues in industry. Yet, this remarkable life became even more notable because Alexander Legge bequeathed his fortune to better the life of the farming and rural populations of this country.

Frank Orren Lowden

"He was a practical, successful 'dirt' farmer, whose views on what the Federal Government should do to aid agriculture were too advanced at the time he sought the Presidency to bring him political support in the East."[37]

—*The New York Times*

Frank Orren Lowden was born two miles outside of Sunrise City in Chisago County, Minnesota, on January 26, 1861. His father, Lorenzo, was a farmer and village blacksmith. His mother, Nancy, was a former school teacher and the mother of three children, who also did much of the farm work while her husband worked at the forge in town.

Frank's father was successful in Sunrise City, but looking for greener pastures. In 1868, the family moved to Point Pleasant in Hardin County, Iowa, where he opened a blacksmith shop and purchased a farm.

Lowden's youth on the Iowa farm was bittersweet. He tremendously enjoyed living in the country, but he did not enjoy farm work. Becoming a farmer or blacksmith were never his career goals. Unlike most boys of his age and time, a portion of the money Lowden earned from agricultural labor was invested in books. It was said that he read and reread his meager library of books until he knew them by heart, and he would walk long distances to borrow books. When he entered school at age eight, he was ready for McGuffey's fifth reader. Lowden's father delighted in his son's precociousness, and they frequently debated issues of the day with each other. At age 12, Lowden participated in a public debate at his school and, a few years later, he gave the Fourth of July oration in nearby New Providence, Iowa.

By his 14th birthday in 1874, Lowden had mastered all of the course work offered in the district schools and begun independent study in subjects not offered by the local schools, such as algebra. He decided to become a teacher in order to earn enough money to attend law school. The regulations at the time stipulated that no one could take the teacher qualification exams before their 17th birthday, so Lowden needed a waiver from the county superintendent of schools. The superintendent ruled that Lowden could earn the teaching certificate only if he made a perfect score on the exam. Lowden met this requirement and was hired by the Meeker school district to teach the three-month winter term beginning in December 1875, for $100. He also took the position of janitor for $1 a month.

The three- to four-mile distance from his home to the school was too far to travel during the winter, so Lowden surrendered $40 of his salary for room and board. Arriving an hour before class, he would sweep out the classroom, wash the blackboards and light the wood stove. Even when the stove nearly "glowed," it was sometimes so cold in the school house that students near the walls saw their breath frost onto their slates. One of the main criteria for being a school teacher in Iowa during this time was the ability to avoid being pushed around by the class bully. Lowden's youth was certainly an issue as he would have to keep discipline in a school room where some of the students were older than he was.

In 1878, Lowden enrolled for a 10-week term at Iowa State Agricultural College at Ames, where his performance was exemplary. He continued to teach in Hardin County until September 1881. That month, he passed the entrance examinations and enrolled in the classics course of the State University of Iowa at Iowa City. He was a member of a fraternity and was well respected by his peers and teachers. In 1885, he graduated class valedictorian and accepted a teaching job in Burlington, Iowa, for $100 a month, saving his money to repay debts and attend law school.

Lowden would stay 10 months at Burlington. While he enjoyed the companionship of the teachers and teaching, he still felt compelled to go into law. He was interested in a law office clerkship and, through mutual contacts, approached the firm of Dexter, Herrick and Allen in Chicago. Although the firm generally only hired lawyers as clerks, they agreed to hire Lowden for $8 a week on the condition that he go to law school at night. Since his teaching salary had recently been advanced to $1,600 a year, this was a considerable reduction in pay. In August 1886, at 25 years of age, Lowden began a career in law.

Success in Chicago. As a clerk, Lowden's responsibilities included typing letters and legal documents and handwriting the office docket, the journal of daily business. In September 1886, he began evening classes at Union College of Law.[38] After preliminary examinations, he placed out of the first-year course work and was able to advance to the second-year courses of the two-year program. This period, while working a low-paying, full-time job and taking night classes, was one of the most difficult of his life, although he excelled in law school. He was elected to the legal fraternity, Phi Delta Phi, and graduated valedictorian of his class. At graduation, he was awarded a $50 prize for oratory and a $50 prize for scholarship. Lowden was exuberant. He was down to his last 40¢ and had been subsisting on coffee and oyster stew.

He passed the Illinois bar examination in July 1887, and became a practicing lawyer at Dexter, Herrick and Allen at a salary of $65 a month. Wirt Dexter, the senior partner, assigned Lowden to be his personal aide. Dexter, Herrick and Allen's clients included the Burlington Railroad and many of the banks and public utility companies in Chicago. Within one year of arriving in Chicago, Frank was not only a lawyer, but was positioned to become acquainted with the business and social elite of Chicago.

Over the next few years, the ailing Dexter served as his mentor and at Dexter's death in 1890, Lowden was faced with a predicament. Many of Dexter's personal clients looked to Lowden to continue their business, but the two surviving partners of the firm, Herrick and Allen, did not wish to adjust Lowden's salary to reflect this. He decided to leave the firm and look for a Chicago lawyer who wanted a bigger caseload.

Lowden approached Emery S. Walker, a promising Chicago lawyer, for a junior partnership, and the firm of Walker and Lowden began business on July 1, 1890. Lowden began to represent his own clients and defend them in court, developing such a reputation that other lawyers began to attend his cases to watch him address the jury and hear his dazzling questioning of witnesses. His social standing increased to the extent that he became a director of the exclusive Calumet Club in Chicago and kept a bachelor's apartment there.

In 1892, Walker and Lowden went their separate ways, probably over Lowden wanting greater compensation. For the next 16 months, he was a junior partner with William B. Keep, whose clients numbered several railways, a major savings and loan, and several prominent Chicago industries. Lowden frequently appeared as counsel in cases before the Federal District Court and the Illinois Supreme Court. He also helped organize the Law Institute with Wallace Heckman, and ran for a seat on the club's first board of managers, although this first venture into politics was unsuccessful.

Florence Pullman. In the summer of 1894, when associates complained he was working too hard and needed a vacation, Lowden relented and agreed to a vacation in Paris and London with Walter Herrick, son of one of his former employers. Sailing on the Normandie, at the first day's breakfast, he caught sight of Florence Pullman, daughter of George M. Pullman, founder of the Pullman Palace Car Company of Chicago. He was introduced to her later that evening. The two were in frequent company during the remainder of the voyage. After arriving in Paris, he and Herrick toured the city for six days under the expert guidance of Miss Pullman. On his departure to London, Lowden sent her flowers and a note asking to see her again when they were both back in Chicago.

Florence Pullman was the daughter of one of the wealthiest men in the United States. The social stratum into which she was born was completely foreign to the farm-bred Lowden. Every aspect of her life—what she wore, where she traveled, who she dated—was reported in the newspaper society columns. She had been educated in the best schools in the United States and Europe. She traveled frequently and enjoyed the use of a private Pullman car equipped with servants to satisfy her every whim. She was rumored to have been engaged to Prince Leopold of Germany, King Alexander of Serbia and the Marquis de Lorme of Spain.

While still in London, Lowden received a reply to his note, asking him to call on her when she was back in Chicago. He returned to his office in September, but it would be six more weeks before Florence was back from Europe. He began visiting her on Sunday afternoons. In November, he began visiting on weekday evenings as well. By late November, he was writing to her frequently. By January 1895, Frank and Florence confessed their mutual love and committed to a secret engagement.

Unfortunately, Florence's father, George Pullman, insisted she not become engaged without his permission. With kings and princes as previous suitors, he was not immediately fond of Lowden and urged his daughter to see him less frequently. Florence obliged him and suggested she and Lowden wait, in the hope that her father would consent. Over the next few months, only a few occasional meetings were arranged by Florence's mother. With Pullman's moratorium and the stress of increased legal work, Lowden suffered grave depression. Florence encouraged him to go overseas. Before leaving for Le Havre, France, in August 1895, he visited the Pullman seaside home in New Jersey. He and Florence agreed to write, but only to post once every two weeks. One of Lowden's letters ran 43 pages.

On his return, Lowden once again visited the Pullmans in New Jersey, and though he wished to ask Pullman for his daughter's hand in marriage, Pullman's attitude suggested what the answer would be. Lowden was further disappointed to learn that Florence was now forbidden to write to him. His return to Chicago brought even more disappointment. Pullman had learned of his daughter's secret engagement and instructed her to write Lowden releasing him from the commitment. Lowden obliged the sorrowful request, taking all blame for not cultivating more goodwill with her father.

Once Pullman had his way, he relaxed his edict and allowed Lowden to visit Florence every Wednesday and Sunday evening from October to Christmas. Sometime in mid-December, walking the four blocks from his apartment at the Calumet Club to the Pullman mansion, Lowden slipped on the ice and was bedridden for several days. When he was able to limp to Pullman's house, the industrialist finally gave his blessing to the marriage. Notification of the engagement appeared in the Chicago papers on January 19, 1896.

Lowden was ill-prepared for the social and financial demands of a society engagement, and the couple half-heartedly considered elopement. In the end, the ceremony took place in the drawing room of the Pullman mansion on April 29, 1896, before more than 200 guests, followed by a reception for almost 1,200. Guests included the Andrew Carnegies, the John D. Rockefellers, former President and Mrs. Benjamin Harrison, the Marshall Fields, the Robert Todd Lincolns, the Philip Armours, Mrs. Ulysses S. Grant, Mrs. Philip H. Sheridan, several Supreme Court justices and many other celebrities, politicians and business titans. The couple honeymooned for 10 days in Washington, D.C., using George Pullman's private car. Later, they visited the Pullmans' summer home, "Castle Rest," in Alexandria Bay, New York. Lowden was 35 years old and had married an American princess.

George M. Pullman

Florence was the favorite of George M. Pullman's four children. Compounding Lowden's courtship troubles and making his success even more remarkable was the fact that 1894 was a particularly difficult year for George Pullman.

When his company's fortunes declined in 1894, Pullman slashed wages by 25 percent. However, he neglected to lower the rents or cost of groceries in the company town. A delegation of workers who met with him to ask him to reduce these costs was fired the next day. Pullman's plant workers began a strike on May 15, which was taken national on June 22 when the American Railway Union, led by Eugene V. Debs, joined the strike in sympathy. After a week, more than 125,000 railroad employees refused to work on any train which employed a Pullman sleeper. Since most railroads used Pullman cars, much of the commerce in the country slowed down. The government sympathized with the railroads, due to the obstruction of mail, and by June 3, more than 2,000 federal troops were in the Chicago area. Over the next few days, the strikers began rioting, setting fires and destroying railroad equipment. The soldiers responded by firing on strikers, killing four and wounding 20. On July 9, President Cleveland outlawed large public gatherings in Illinois, and the union leaders were jailed. By September 6, the strike was officially over and the union was broken. All Pullman employees were required to sign a statement that they would never attempt to join a union.

George Pullman's reputation was savaged in the press. He went from being an industrial hero who made long-distance rail travel practical to being a greedy and heartless robber baron. He died of a heart attack three years later at age 66. The family was so fearful that his body would be stolen for ransom or defaced that the coffin was covered in tar paper and asphalt and then sunk into a concrete block the size of a small room. The top of the block was overlaid with railroad ties and more concrete.

Lowden's relationship with his father-in-law improved after the wedding, and in succeeding years, with Pullman's assistance, he assumed positions and trusteeships with several businesses and corporations. Between his wife's fortune and his own success, he soon had a considerable income. When Pullman died in 1897, Lowden became the de facto head of the family and helped oversee the disbursement of the $17.5 million estate.

Lowden Enters Politics. Lowden's interest in law did not wane. In 1898, he was named a senior partner in the firm of Lowden, Estabrook and Davis. His reputation for public speaking grew, and he was asked to speak on a wide variety of topics. He became increasingly involved in his university alumni associations and civic activities in Chicago.

Lowden also became more involved in politics. Sometime after moving to Chicago, he had switched his affiliation from the Democratic to the Republican Party. Certainly his switch was motivated by the fact that many of his legal and business associates were Republicans, and he was also influenced by his membership in the Union League Club. Hutchinson notes, "Its members fostered the spread of the myth, which thousands of voters believed by the 1880s, that the Republicans alone had won the Civil War, saved the Union, and abolished slavery."[39] These were ideas Lowden firmly believed.

His first formal involvement in city politics was in 1893 when he assisted in a mayoral campaign. Throughout the 1890s he became increasingly involved in the local party organization through the Political Action Committee of the Union League Club. His first crusades were against corruption and machine politics.

His efforts were interrupted in 1898 by the Spanish American War. After a rousing speech, Lowden was selected to head the Union League Club's efforts to raise and equip three regiments of volunteers. Although he had minimal military training, he was elected a lieutenant colonel of the First Regiment, Illinois National Guard. With his lack of experience, Lowden wisely attended to the more ceremonial duties and worked with the Illinois legislature to construct an armory and parade ground. Although the unit was never called on for combat, Lowden's service furthered his prominence in the community.

His political activities increased. With other members of the Union League Club, he formed the "Roosevelt, 1904 Club" in the late 1890s to espouse a presidential candidacy for Theodore Roosevelt. He was named a delegate to the Republican National Convention in 1900. After the convention, he was selected as a member of the Committee of Notification to inform President William McKinley of his re-nomination. He canvassed Illinois for six weeks before the election, speaking in support of the local and national candidates. For his services to the party, President McKinley offered Lowden the position of assistant postmaster-general of the United States, which he declined.

Lowden began to have political aspirations of his own and slowly tested the waters. He put his hat in the ring for the 1904 Illinois gubernatorial nomination, but lost a tough convention battle. He served as a delegate to the Republican National Convention and managed Theodore Roosevelt's presidential campaign in Illinois. Traveling the state in his private Pullman car, he spoke at least 40 times in support of Roosevelt in the month before the election.

In 1905, he declined a presidential judicial appointment for the Federal District Court in Illinois. His legal career had been supplanted by one in politics. He changed his voting address from Chicago to his farm estate, "Sinnissippi," 90 miles west of the city, and began listing his occupation as farming. When his local congressman announced his retirement, Lowden announced his intention to be his successor. He survived a tough primary battle, withstanding charges of being a "carpet bagger" too rich and privileged to represent such a rural district. By a margin of 2,000 votes out of 31,372 cast, Lowden was elected representative of the 13th Congressional District of Illinois.

Lowden entered office counting as friends President Theodore Roosevelt, Speaker of the House Joseph Cannon, several members of the Cabinet, Supreme

Court justices, and other members of Congress. Although this member of the Republican National Committee and son-in-law of one America's business titans considered himself a "farmer," he was assigned a seat on the Committee on Foreign Affairs.

As a junior member, Lowden was not overly visible. He was conscientious to the needs of his predominately rural constituents and an advocate for agriculture, agrarianism, and limiting graft and corruption. His legislative accomplishments mirrored his committee selection—foreign affairs. As a congressman, Lowden was less than fully satisfied. Hutchinson notes, "For a man of his nervous temperament, accustomed to prominent participation in important civic and business projects, it was singularly frustrating to be only a junior congressman, spending hours in committee meetings debating petty matters and rarely 'making the news' except in its society columns."[40]

Yet, Lowden's political star continued to rise. In 1909, he was strongly considered as a senatorial candidate from Illinois, although not selected due to a messy fractional fight.[41] Efforts were undertaken to promote him for the presidency and the speakership. When he became embroiled in a Republican effort to curb the power of Speaker Joseph Cannon, Lowden balanced his progressive leanings with the need to preserve party loyalty and the support of fellow Illinoisian Cannon.

The strain and anxiety of political life took their toll. Lowden's health declined to the point that his doctor recommended resting for at least a year. Thus, he decided against standing for re-election in 1910. His Republican successor was elected, but the GOP lost control of the House of Representatives for the first time in nearly 15 years.

Farming at South Bend and Sinnissippi. Lowden returned to his farm estate, Sinnissippi, to recover his health and look after his business interests. His investments included a newspaper, mining operations, international agricultural operations, large tracts in Idaho and Michigan, a 17,000-acre ranch in the Panhandle of Texas, and several properties in Arkansas, including the 20,000-acre South Bend plantation along the Arkansas River. Although he tended to be very involved in their operations, few of his investments were profitable.

Lowden took great interest in South Bend. He viewed it as an experiment in diversifying southern agriculture and improving the lot of tenants through new crops and crop rotation. Never satisfied with cotton alone, "he experimented with rice, corn, wheat, cowpeas, timothy, red clover, alfalfa, and lespedeza."[42] He also raised hogs and cattle there. Hutchinson reported, "By 1913, on this tract lived 150 tenant families, comprising 250 adults and 204 children, and, in addition, 21 employees ranging from managers and assistant managers to house servants."[43] The large plantation house was updated with modern conveniences for Lowden's spring and autumn visits. At his death in 1943, South Bend was deeded to Farm Foundation.

Sinnissippi,[44] Lowden's farm along the Rock River near Oregon, Illinois, held his true affections. He ran it as a demonstration farm for such concepts as crop rotation, fertilizer, cover crops, field drainage, the scientific method in research, and bookkeeping. The bulls in his Shorthorn herd were "among the best of their generation anywhere."[45] He also raised hogs, sheep, horses, goats and chickens. To prove that Illinois farmers could plant and harvest timber and to demonstrate that trees retard erosion, Lowden planted nearly 130,000 seedlings between 1902 and 1910. More than 70 percent were white pine with other conifers making up the remainder. The operation was such a success by 1910 that he increased the yearly planting to 50,000 seedlings, and eventually the plantings covered one-third of his estate.

Lowden firmly believed in the benefit of cutting-edge technology and reliable information. When he decided to enter the dairy business in 1913, he first spent two months visiting farms in Europe. The next year he built a creamery, purchased milking equipment, and assembled demonstration herds of Holsteins, Guernseys, Jerseys and Milking Shorthorns. In 1917, judging the Holsteins to be the most profitable, he sold the other breeds and joined the Holstein-Friesian Association of America. By 1921, he was the organization's president and served in that capacity for nine years.

One of Lowden's greatest interests was tenancy. By 1917, about three-quarters of his 4,400 acres at Sinnissippi was farmed by tenants. He developed three different lease arrangements for his tenants depending on their resources and preferences. Finding reliable tenants, though, proved to be difficult as the more hardworking and forward thinking the tenants, the less likely they were to remain tenants. Frequently, Lowden was left with contented tenants who generated little financial return.

Return to Public Life. Although he was satisfied to manage his farming interests, the allure of the political arena slowly drew Lowden back into the fray. He positioned himself as the Republican candidate for governor of Illinois, and after a spirited campaign won a decisive election in 1916. Hutchinson relates: "His majority was nearly 150,000 in a total of about 1,260,000 votes cast. He carried seventy-nine counties, including Cook County, and thirteen out of fifteen downstate congressional districts. Three out of four of the voters in his own county and four out of five of those in its county seat marked their ballots for him."[46]

Governor Lowden immediately began efforts to reform the state government. One of his first and probably greatest accomplishments was to streamline the Civil Administrative Code—which combined more than 100 largely independent boards and commissions—into nine government departments. Although modified over the years, "...the imprint of Lowden's work is still deep and clear at Springfield."[47] He also supported women's suffrage and pushed for a revision of the Illinois Constitution in order to establish an income tax.

World War I dominated Lowden's tenure as governor. He oversaw thousands of war-related tasks, from leading Liberty Bond campaigns and making patriotic speeches to ensuring Illinois receive its fair share of government contracts. The war increased racial tension in the state after thousands of African Americans migrated to Illinois in search of jobs. Lowden dispatched the Illinois National Guard to East St. Louis in 1917 and personally intervened in Chicago in 1919 to put down race riots. His tenure was also known for passing a bond issue to improve Illinois roads.

Lowden's accomplishments as governor have not been forgotten. A 2003 *Chicago Sun-Times* commentary ranked him second in its list of the 10 best governors in the history of Illinois.[48]

As governor, Lowden patterned his pro-war speeches after Theodore Roosevelt's. Drawing on his 20 years of association, he met with the former President in Oyster Bay, New York, in 1918, and hosted him in Springfield. When Roosevelt died in 1919, the Bull Moose faction of the Republican Party was left leaderless and Lowden attempted to assume that position. By the spring of 1919, Lowden allowed his supporters to include his name in the growing list of Republicans seeking the presidency.

As the campaign intensified, General Leonard Wood emerged as the Republican front-runner, with Lowden a distant second. Hiram Johnson of California and Warren G. Harding of Ohio were the most notable contenders in the remainder of the pack. Wood was a popular general who had commanded the 1st Volunteer Cavalry, the "Rough Riders," at Las Guasimas and San Juan Hill in the Spanish American War. (Theodore Roosevelt, the former Assistant Secretary of the Navy, had been second in command.) Wood had also served as Chief of Staff of the Army. Hiram Johnson had served as governor of California and as a U.S. senator. Warren Harding was a U.S. senator from Ohio.

Throughout the campaign, Lowden trailed Wood in the East and Johnson in the West. His hopes were that the convention delegates would be deadlocked and he would win the nomination as the compromise candidate. As he surged late in the primary campaign, there was optimism he might even win the nomination outright.

The Republican National Convention met in Chicago in June 1920. In the first ballot, Wood failed to receive the necessary 471 votes for the nomination. In succeeding ballots, Lowden's count rose until he was tied with Wood at around 310 votes each. After eight ballots, the convention was deadlocked. According to legend, with Wood, Lowden and Johnson unable to capture enough delegates to win the nomination, a group of senators and party leaders met in a suite of "smoke-filled rooms" at Chicago's Blackstone Hotel and selected Harding as an acceptable compromise choice. Lowden agreed, and his delegates shifted. Harding, a personal friend of Lowden's, was selected on the 10th ballot. He went on to defeat Democrat James Cox and become the 29th President of the United States in 1920.

After his defeat, Lowden fell into a slough of exhaustion and depression. With the Illinois gubernatorial primary less than three months away, he choose not to run again. He declined several posts offered to him in the Harding administration. He completed his term as governor and returned to Sinnissippi.

Lowden's return to agriculture coincided with the disastrous agricultural depression of 1921. Previously, his interests in agriculture had been confined to conservation, purebred livestock and promoting rural life. He believed rural America's greatest challenge was increasing productivity to meet a growing urban population. He did not believe surplus production would be a recurring problem. Consequently, when farm leaders encouraged him to become more involved, he was reluctant, believing the crisis would quickly pass.

While conditions were severe enough nationwide to garner his attention, they soon struck at home. At his Arkansas plantation, South Bend, the losses from 1920 to 1924 completely offset the profits from 1914 to 1920. The plantation was profitable in only one year during the decade and suffered a calamitous flood in 1927. At Sinnissippi, Lowden adjusted the lease arrangements so his tenants could survive. From 1921 to 1923, his prized cattle were ravished by tuberculosis, compounding his losses. The farm office building, along with Lowden's records and trophies, burned to the ground in 1924.

From 1921 onwards, Lowden became a spokesman for the agricultural situation to a doubting urban and industrial nation. Hutchinson notes: "When corn or cotton prices rallied, as in 1922 and 1924, he declined to cheer. It is a sorry situation, said he, when planters erect a statue to the boll weevil for keeping them out of debt and when Kansas farmers give thanks to the Almighty because the Iowa corn crop is far below normal in size. Something was desperately out of kilter when the nation's fundamental industry depended for its solvency, year after year, upon the failure of many of its members. To make this lamentable condition clear, he frequently spoke to groups of eastern newspapermen, bankers, and manufacturers and published a half-dozen articles in magazines with many urban subscribers."[49]

At first he advocated no explicit solution, stressing that agriculture's future depended upon the support of its urban brethren. However, as he investigated the problems further, he began to advocate marketing cooperatives to make farmers' bargaining powers more equal with buyers. In October 1923, he helped establish the Wheat Growers Advisory Committee. Its membership included Clifford V. Gregory, Dan A. Wallace and Bernard Baruch, all of whom would later be founding Trustees of Farm Foundation. Also invited was Alexander Legge, who declined to attend but expressed his full support. The Wheat Growers Advisory Committee developed a complicated scheme to pool crop marketing, but after a failed campaign to win acceptance by the nation's farmers, the project was abandoned in October 1924.

No matter how much he insisted otherwise, Lowden's efforts to promote the cause of agriculture were viewed skeptically as a political ploy. Furthermore, although he claimed he was through with politics, opportunities were rife. He was encouraged to run again for governor or the Senate. As scandals in the Harding administration broke, friends encouraged him to run again for the presidency. When President Harding died in August 1923, many looked to Lowden, but he was reluctant to run again.

Calvin Coolidge stepped into the presidency and indicated his willingness to run in 1924. Fearing an electoral battle, he first offered Lowden an ambassadorship to Great Britain then asked him to be his running mate. Lowden firmly declined the offers, but was nearly drafted at the convention anyway. He explained his decision, "They denied me the Presidency in 1920. I will not take it now if I have to get it by slowly walking behind the hearse of some other man."[50] Florence Lowden wrote in her diary, "Having turned down a governorship, senatorship, a cabinet position, the ambassadorship to the Court of St. James, and now the V.P., it would seem as if there was little left in the way of public office to offer."[51]

Lowden returned his attentions to encouraging cooperative marketing in agriculture. As an enthusiastic supporter of the proposed McNary-Haugen Farm Relief Bill, he began to be viewed as the farmers' champion, striving to raise the plight of agriculture above partisan bickering. He frequently spoke across the country on agricultural issues and his input was consulted for agricultural policy proposals.

While he suggested otherwise, he did retain political ambitions. His chances for the presidency were boosted again when Coolidge announced in 1927 that he would not seek re-election. Once again, with his friends' encouragement, Lowden decided to run. He faced two strong candidates for the nomination, Vice President Charles Dawes of Ohio and Secretary of Commerce Herbert Hoover. After a modest campaign, Lowden accepted that Hoover would win on the first ballot at the party convention in Kansas City. At the convention, he tried but failed to insert an agricultural policy plank based on the McNary-Haugen proposal. Lowden's quest for the highest office in the land was over. However, his efforts brought the agricultural situation into the campaign and ultimately led to the creation of the Federal Farm Board.

After the election, he and Florence began to spend more time at Sinnissippi. His interests continued to expand. In 1926 he joined the board of directors of the American Country Life Association and became the organization's president in 1929. He also became interested in social science research, interacting with many political scientists and economists.

His interest in agriculture continued as the Great Depression took hold and agriculture's condition deteriorated further. "Lowden had warned for years that the eventual outcome of the agricultural distress would be a disaster involving everybody. Columnists and industrialists who had once scoffed at his prophecies hailed him now as a leader of extraordinary foresight. They listened with unaccustomed respect when he declared that there would be no general economic recovery until the American farmer had been lifted back upon his feet."[52] In 1930, he met with President Hoover at the White House and Alexander Legge at the Federal Farm Board about the agricultural situation.

During the late 1920s and early 1930s, it could be argued that Frank Lowden was one of the most prominent agricultural leaders in the United States. It is not surprising, then, that he would be actively involved in the founding of Farm Foundation and bequeath part of his legacy to that endeavor.

Lowden Postscript. The last 10 years of Lowden's life were spent in semi-retirement. Although he never again ran for public office, he remained active in politics. He initially supported the New Deal policies but, as the years advanced, became an opponent. At an Alfred Landon campaign rally in 1936, he proclaimed, "You cannot maintain the morale of a people by making relief rolls more attractive than pay rolls."[54] Although Roosevelt's policies were not totally effective, Lowden realized they were more successful than the Republican policies of the 1920s. He tried to steer his party toward that acknowledgment and to develop strategies for Republican victory.

In 1937, Roosevelt's efforts to modify the judiciary system incensed Lowden. In the late 1930s, as the Nazi menace grew in Europe, his primary interest shifted from agriculture to foreign affairs. As an isolationist, he feared Roosevelt would try to involve the United States in a foreign war. Yet, after Pearl Harbor he wired Roosevelt, "If you can use an infirm old man I tender you my services to the very limit of my strength."[55]

Lowden died at age 82 in Tucson, Arizona, on March 20, 1943. He served as chairman of the Board of Trustees of Farm Foundation from 1933 to 1943.

One of the most insightful contemporary assessments of Frank Lowden is his 1943 obituary in the *Des Moines Register*:

> "The story of Frank Lowden is a saga of not just one generation but two, of pioneering and of modern social and industrial problems, of the best of conservatism and the best of progressivism. It is a strange story in which a great leader of political forces sometimes declined high office, sometimes was denied it because of his allegiance to high principle, but all the while carried enormous "political weight" because of the respect which his character commanded.
>
> "The facets of this man's interests and achievements seem almost to be limitless. We dare say that even few who thought they knew him intimately ever stopped to appraise the multitude of causes to which he devoted time and energy and money.

"Of course here in the middle west, Governor Lowden was known as an agricultural leader. Back in the early '20s he was a forceful advocate of the "equalization fee," of the McNary-Haugen bill, of scientific soil and seed grain development, of blooded livestock raising, and so on. He understood the basic *social* implications, as well as the economic, of agricultural stability. This was a vital part of his philosophy about maintaining a strong democracy.

"But among public administrators, Governor Lowden was known as a progressive and practical reformer. He made Illinois' antiquated budget and administrative machinery into an efficient, modern system. Subsequent savings brought about the lowest tax rate Illinois had enjoyed for years. He modernized the state's penal system in many ways. He started the state's hard-surfaced highway network. He started the Great Lakes-Mississippi waterway system. He pressed for reform throughout the old county system of government. And so on.

"In the professional world Mr. Lowden was known as a lawyer of great talent. In the business world he was a head of numerous large corporations. Yet as a member of Congress he had vigorously supported the income tax principle, labor legislation, and the exposure of corporate practices.

"In the field of education, where here in Hardin County, Iowa, he got his professional "start," Mr. Lowden was always a zealous advocate of modernization. He taught law and served as a trustee on several university boards.

"In politics, he was never stigmatized with a "small" act done for personal advantage. He declined a whole list of jobs, many of them promising political advancement, because he was afraid his conscience wouldn't "fit." But because he believed that the two-party system made for the success of modern democracy, he was loyal to the Republican party throughout his life, and spent his energy toward bringing it to a constantly higher level of public responsibility.

"Few men so "big" intellectually and spiritually come along in an ordinary lifetime. Few men who have achieved or accepted so little in the way of political preferment touch as many common men with their good influence as Frank Lowden has.

"We in Iowa may properly be proud that his formative years were spent here among us, and that to this degree he "belonged" to us."[53]

Chapter 2

Events Leading to the Founding of Farm Foundation

"I wonder if agricultural conditions might not have developed somewhat differently if the Agricultural Foundation had been organized early in 1929 and had vigorously gotten underway in its study of certain phases of the agricultural situation and in the widespread publication of its findings? I wonder whether the Congressional Act creating the Federal Farm Board might have been written differently? I wonder whether the actions of the Agricultural Foundation (always assuming that it would have done vital work in an efficient manner) might not have proved a valuable aid to the Federal Farm Board and might not have helped toward a better adjustment of the relationship of agriculture to industry in the United States and brought about a different attitude on the part of the agricultural leaders than exists now, and of Congress in the attention which it will give to this matter in the near future?"[1]
—Magnus W. Alexander, National Industrial Conference Board, 1931

Although Farm Foundation acknowledges two principal founders, Alexander Legge and Frank Lowden, dozens of individuals were involved in its organization, including some of America's most prominent "A-list" citizens. The organizers were brought together by mutual agreement on the need for an organization such as Farm Foundation, yet disagreed on what activities it should undertake. They grappled with difficult questions for seven long years. The formation of Farm Foundation was not easy, and unfortunately, would come to fruition in some of the most difficult times the U.S. economy and agriculture had faced.

It is not known who first proposed the idea of a private foundation devoted to agriculture. In 1920, there were only 54 foundations[2] established in the United States, mainly to promote urban and social concerns. Although the number of foundations would more than triple by 1930, until the establishment of Farm Foundation, there were no private agencies dealing specifically with agricultural or rural matters. The Foundation was conceived as a response to the agricultural conditions of the 1920s.

Murray R. Benedict's book, *Farm Policies of the United States 1790-1950,*[3] notes that the decade before the U.S. entry into World War I was a prosperous period for U.S. agriculture. Land values and the number of farms had steadily increased. Surplus agricultural production was exported to Europe. Government intervention in the agricultural sector was minimal. Two of the major concerns—the need for an agricultural extension service and the lack of agricultural credit—were addressed, respectively, with the passage of the Smith-Lever Agricultural Extension Act in 1914 and the establishment of the Federal Land Bank System in 1916.

During World War I, Great Britain was heavily dependent on food imports, and France lost control of much of its food producing area. They looked to the United States for greater agricultural imports. As demand increased, prices rose rapidly. The Chicago wheat price increased to $3.40 in May 1917 from $1.06 in June 1916.[4] While the United States enacted policies to increase agricultural production, the short period of actual U.S. participation in the war (April 1917 to November 1918) and several poor crop years meant that most of the increased U.S. supply was from conservation efforts and more efficient distribution. During the war, production was hampered by several factors, such as a shortage of seed corn, labor shortages and adverse weather. Net farm income, which ranged between $3.4 billion and $4.6 billion during the prosperous period 1910 to 1916, soared to between $8.3 and $9.1 billion from 1917 to 1919.[5]

In the immediate postwar period, U.S. agriculture found itself supremely overconfident. Factors such as increased mechanization, better weather and a government-sponsored expansion of county agents meant that, by 1920, agricultural production would reach record levels. According to the 1920 report of the Secretary of Agriculture:

> "The farmers of America have again justified the faith of the Nation in their ability to meet its requirements of food, feed, and raw materials for clothing. They have produced this year, in the face of enormous difficulties, the largest harvest in the history of American agriculture, with a single exception. The combined yield of the 10 principal crops is 13 percent above the average for the five years preceding the outbreak of the World War.
>
> "The corn crop of 3,199,000,000 bushels is unprecedented, representing more than four-fifths of the world's production. The sweet-potato crop of 106,000,000 bushels is the largest ever produced

and far in excess of that of any other year except 1919. The rice crop of 52,000,000 bushels is one-fourth greater than the largest crop ever before harvested. The tobacco crop of 1,476,000,000 pounds considerably exceeds any previous yield. The sugar-beet crop is more than one-third larger than the largest ever before recorded. The grain sorghum crop of 149,000,000 bushels is 18 per cent above that of 1919, which was itself a record crop. The potato crop of 421,000,000 bushels has been exceeded only once, and then by a very narrow margin. The oat crop of 1,333,000,000 bushels has been exceeded only three times, and the tame hay crop of 88,000,000 tons only twice. The apple crop of 236,000,000 bushels has been exceeded only once, in 1914. The yields of wheat, barley, buckwheat, peaches, peanuts, edible dried beans, flaxseed, and cotton are slightly below the average, but they, nevertheless, represent an enormous volume in the aggregate. The number of all classes of livestock on farms, although less than the number in 1919, exceeds by 18,214,000 the average for the five years preceding the outbreak of the European war."[6]

Besides producing record agricultural surpluses, another factor worsened an already serious problem for U.S. agriculture. Until World War I, the United States had been a debtor nation to the war powers, able to export more than it imported without disturbing the trade balance. After the war, the United States became the world's largest creditor nation. In order for the United States to export at the same level it had before the war, it would have to provide credit or assume more imports. The United States did neither, and U.S. farm prices dropped precipitously. By 1920, the United States had entered a severe agricultural depression.

As the crisis intensified, the federal government began to look at a legislative solution. The McNary-Haugen Farm Relief Bill achieved the most prominence. After being considered four times, it was finally passed in 1927 and then vetoed by President Coolidge. It was passed a second time in 1928 and vetoed again. The McNary-Haugen bill proposed that the federal government increase agricultural prices by buying up surpluses at a fair price level, disposing of them overseas at a loss, and recovering that loss through a fee assessed against farmers. Coolidge based his vetoes on his belief that the legislation would perpetuate, rather than solve, the core agricultural problem of overproduction.

Business Men's Commission on Agriculture Report. During the 1920s, many studies were undertaken to understand and propose remedies for the farm problem. Farm Foundation can trace its lineage to the conclusions of one of them, the 1927 report of the Business Men's Commission on Agriculture.[7] The Commission was a joint project of the National Industrial Conference Board and the Chamber of Commerce of the United States. Over a four-month period, the

Commission conducted hearings in New York, Chicago, Minneapolis, Des Moines, Memphis, Kansas City, Dallas, Atlanta, Greenville and Washington, D.C., and invited the participation of farmers, businessmen, bankers and economists. The 273-page report summarized the agricultural situation at the time and offered suggestions for improving the conditions of the farm sector.

One of the suggestions was to establish "an agency which is entirely independent of the Federal government, the state governments and of all business interests of a regional or local character...Such an organization, which might be called the 'National Agricultural Foundation,' should be the agency for a variety of activities which for one reason or another cannot well be undertaken by the Federal government or by organizations of farmers, and which are directed toward the promotion of agriculture as part of the national economy."[8]

The National Industrial Conference Board, under the leadership of Magnus W. Alexander, took measures to organize the foundation. In 1931, Alexander related:

"As you may recall, I interested Ex-Governor Frank O. Lowden, Mr. Owen D. Young, and others in the idea and it seemed as if progress was at hand. It was then November of 1928 and Mr. Hoover had just been elected President of the United States. Since he had expressed a definite intention to deal comprehensively with the agricultural problem, my advisors suggested that he would have an opportunity of counseling delay, if he so desired, until after he had submitted an agricultural relief plan to the Congress and to the public. Accordingly, Hon. Charles Nagel, Chairman of the Business Men's Commission, wrote Mr. Hoover who had meanwhile left for a South-American trip. Soon after his return, however, Mr. Hoover replied by stating that he had referred the matter to Mr. Hyde who was to be the Secretary of Agriculture; and Mr. Hyde requested a copy of the Business Men's Commission report for his perusal. There the matter rested."[9]

Although it failed to attract the attention of the Hoover administration, the idea of a national agricultural foundation intrigued Alexander Legge. He began discussing his ideas with others. Dan A. Wallace, editor of *The Farmer*, recalled in 1943:

"For a number of years, Mr. Legge had been wanting to render a service to agriculture, with which his life long interests had been connected. He hoped that other men similarly situated and interested would wish to join him in setting up some endowed institution that could serve the farmer, the farm family and the farm enterprise.

"To that end, Mr. Legge had been working with the Chicago University in setting up a Farm Foundation. However, he was reluctant in turning it over to an education group because he wanted the Foundation to be very practical in its service. On this point, he seemed to fear the theories of the educators. He wanted to make the farmer more prosperous because he held that if the farmer made sufficient income, he would automatically improve his social status. It was at about this stage in his thinking that I first talked with him about the Foundation idea."[10]

Legge formulated his ideas and instructed William S. Elliott (see box page 34), general counsel for International Harvester, to develop a legal constitution for an Agricultural Service Foundation. A seven-page draft of the proposed plan was prepared in 1928, and listed the objective of the foundation as "... the improvement of the economic and social conditions and general welfare of that part of the population of the United States of America which derives its main support from agriculture, using this word in its broad sense to include stock raising, dairying, and other farm activities, as well as cultivation of the soil."[11] The document offered few specifics, mainly focusing on the legal organization of the proposed foundation.

In 1929, Legge asked George N. Peek,[12] a former Deere & Company and Moline Plow Company executive, to comment on the foundation plan. In his nine-page reply, Peek observed: "As I understand it, your thought is not so much to create a new agency for scientific research, as to set in motion a new force which is closer to the farmer and more alert to practical problems than are existing institutions and which is more concerned with the application of best principles than with academic investigation. The Foundation, for the most part,

---

Dan A. Wallace

Organizer, Farm Foundation Board Member 1933-1940

Dan Wallace was a member of one of the 20th century's most notable agricultural families. His father was Henry "Uncle Henry" Wallace (1836-1916), founder and editor of the influential weekly Iowa farm magazine, *Wallaces' Farmer*. His brother Henry C. Wallace (1866-1924) served as U.S. Secretary of Agriculture from 1921-1924. His nephew Henry A. Wallace (1888-1965) founded Pioneer Hi-Bred in 1926, served as Secretary of Agriculture from 1933-1940, Vice President from 1941-1944, and Secretary of Commerce from 1945-1946. Both Henry C. Wallace and Henry A. Wallace served as editors of *Wallaces' Farmer*.

Dan Wallace served the Webb Publishing Company in St. Paul, Minnesota, as directing editor of *The Farmer*, 1905-1935, and *The Farmer's Wife*, 1919-1935. He chaired the 1931 organization committee, coordinated the 1933 organizational meeting, and was an original member of Farm Foundation's Board of Trustees, serving from 1933 to 1940.

William S. Elliott

Organizer, Farm Foundation Board Member 1934-1951

William S. Elliott, general counsel of International Harvester (1924-1946), assisted Alexander Legge in the organization of Farm Foundation and represented Legge in his absence. Along with William J. Donovan, Elliott drew up the Farm Foundation Trust Agreement. Elliott was the first secretary of Farm Foundation's Board (1933-1942). He was elected to succeed Bernard Baruch on the Board, serving from 1934 to 1951. Elliot was chairman of the Executive Committee (1934-1944) and presided at the 1942 and 1943 Board meetings.

---

would seek to hasten the general adoption and application of the fruits of research by others, rather than to undertake original and independent research of its own."[13]

He went on to describe seven areas in which he believed the foundation could make a difference to agriculture: production, marketing and distribution, land policies, taxation, standard of living, other national policies affecting agriculture, and uses for farm by-products. Furthermore, he listed 16 individuals with expertise in these areas, one of whom was Frank Lowden.

Legge wrote to Lowden on July 11, 1929, enclosing his rough draft of the plan and Peek's letter:

> "I think our mutual friend, Mr. George N. Peek, has talked to you about a dream that I have been indulging in for some time past, and that is the forming of some kind of a business organization that might be helpful in the big problem of agriculture. The underlying thought was that there were many things that a business organization, if a live institution could be set up, would be able to do that probably cannot and certainly will not be done by government or state operations.
>
> "I am not approaching you with a financial touch. I am confident that if a workable organization is set up I will be able to go out and get together enough money to give it a fair trial. I do feel very strongly that the question of whether it is worth while or not depends far more on the type of the organization or the kind of a set-up we get than it does upon the financing of it."[14]

Lowden replied the next day that he was "...tremendously interested in this proposed undertaking."[15]

With Legge's time monopolized by chairing the Federal Farm Board, the foundation matter rested somewhat. In early 1930, he had William Elliott incorporate suggestions and print a formal *Constitution of the Agricultural Service Foundation*. The document amplified the purposes of the foundation:

"1. To conduct research and experimental work for the study of any social, mechanical, physical or economic problem of importance to any substantial portion of the agricultural population of the country, including problems of production, marketing and purchasing, the sound coordination of the agricultural with the industrial and mercantile life of the country, living conditions and human, animal and plant diseases.

2. To finance any such research or experimental work conducted by the staff of any university or college, or other institution, corporation or person calculated, in the judgment of the Board of Trustees, to lead to useful results.

3. To disseminate education and useful information developed as a result of any such study, research and experimentation, or otherwise, in such manners to be of practical value to the farming population."[16]

On receipt of a copy, Lowden replied: "I have tried to find flaws in it but without success. It seems to me that you have covered the ground thoroughly and have anticipated with great care new conditions that might arise. I am tremendously impressed with the possibilities of this Foundation."[17]

Legge wrote back:

"I am meeting with some encouragement on this foundation matter, and hope in the course of the next few months to make a start at it. In doing so, I would like to include you as one of the organizers. This is not a bid to try to get you to finance it. We would be glad to have you go along with us on the financing in a modest way, leaving you to write your own meal ticket in that respect. What I am interested in in your case is to have you give the movement your blessing, and the most effective way to do this is for you to appear as one of its original organizers. I trust it will be agreeable for you to do so."[18]

Lowden's reply two days later illustrates the effect economic conditions would have on the project: "Just at present I am unable to help finance anything. What ready funds I have are being rapidly depleted in helping friends to avoid bankruptcy. Maybe later I shall feel solvent again. If, notwithstanding this, you wish me to appear as one of the organizers, I shall be glad of course to have you do so."[19]

Legge also approached Cyrus H. McCormick Jr. for support. In a letter to his sister, Anita Blaine, McCormick noted: "Long ago Alex Legge told Harold [McCormick] and me he was making a foundation in Washington for a board to study the farmers' interests continually, and gain such light on the subject that some plan could finally be devised for practically helping the farmers...In the meantime the Federal Farm Board was organized and Alex was called to be its chairman, and they have been successfully battling with this most difficult subject."[20]

Understanding that Legge was not asking for financial support but only gauging interest, McCormick wrote:

> "...I find that while the plan legally is excellently set forth in the pamphlet which I am now enclosing to you, the practical part of the organization has not yet been reached. So I have suggested to Will Elliott that Alex [Legge] should select some practical man, not a member of the Harvester Company and certainly not himself, to start making a quiet canvass of investigation to find out who is ready to make the start, by financial contribution and by personal service. And also that Alex should indicate to someone the kind of men he would like to have for founders and the type of men he would like to have as trustees. Then if he could give me that information I would decide very soon how much money I would like to put into the effort, for I have already told Alex Legge that I wanted to join him in some way. As soon as I can get that information I will pass it on to you and Harold and you can then decide, each for yourself, what you want to do. I can say without hesitation that I think it would be lovely and appropriate if we three (who are all that are left of the McCormick clan who could take up a sympathetic work of this kind with Alex Legge) could signify what financial and what personal support we desire to give or can give.
>
> "It would be only natural that if Alex is starting a movement of this kind, all the outside world would like to know whether or not we, his partners, are with him, or whether we are indifferent to the proposal."[21]

McCormick continued, "I told Elliott that I would not be able to take any official position which would require attendance of the meetings like a board of trustees, but that I would be glad to lend my name in any way that could help, and also to subscribe financially, and the amount that I thought of subscribing (assuming that the money would not have to be paid immediately) was One Hundred Thousand Dollars."[22]

Mary Harriman Rumsey. While Alexander Legge worked on his foundation idea, the worsening plight of agriculture and rural people attracted the attention of Mary Harriman Rumsey (see box), daughter of railroad magnate Edward H. Harriman. Her interest in "fostering ideal rural and urban communities and a sympathetic understanding between them"[23] lead her to join the American Country Life Association, of which Frank Lowden was president.

In 1930, Rumsey organized an eight-month nationwide lecture tour for George W. Russell of Ireland. An advocate of "rural civilization," Russell "...fostered the agricultural cooperative movement in his homeland as a means of spiritual growth and a spur to nationalism."[24] Rumsey was greatly influenced by Russell's book, *The National Being: Some Thoughts on an Irish Policy,* and hoped the

Mary Harriman Rumsey

Organizer, Farm Foundation Board member 1933-1934

Mary Harriman Rumsey was the daughter of railroad tycoon Edward Henry Harriman and sister of Averell Harriman. Always socially conscious, in 1901, at age 19, she founded the Junior League for Promotion of the Settlement Movement in New York (now the Junior League). While her father had built an empire based on competition, she believed in cooperation, assisted countless social organizations in New York and is credited with opening approximately 500 playgrounds in the city. She was greatly influenced by *The National Being: Some Thoughts on an Irish Policy* by George Russell. "In that book, I found my nebulous ideas put into practical form. Here was a man who believed that it was not possible for a country to advance without cooperation and who described how the best sort of community life could be built up through it."[53] She was involved in organizing Farm Foundation and was a member of its first Board.

lecture tour would introduce his ideas to America.

Russell, a multi-faceted man better known outside agricultural circles, was an accomplished artist, poet and writer who used the pseudonym Æ, and a self-described "mystic." His mysticism would probably be diagnosed as mental illness today. It was said, "He lived in two worlds. In everyday life he was a practical man, but behind it he lived in a land of elves and of the little people whose language he understood and spoke. He did not create them by an act of will or stimulated imagination; they were *there* to greet him and he opened his house and heart to them."[25]

Regardless, Russell's poetic blending of economics and spiritualism resounded with many people of wealth and influence in the United States and inspired near-religious devotion to his ideas. Rumsey organized 66 prominent citizens from across the country as the Committee of Welcome for George Russell Æ Lecture Tour, many of whom would soon be involved in the formation of Farm Foundation. At Frank Lowden's invitation, Russell gave the principal address at the October 1930 meeting of the American Country Life Association in Madison, Wisconsin, beseeching his audience "...to get the reformers and foreseers in your country to think of building up a rural civilization, something which the world has never yet seen."[26]

A few months later, Rumsey called on members of the lecture tour committee and others interested in the agricultural situation to discuss the possibility of establishing a "foundation for agricultural and community development." The meeting in New York City on December 9, 1930, was attended by: O.H. Benson, Judge Richard Campbell, Frank Lowden, Julian Mason, George McDonald, Frank E. Mullen, Phillip A. Parsons, Clarence Poe, Dan Wallace and John P. Wallace. With Lowden presiding, the group discussed "how they might help to build up a rural civilization which would make life more satisfying to the farmer, both economically and culturally."[27] Dan Wallace spoke of his efforts to organize an agricultural foundation utilizing the radio.[28] The work of Legge was also mentioned. The conferees adopted a statement, "That we proceed at once to form a temporary organization for the purpose of developing a permanent Foundation and to elect officers."[29]

Invitations to join a temporary organizational committee were extended to Magnus Alexander, Bernard Baruch, J.C. Cullinan, Colonel William J. Donovan, Mrs. John Greenway, Alexander Legge, Mrs. Medill McCormick, Eugene Meyer, Dr. Henry Pritchett and Owen D. Young. The temporary officers selected were: Dan Wallace, chairman; Julian Mason, vice chairman; George McDonald, treasurer; and Mary Harriman Rumsey, secretary. MacDonald and Rumsey jointly offered a contribution of $60,000 to be used by the future organization.

The group met again on January 15, 1931, to discuss a charter, constitution and bylaws. In attendance were Magnus Alexander, O.H. Benson, Judge Richard Campbell, Colonel William Donovan, Julian Mason, Leland Olds and Mary Harriman Rumsey. At this meeting, the group further defined their objectives for the proposed foundation with a focus on George Russell's philosophy. Judge Campbell, who presided over the meeting, stated: "...It is important that Æ's central idea of establishing and promoting community and neighborhood groups should be stressed in whatever policy is adopted. That the project to build up a rural civilization should be a major consideration and that the charter should provide, amongst other things, in concrete terms for a program that would call for the gradual equalization, as far as may be, of economic and cultural advantages between city and country."[30]

Leland Olds, who had accompanied Russell on his tour, added:

> "In defining the objectives for the proposed Foundation, what Æ has said to people all over the country must be taken into account. His plan called for the creation in villages and in rural communities, of little economic republics through the adoption of the cooperative principle. He has suggested following the lines of the Irish Cooperative Movement as laid down by Sir Horace Plunkett...
>
> "Sir Horace established the principle that through his own organizations the farmer should be master in his own house. He felt that it was necessary to change the mood of the farmer from one of individualism to cooperative effort. The principle of cooperation should be considered as a basis of local organization... Æ suggests that the most successful way to go at this thing is to try it experimentally in a few communities that can be interested, and that as the experiment succeeds in these communities others will be anxious to follow their example, and the movement would grow normally not starting with too big an undertaking."[31]

By early 1931, there were three separate groups advocating an agricultural foundation. The first, led by Legge, espoused a foundation which would "...seek to hasten the general adoption and application of the fruits of research by others, rather than to undertake original and independent research of its own."[32]

The second, led by Rumsey, championed the philosophy of George Russell and consisted primarily of concerned New York socialites whose basic interest was promoting "rural civilization" through cooperative community organization.

The third group, only loosely organized, included men who were much closer to the problem, such as Lowden, Mullen, Poe and Wallace. Lowden served as a bridge between the two other groups. Wallace and Mullen agreed with Rumsey's social concerns, but had additional ideas of their own. For instance, in 1929 they developed a prospectus for an agricultural foundation utilizing technology to reach rural America. "The first project contemplates the establishment of a series of radio broadcasting programs over a period of five years. The second project deals with the establishment of a National Agricultural Foundation. Both the broadcast program and the Foundation idea are proposed on the basis of promoting the educational and social welfare of rural life."[33]

Now, as chairman of the New York group's organizing committee, Wallace began working with other agricultural journalists to develop a prospectus for Rumsey's proposed foundation. He requested assistance from Edward M. Tuttle, editor-in-chief of *The Book of Rural Life*, who developed an outline in late December 1930 of the types of organization and services an agricultural foundation could undertake.[34] The report would also benefit from the work of Carroll P. Streeter, Bess M. Rowe, Dr. John W. Holland, and Dillon P. Tierney. In his prospectus, Wallace managed to bridge and expand the ideas of the Legge and Rumsey camps.

By early 1931, the 29-page prospectus included sections on the present agricultural situation, the need for a farm foundation, and possible foundation activities. Proposed activities included: a program for community organization, a rural health program, a program of rural education, a national program for farm women, a program for rural churches, and a rural beautification program. The report called attention to the worsening agricultural situation:

"Last year, 1930, was probably the most disastrous year American agriculture has ever known. The drought over a large section of the country was the worst ever recorded in the annals of the United States Weather Bureau. At the same time, prices of farm commodities dropped to the lowest levels in a generation. The aggregate value of farm crops in 1930 was nearly two and one-half billion dollars less than the previous year, combined with a comparable reduction in the value of livestock products. Add to these conditions a constantly diminishing level of land values and a 65-cent purchasing dollar, and the need of some agency to foster and encourage the perpetuation of American rural life becomes apparent."[35]

It went on to state: "Following the New York conference the temporary chairman [Wallace] called upon several high officials in the government service, all of whom expressed great interest in this idea of a new and distinctive service to rural civilization. Subsequent letters to various agricultural leaders throughout the country have elicited a profoundly interested response to the same idea and an urgent hope that such Foundation will be speedily established."[36]

One letter, from Charles Nagel, was particularly encouraging:

"I am delighted to see that the suggestion for a foundation has finally been seriously undertaken. As you know, that was the chief recommendation of the Agricultural Commission, of which I was Chairman, and which made its report some years ago.

"I am familiar with Mr. Legge's pamphlet, and take it that it follows virtually the same lines. It is a great satisfaction to know that President Hoover is in sympathy with the movement, particularly since at an earlier stage I entertained some doubt as his attitude upon the subject."[37]

Due to conflicting schedules, two follow-up meetings were planned for Chicago on February 15, 1931, and Washington, D.C., on February 16, 1931. Participants at the first meeting would take the train to Washington to meet with Legge and other East Coast members who could not be present in Chicago.

The Chicago meeting took place at Frank Mullen's office in the Merchandise Mart. In attendance were Lowden, Clifford Gregory, Mullen, Poe, Tait Butler, George Russell, Rumsey, Judge Richard Campbell, Dan Wallace, Henry A. Wallace, John P. Wallace and William Elliott representing Alexander Legge. The differences in philosophy between the Legge and Rumsey camps were evident.

The meeting began with a discussion of the general goals of the foundation. Dan Wallace recounted his discussions with Legge following the New York meeting in December: "I talked with Mr. Legge, asking for his views about things we discussed in New York, and asking if he would be willing to go on with some further conferences. He assured me of his very great interest in the whole idea, because it was along the idea he had been working on for several years."[38]

Speaking for Mary Harriman Rumsey, Richard Campbell was more confrontational. "Mrs. Rumsey asked me to bring to your attention today that her interest primarily is community organization among the farmers...In a rather vague way, Mrs. Rumsey's idea is, to use her own formula, to equalize the advantages as far as possible, between the cities and the country—to bring the country to the city and the city to the country—and in that way build up a

The "New York Group" and the Farm Press

Many who attended early organizational meetings were acquainted to some degree with Mary Harriman Rumsey or were members of the farm press:

Magnus Alexander was a New York engineer and economist. He organized the National Industrial Conference Board in 1916 and served as its managing director/president until his death in 1932. He attended the organizational meetings on January 15, February 16, and April 25, 1931.

O.H. Benson was head of Boys' and Girls' Club Work (4-H) for 33 northern, central and southern states at USDA,1910-1920. He is credited with originating the 4-H clover emblem and motto and the federal-state-county partnership under which 4-H is organized. He attended the organizational meetings on December 9-10, 1930, and January 15, February 16, and April 25, 1931.

Tait Butler was editor and assistant publisher of *Progressive Farmer*. He attended the February 15, 1931, organizational meeting.

Judge Richard Campbell was a New York attorney with the firm Gilbert, Campbell & McCool and a former judge in the Court of First Instance (1908-1917). He attended organizational meetings on December 9-10, 1930, and January 15, and April 25, 1931.

Colonel William J. Donovan was a Medal of Honor winner in World War I and an influential Wall Street lawyer. During World War II, he was promoted to the rank of general and headed the Office of Strategic Services, precursor to the Central Intelligence Agency. He attended the January 15, and April 25, 1931, organizational meetings.

Julian Mason was managing editor of *The New York Herald Tribune* from 1922 to 1926 and *The New York Evening Post* from 1926 to 1933. Mason attended organizational meetings on December 9-10, 1930, and January 15, and February 16, 1931.

Charles Nagel, a St. Louis, Missouri, lawyer, was Secretary of Commerce and Labor under President Taft (1909–1913). He founded the U.S. Chamber of Commerce and chaired the Business Men's Commission, which produced the 1927 report advocating an agricultural foundation.

Leland Olds was secretary of the Committee of Welcome for George Russell Æ Lecture Tour and accompanied Russell on his 1930-1931 tour. He would later become chairman of the Federal Power Commission (1939-1949). He attended the January 15, and February 16, 1931 organizational meetings and also represented Rumsey at the July 21, 1933, Farm Foundation Board of Trustees meeting.

Phillip A. Parsons was a sociologist and dean at the University of Oregon. He attended the December 9-10, 1930, organizational meeting.

Henry A. Wallace was the son of Henry C. Wallace and grandson of Henry Wallace. He was editor of *Wallaces' Farmer* from 1921 to 1933. In 1923, he developed the first commercial hybrid corn and in 1926, with two partners, founded Pioneer Hi-Bred. He served as Franklin Roosevelt's Secretary of Agriculture (1933-1940) and Vice President of the United States (1941-1944), then was Secretary of Commerce (1945-1946). He was the Progressive Party candidate for President in 1948. He attended the February 15, 1931, organizational meeting.

John P. Wallace was a brother of Dan Wallace, a son of Henry Wallace, and a co-founder of *Wallaces' Farmer*. He attended the December 9-10, 1930, and February 15, 1931, organizational meetings.

rural civilization, and that is what she is primarily interested in."[39] He implied Rumsey would not be interested unless the foundation had a focus corresponding to her views.

Elliott responded for the Legge camp:

"I think it is rather fundamental that we settle at the start this one thing — the primary idea.... [Alexander Legge] felt it would be a mistake to extend it beyond the rural field. That is a tremendous field in itself, and while planning that, we are all working for Mrs. Rumsey's idea of equalizing conditions in and out of the city. The fact is there are a great many people giving money besides those who are going to give it to this foundation, and if they are centering it by giving it to the city, she may have to bring that equalization about by throwing hers into the country problem.

"Mr. Legge feels quite clear there. He also feels the foundation will attract more money, because you can not attract people to turn over money to you for the general good of the whole world. They want something specific. That is the way city foundations get their money; it is a specific hospital, project, this or that or the other thing; but when you cover improving the city and country life too, you have the whole life of the country in one foundation."[40]

The next item on the agenda was to "take up the proposed articles of incorporation which have been prepared by Mr. Donovan and Judge Campbell and also outline the things that the agricultural representatives of the Committee want done."[41] Elliott introduced the legal constitution he had developed for Legge in 1930. While the Rumsey proposal advocated promoting the cooperative organization of farmers and equalizing the advantages of urban and rural areas, the Legge proposal focused on encouraging research.

The group conferred to bridge their differences. Under Elliott's direction, five objectives were agreed on:

"1. To encourage and develop cooperative effort and community organization and consciousness, as means for improving the economic, social, educational and cultural conditions of rural life.

2. To stimulate and conduct research and experimental work for the study of any economic, social, educational or scientific problem of importance to any substantial portion of the rural population of the country, including problems of production, marketing and purchasing, and the sound coordination of the agricultural with the industrial, financial and mercantile life of the country.

3. To encourage, aid or finance any research or experimental work conducted by the staff of any university or college or other institu-

tion, corporation or persons calculated, in the judgment of the Board of Trustees, to lead to useful results.

4. To disseminate educational and useful information developed as a result of any such study, research and experimentation, or otherwise, in such manner as to be of practical value to the farming population.

5. To promote and enlarge the intellectual and cultural interests and opportunities of the rural population through community action."[42]

The second, third and fourth objectives were modified from Legge's 1930 *Constitution of the Agricultural Service Foundation*. The first and fifth objectives promoted the ideas of the New York group, somewhat modifying what was originally a much stronger social and cultural focus. C.V. Gregory noted that the fifth objective "...made no mention of promoting cultural opportunities in art, literature, music, etc." Elliott responded, "I just had a little hesitation about putting art in as a named object at this time; not that I am not for it in the beautification of highways, but when the farmer is wanting bread and you give him art, you are going to get a little satirical reaction..."[43]

After a sometimes tense meeting, the conferees traveled to Washington to meet at Legge's Federal Farm Board office. In attendance were Magnus Alexander, O.H. Bensen, W.C. Lassetter (representing Clarence Poe), Legge, Julian Mason, Mullen, Leland Olds, Rumsey and Dan Wallace. Lowden was absent due to other commitments.

A few days later, Wallace wrote Lowden: "Mr. Mullen and I expected quite a debate with Mrs. Rumsey on the question of devoting the work of the Foundation entirely to rural affairs. We also expected some protest because of the strong emphasis placed upon the economic rather than the social aspects of the rural problem. To our surprise, both Mrs. Rumsey and the others present agreed enthusiastically with all the conclusions reached at our meeting of last Sunday [Chicago]. After all of the meetings that have been held and the discussions back and forth, the New York group have apparently changed their viewpoint to a marked degree. At the Washington meeting practically all of our discussion was based on our report of the Chicago meeting. The report was accepted and approved unanimously."[44] Wallace also stated that Legge, Alexander, and Henry Robinson were "all thoroughly sold on the idea of a Foundation...All in all, it would appear that the Foundation which we have discussed so frequently bids fair to become an actuality within the next two months."[45]

Wallace also confided his concerns:

"There are one or two things about the procedure of this week that give me some concern. I realize fully the importance of the economic slant to the farm problem, but I do feel that we should not in any way neglect the social and educational work which the Foundation might undertake. It seems to me that the biggest work of the Foundation is to sell the idea of a new social order to the American people: the idea of complete organization coupled with abundant cultural opportunities in rural districts. In selling this idea the Foundation would have two splendid avenues of approach, through the farm press and the radio. I was rather disturbed in the discussions of this week which centered largely around research and economic investigations. The discussion centered around these themes probably because both Mr. Alexander and Mr. Legge have been so absorbed in these very questions during recent years. This is quite proper, but I sincerely hope that the social and educational problems will not be neglected."[46]

On April 25, 1931, the executive and legal committees met. Judge Richard Campbell, William Donovan and William Elliott completed *A Constituent Agreement Creating The American Farm Foundation*,[47] which, along with a revised prospectus, was to be distributed to prospective donors. Some members apparently thought the organizers' work was done. Elliott thought otherwise:

"As I see it, this Executive Committee cannot be discharged and the biggest job that we have is between the signing of the Trust Agreement and this time. There isn't anywhere near the amount of money in sight today which the Foundation ought to have when it is organized. It will be a flop if it comes out with all of these tremendous purposes, what it thinks it can do with the farmers, and there is just a little bit of money in sight.

"It seems to me that we have gotten through only the first stages when we agree that there ought to be a Foundation, and when we agree on its purpose and organization. The big job now is ahead for this committee. They should take hold of the prospectus in a persuasive way for the one purpose of getting money."[48]

The organizers began working to secure other donors. In May 1931, Rumsey wrote: "Now is the time when every one must make the greatest effort to secure more Founders and more members of prominence for the Organization Committee. It was suggested that each member of the organization group should approach prospective donors armed with the Prospectus and Trust Agreement."[49] This effort, though, generated little success.

The slow progress clearly irked Legge. He wrote Lowden on July 24, 1931: "I assume that you have at last received from Mrs. Rumsey the revised edition of the prospectus on the American Farm Foundation. Just why Mr. Mason should have spent four months in the revising of this dope is hard for me to understand, but anyhow that is what has happened. We are now in position to go ahead with the organization and the soliciting of support."[50] Lowden replied: "...this is the most difficult time I have ever seen for approaching men for subscriptions. I would not know myself to whom to go under the circumstances...Of course, personally I shall make a small subscription to the Foundation—just how small I have not yet determined. The most important part of my correspondence these days is receiving notices of reduced or omitted dividends or defaulted interest, and I fear the worst is yet to come. And so I prefer waiting a little while before deciding upon just what I can do."[51]

Having resigned from the Federal Farm Board, Legge's time was once again occupied by International Harvester. With business conditions deteriorating, it was a terrible time to solicit financial support. The near futility was echoed by Magnus Alexander in a letter to Dan Wallace in December 1931: "As you may recall, I had some misgivings that so big a project as is planned by your group could be put under way quickly, when some of those who are to take a leading part are so tremendously occupied with their own business problems, created or intensified by the prevailing economic depression."[52]

Legge took personal action to move the project along. On October 12, 1931, he created a trust containing securities and cash valued at more than $400,000 with himself, Addis E. McKinstry, George A. Ranney, William M. Gale and William Elliott as trustees. The trust agreement provided for the transfer of the trust fund to a foundation to be created for the general welfare of the rural population of the United States. Legge also prepared his will to include a $500,000 bequest to the foundation at his death.

The optimism the founders felt in February 1931—that the project was near completion—had long passed. As 1932 waned, little progress had been made, and economic conditions were worse than the 1920-21 depression. Yet, conditions in agriculture would get even worse before they got better.

Chapter 3

Creating Farm Foundation

"We have perused the printed trust agreement, but the five objectives therein named are necessarily so general in scope that there is little clue to the plan which the founders have in mind. For example, is it at all likely that the Foundation will set up anything in the way of a new or independent program of work or is it more likely that it will make possible by financial support the undertaking of additional projects by existing agencies, such as the Agricultural Extension Service, Farm Bureau, 4-H Club movement, etc."[1]
—C.E. Woodward, *Northwest Farm Equipment Journal*, 1934

As 1932 drew to a close, Farm Foundation was in no greater financial position than it had been when it was founded in 1930. Instead of providing greater resources, the New York group's activities had been a three-year detour with no obvious accomplishment. The no-nonsense, pragmatic Legge must have been skeptical of the group's notions of "rural civilization." His social awkwardness and practicality made him much more comfortable with farmers and businessmen than with New York socialites and Irish mystics.

By the end of 1932, Legge believed it was time to formally organize the Foundation. He wrote Lowden on December 22, 1932, "I think the situation has cleared sufficiently so that we should be getting a start on that Agricultural Foundation matter."[2] William Elliott and Dan Wallace then contacted prominent citizens soliciting their support and inviting them to join in incorporating the Foundation. Although general economic conditions had improved, Wallace noted in his invitation to George MacDonald: "Mr. Legge feels that we should go ahead with a formal incorporation of the Foundation at this time, even though it may be necessary to proceed in a modest way, rather than along the ambitious lines we first contemplated. Accordingly, he has secured the promise of a comparatively small group of gentlemen who will be asked to take definite action at this time, if, in their opinion, such action appears to be desirable."[3] To C.C. Webber he said, "...the original funds turned over to the Foundation are more limited than were first proposed."[4]

Wallace also stressed the urgency of launching the foundation in "...a time when the entire nation is in a state of bewilderment over the puzzling problems of our times."[5] He told Frank E. Mullen of NBC: "Confidentially, some of the most important business men of the country are very much concerned at this time about the social unrest in the country. They have a right to be concerned, and they want to do something about it. I think we can show them one way to do some good."[6]

Executing the Trust Agreement. A February 10, 1933, meeting was called "... to bring together a number of persons who have indicated a willingness to be contributors and others considered as trustees, with the idea of agreeing on a final organization and executing a trust agreement which will create the Foundation."[7] Attending were: Ralph Budd, Chicago; William S. Elliott, Chicago; Clifford B. Gregory, Chicago; Alexander Legge, Chicago; Frank O. Lowden, Oregon, Illinois; Cyrus H. McCormick, Chicago; George MacDonald, New York; Frank E. Mullen, Chicago; Henry M. Robinson, Los Angeles; Arch W. Shaw, Chicago; John Stuart, Chicago; Charles C. Teague, Los Angeles; Melvin A. Traylor, Chicago; and Dan A. Wallace, St. Paul.

Those invited, but unable to attend included: Bernard Baruch, New York; Burridge Butler, Chicago; Edward N. Hurley, Chicago; Harold McCormick, Chicago; Charles Nagel, St. Louis; Arthur R. Rogers, St. Paul; Mary Harriman Rumsey, New York; Charles C. Webber, St. Paul; Robert E. Wood, Chicago; and Owen D. Young, New York.[8]

At this meeting, the founders appointed an organization committee consisting of Lowden, Wood, Stuart, Wallace and Legge. The organization committee had three tasks:

1. Complete the membership of the 21-person Board of Trustees.
2. Designate terms of office of all members of the Board.
3. Call the initial meeting of the Board.

The organization committee selected Lowden as chairman of the Board. Of those present at the meeting, "at large" positions were allocated to Gregory, Legge, MacDonald and Stuart. Lowden and Teague were appointed as "farmer members." Robert Wood was appointed "merchant member," Traylor as "finance member," Budd as "transportation member," Wallace as "farm press member," and Mullen as "radio member." Baruch, Clarence Poe and Rumsey were assigned the three remaining "at large" positions. Young was selected as a "manufacturer" member in absentia. Only Legge, Lowden, MacDonald, Mullen, Poe, Rumsey and Wallace had been involved in any prior meetings. Both Poe and Rumsey were absent.

Over the next four months, the committee completed the Board with three additional farmer members—Roy Johnson of Casselton, North Dakota, W.E.

Riegel of Tolono, Illinois, and R.E. Lambert of Darlington, Alabama—and three university members—Chris L. Christensen of the University of Wisconsin, A.R. Mann of Cornell University, and F.D. Farrell of Kansas State College of Agriculture.[9]

The committee also fixed and assigned terms of office for all 21 Trustees:

- Serving until the annual meeting of the Board in 1934: Bernard Baruch, John Stuart, Charles Teague, W.E. Riegel and Robert Wood.
- Serving until the annual meeting of the Board in 1935: Alexander Legge, Frank Lowden, Roy Johnson and Dan Wallace.
- Serving until the annual meeting of the Board in 1936: George MacDonald, Clifford Gregory, R.E. Lambert and F.D. Farrell.
- With terms until the annual meeting of the Board in 1937 were: Melvin Traylor, Owen Young, Frank Mullen and Chris Christensen.
- Serving until the annual meeting of the Board in 1938 were: Clarence Poe, Mary Harriman Rumsey, Ralph Budd and A.R. Mann.

Specifics of the Trust Agreement. Article I of the Farm Foundation Trust Agreement states its objectives:

> "Recognizing the importance to the national welfare of improving and at all times maintaining healthy and satisfying conditions of life for the farming and rural population of the country with adequate economic returns and social, educational and cultural advantages, a continuing foundation, to be known as the FARM FOUNDATION, is hereby created. The purpose of the Foundation is to administer all funds and property now or hereafter contributed by the Founders or others and to use and devote the same and the income thereof to the general welfare of the rural population of the United States of America in such ways as the Board of Trustees may from time to time determine. As an amplification of said purposes and without in any way limiting the same or the discretion of the Board of Trustees, it is contemplated that said funds may be expended,
>
> 1. To encourage and develop co-operative effort and community organization and consciousness as means for improving the economic, social, educational and cultural conditions of rural life.
> 2. To stimulate and conduct research and experimental work for the study of any economic, social, educational or scientific problem of importance to any substantial portion of the rural population of the country, including problems of production, marketing and purchasing, and the sound coordination of the

agricultural with the industrial, financial and mercantile life of the country.

3. To encourage, aid or finance any university, institution, corporation or persons in the conduct of any such research or experimental work.

4. To disseminate educational and useful information developed as a result of any such study, research and experimentation, or otherwise, in such manner as to be of practical value to the farming population.

5. To promote and enlarge the intellectual and cultural interests and opportunities of the rural population through community action."[10]

The Trust Agreement called for a Board of Trustees of not fewer than 21 members, which would designate a trust company to manage all funds and securities. The First National Bank of Chicago was chosen as Corporate Trustee. The agreement also stated:

"For the purpose of insuring sound and effective management based upon broad information and consideration of all viewpoints, seven of the said Trustees shall be chosen at large and fourteen shall be chosen on account of their special experience in different fields of activity and as representing the viewpoints of persons engaged in such fields respectively, as follows: Five members experienced in and representing farming, one member experienced in and representing finance, one member experienced in and representing manufacture, one member experienced in and representing merchandising, one member experienced in and representing transportation, one member experienced in and representing the farm press, one member experienced in and representing radio as a means of education. Three members from the executive, teaching, experimental or extension staffs of three Land Grant universities or state universities maintaining agricultural departments."[11]

The remainder of the Trust Agreement dealt with election of Trustees, meetings, approval and supervision of investments, expenditures and accounts. It authorized the Board to elect not more than seven additional Trustees, and to accept additional contributions either for general or specific purposes within or consistent with the general objectives of the Foundation. Foundation projects were to be financed out of income; after February 10, 1938, and with a vote of three-fourths of the Board, a portion of the principal funds not exceeding five percent in any one year was to be used.

Reactions. The establishment of Farm Foundation was kept a near secret. "No announcement of the Farm Foundation was made at the time that it was formed in February 1933. It was Mr. Legge's idea that the first and most important task was to bring together a substantial sum of money. He talked about a sum between five and ten million dollars."[12]

Most of the New York group offered only lukewarm support. Only George MacDonald had been present at the founders' meeting. However, Mary Harriman Rumsey, who had been absent due to her son's illness, wrote Wallace: "Since writing this I talked with Mr. Legge. I am more enthusiastic than ever. He said the 'objects' drawn up in New York were adhered to. I am so glad."[13] Wallace replied: "In looking over the Trust Agreement you will note that all of our original ideas are included. The Board of Trustees is given authority to undertake almost any useful service to agriculture. This service will be directed at the social as well as the economic problems of agriculture."[14] It was hoped Rumsey's enthusiasm would bring in additional donations.

George MacDonald was another key fundraising target. Legge instructed Wallace: "With business breaking as hard as it is, it is going to be tough sledding for us to get financial support. I am satisfied that [MacDonald] is one of the subscribers that can come across with something worthwhile and I am wondering what his reaction was when you saw him. Please do all you can to follow this up, and also others who should come along and help in the movement. Where financial conditions are such that they cannot see their way clear to subscribe very heavily at present try to get them to come along for a small amount. It is always possible for them to increase their subscription later when they feel better able to do so."[15]

Any momentum the founders may have had was quickly overwhelmed by events. Farm Foundation's establishment coincided with one of the most trying economic periods in U.S. history. When President Roosevelt assumed office in March 1933 "a quarter of the nation's work force was jobless. A quarter million families had defaulted on their mortgages the previous year. During the winter of 1932 and 1933, 1.2 million Americans were homeless. About 9,000 banks, holding the savings of 27 million families, had failed since 1929—1,456 in 1932 alone. Farm foreclosures were averaging 20,000 a month."[16]

Roosevelt called for a "New Deal." For the wealthy, it meant an unprecedented and massive redistribution of wealth. Clearly, if Depression conditions had not already deterred potential Farm Foundation donors, Roosevelt's plans did. Fifteen major bills were drafted to address economic and social conditions. The Agricultural Adjustment Act (AAA) of 1933 was signed on May 12 to help agriculture cope with the economic and social strain it faced as part of the overall economic crisis. Against this backdrop, the founders set the first meeting of the Farm Foundation Board of Trustees for July 21.

First Board of Trustees Meeting. Farm Foundation's first Board of Trustees meeting took place at the Palmer House Hotel in Chicago. The Board accomplished three objectives: selected a chairman (Frank Lowden) and secretary

(William Elliott); completed the Board membership and set terms of office; and approved bylaws. The bylaws included a provision for the hiring of a managing director. The meeting concluded with an informal discussion on the direction of Farm Foundation.

Death of Alexander Legge. Legge spent the morning of Saturday, December 2, 1933, at his office in the International Harvester Building in downtown Chicago. As part of Roosevelt's New Deal, businesses were being organized under the National Recovery Administration (NRA) fair trade codes drawn up by trade associations and industries. Legge was working on the codes for the agricultural machinery industry.

Legge was visited that morning by his friend, Arch Shaw, and Shaw's son. They expected to spend only a few minutes with Legge. Shaw recounted: "He said he was tired, and lay back in his big chair and put his feet on the table. He kept talking about the NRA and how much he had to do and how tired he was. No matter what the momentary subject of conversation was, it always wound up with the NRA and the codes, as though the pressure of that problem rested heavily on him. We were there an hour and a half, and had to be rather insistent when we left. It seemed as though he didn't want us to leave—as though he wanted someone there with him."[17]

That evening, Legge drove out to his Hinsdale, Illinois, home. The next morning, he visited his farm. He started setting out some lilacs in the garden. At ten o'clock he felt so ill he asked his close friend and the company's chief medical officer, Dr. James A. Britton, to come out at once. His symptoms rapidly grew more alarming and he was taken to his home in Hinsdale and a neighborhood doctor was called. At 11:15 a.m., before either of the physicians had arrived, Alex Legge died at age 67. His cause of death was a blood clot near the heart.[18]

In this will, Alexander Legge left Farm Foundation $500,000, making his total contribution more than $900,000. In terms of financial support and effort, most of the credit for establishing Farm Foundation must go to Legge. As founding Board member Chris Christensen noted, "While several people worked closely with Mr. Legge in this development, it was Mr. Legge's persistence, vision and desire to bring about the Farm Foundation which led to its final creation."[19]

With the abrupt passing of Legge, the full reigns of leadership of the Foundation passed to Frank Lowden, who remarked: "I do not know when I have been so shocked as I was when I heard of Mr. Legge's death. I had luncheon with him only the Wednesday before and of course, we talked of nothing but the Foundation. That was nearer his heart than anything else."[20] Lowden now began efforts to publicize the Foundation. A press release was issued on December 6, 1933, describing the formation of the Foundation and the ultimate intention of securing additional donors. News of the new Foundation was reported widely. Coming at the height of the Great Depression, the publicity generated scores of requests for assistance from individuals and organizations across the country. Lowden's standard reply was:

"It was Mr. Legge's intention, if he had lived, to attempt to secure other substantial contributions to the Foundation before any definite program was adopted. He felt that there were other people of wealth in the country who could be interested in this project. Those of us who are charged with the responsibility of carrying on the work of the Foundation are of the opinion that our first duty is to attempt to do what he would have done if he had lived; namely interest others in contributing to the endowment of the Foundation. Indeed, until we know in a general way the probable income of the Foundation, it will be impossible to form a program intelligently. For whatever program is adopted must, of course, depend upon the income of the Foundation. Therefore, in accordance with what we believe would have been Mr. Legge's wishes, we shall postpone the consideration of a program until we know what our probable income will be."[21]

Many others assumed the Foundation would create jobs and hire staff. Chris Christensen reported: "I am having a great number of inquiries both through mail and personal call from individuals interested in securing employment with the Farm Foundation. In each case, I am telling them that their inquiries are premature as the newly created Farm Foundation has not as yet been placed on an operational basis."[22]

Farm Foundation's executive committee met on April 27, 1934. In attendance were Frank Lowden, Ralph Budd and Chris Christensen. Also present were Trustees John Stuart, Robert Wood, Frank Mullen and C.V. Gregory. In this time of uncertainty, the committee reached four decisions:

"1. That it as not advisable at this time to determine upon any immediate field of work;
2. That, consequently, the type of Director needed could not be well determined at this time and the selection of a permanent Director should be postponed;
3. That a substantial increase in the endowment would be necessary if the Foundation is to become an effective force, and that such increase should be possible if the matter were properly presented to other possible contributors; that is, persons of means interested in the improvement of farm life;"
4. That Charles L. Burlingham, favorably known to a number of the Trustees, should be employed for a period of two months to assist in presenting the Foundation project to prospective donors."[23]

Charles Burlingham was hired for two months at a salary of $500 a month.

Second Meeting of the Board. The second meeting of Farm Foundation's Board of Trustees was June 22, 1934, at the Chicago Club. The minutes note the value of the trust at $635,000, including the market value of the portfolio and cash on hand. In honor of Alexander Legge, the Board adopted the following resolution:

"At this meeting of the Board of Trustees of the Farm Foundation, being the first session held since the death on December 3, 1933, of Mr. Alexander Legge, we desire to record our reverent tribute of respect to the memory of this good and great man who meant so much to the Farm Foundation, and to whom the Foundation meant still more. In advancing the idea and need of a Farm Foundation, Mr. Legge was a leader and his generous personal contributions to the endowment have made a reality the first permanent and privately endowed institution for improving the conditions of farm and rural life in America. It was intended by him to be the practical and broadly useful expression not only of his own life-long sympathetic interest in the welfare of our farmers, but of the sympathies and desires of others who shared his views regarding all those who till the soil.

"The sudden death of Mr. Legge soon after the establishment of the Farm Foundation leaves to us as his fellow Trustees an added responsibility toward this undertaking. It will be our task and our best tribute to our friend and fellow worker to build for the Foundation over a period of years a record of real service and accomplishment."[24]

The Board also passed a resolution noting the death of Melvin Traylor on February 14, 1934. To fill the two vacancies, Bernard Baruch (whose term had expired at this meeting) was re-elected to fill Legge's term, and Arch Shaw was elected to fill Traylor's.

Charles Burlingham gave a report about canvassing business leaders in Chicago and Detroit who were, without exception, interested in Farm

---

Charles L. Burlingham
Farm Foundation Assistant Secretary, 1934

Farm Foundation's first employee, Charles L. Burlingham, received an undergraduate degree from Iowa State College and a master's degree in dairying from the University of Missouri. He came to Farm Foundation after a career with USDA, the dairy industry and publishing organizations.

Foundation, willing to contribute, but also "desirous of delaying contributions." They "want to know what work is to be undertaken before they consider making funds available."[25]

Since his research indicated that defining a program of work was necessary for soliciting funds, Burlingham identified five programming areas of general interest to those surveyed: land utilization, investigating market structure in agriculture, cooperative marketing in agriculture, coordinating agricultural research, and supporting the betterment of rural life. He recommended the Foundation begin work right away to "preserve the enthusiasm and inspiration" which had brought it into being. "The Foundation's first work might be to study what is now being done, whether present activities can be coordinated to advantage, what new work may wisely be undertaken and what forces can be brought together in giving Agriculture the best use of the present available equipment and personnel."[26] He suggested organizing a two-day conference of leaders from USDA, colleges and universities, state departments of agriculture and producer organizations to assist in developing a plan of action. Burlingham also proposed Farm Foundation study land tenure and sponsor country life clubs and community cooperatives. The Board minutes noted:

> "It was generally agreed that it was inadvisable at this time to direct any special efforts towards increasing the Foundation endowment and that presentation of the matter to individuals or companies who might be expected to be sympathetic could better be postponed until financial conditions become more certain. The view was also expressed by a number of Trustees that it would be easier to obtain support from time to time after the Foundation had entered upon or carried through some definite projects. It was recognized, however, that if the Foundation is to fill the place envisioned by its Founders, it will have to build up its endowment over a period of years, increasing its funds as it broadens its work; and while no endowment campaign is now undertaken, it was understood that this did not preclude any Trustee from presenting the Foundation project to any prospective donor if and when the opportunity may seem favorable.
>
> "It was the prevailing opinion that the Foundation would not be justified at this time in employing a permanent Director or setting up an office and organization to carry on any work, first, because of the present limited income and, second, because it was not clear at the present time in what field the Foundation could best employ its resources. It was pointed out by several Trustees that the Foundation was a permanent institution, that it was not so important that it spend its income at once as that it proceed on a course which would lead to the greatest usefulness over a period of years, and that in view of the greatly

expanded activities of the Federal Government and present <u>economic conditions</u>, it was not clear what would be the most appropriate and useful field for the Foundation activities."[27]

The Board passed two resolutions. The first was to sponsor a series of educational NBC radio broadcasts on conservation. The second directed Chris Christensen and the executive committee to study the matter of Foundation activities.

Misgivings and Economic Necessity. For a variety of reasons, some early proponents of the Farm Foundation concept were less supportive after its formation. For instance, "Although Mrs. Ramsey consented to be a trustee, her enthusiasm waned after the Washington meeting [February 16, 1931]. During the few remaining years of her life she never again prominently associated herself with the project."[28] She died in an equestrian accident December 19, 1934.

George MacDonald, the only other member of the New York group to serve as a Trustee, attended only the organizational meeting and three of five Board meetings during his term. Although Rumsey and MacDonald had jointly pledged $60,000 to the project in 1930, Dan Wallace learned later from Farm Foundation Managing Director Henry C. Taylor "...that there is no record of funds turned over by the New York group to the Foundation. At least the Trust Company so reports. On that point, I could not be informed just as I do not know how much cash was turned in by the other Founders. I do know that most of the endowment fund came from Mr. Legge and the McCormicks. I also know that Mrs. Rumsey and Mr. MacDonald were apparently quite willing to turn over considerable funds to the cause if they approved of the final set-up and the conduct of the Foundation."[29]

Some of the first Board members were too involved in their own affairs to give much attention to the Foundation. Taylor later said: "Of the first Board, there were four who did not serve. They simply allowed Legge to use their names in starting. [Charles C.] Teague was nasty about it. [He] was in the East and left Chicago for California the day before the meeting then knocked what others did. I would ignore him. As for [Bernard] Baruch and Owen D. Young, they simply never participated in any activity."[30] Others were discouraged by the economic conditions of the time. Chris Christensen noted in 1935: "The uncertainties which have surrounded the economic situation in the United States the past two years of course have not been favorable for the securing of contributions, and consequently we have made little progress in this direction, although there [are] a number of good prospects."[31]

The change in Cyrus McCormick's support is a striking illustration. In July, 1931, his secretary, F.A. Steuert, wrote: "...Cyrus McCormick told me that he had an idea of giving $100,000 to Mr. Legge's foundation and he hoped that his brother Harold and Mrs. Blaine would do the same; that he would like to consider the advisability of giving Harvester Preferred stock—that Mr. Legge thinks that would be the best security they could give and it would be better than cash."[32] In April, 1933, Steuert wrote: "In talking with Mr. Judson F. Stone over the telephone this morning in regard to Mr. Legge's 'Farm Foundation,' he expressed a desire to talk with Mr. McCormick before he committed himself on the question of his contribution toward the endowment. Mr. Stone is thinking about common instead of preferred stock."[33] Cyrus and Harold McCormick each transferred 1,000 shares of Harvester common stock to Farm Foundation on May 5, 1933. In the end, the book value of Cyrus McCormick's donation was $13,782.53,[34] but as a reflection of prevailing economic conditions, it was one of the few substantial early donations Farm Foundation would receive beyond the Legge bequest.

After seven years of effort, despite the loss of its principal founder and the advent of the Great Depression, Farm Foundation was organized and preparing to initiate projects and programs "...devoted to the general welfare of the farming population of the United States and improvement of the conditions of rural life."[45] The difficult question remained. What type of programming should it be?

*   *   *   *

Farm Foundation's First Board Members. Many of Farm Foundation's first Trustees were notable captains of industry, philanthropists and luminaries. Besides Legge, Lowden, Rumsey and Wallace, the roster included:

- **Bernard M. Baruch,** a self-made millionaire and legendary stock trader, was an economic advisor to American Presidents for 20 years. He was a member of the Board from 1933 to 1938.
- **Ralph Budd,** as president of the Great Northern Railroad until 1932, oversaw many epic construction projects in the Northwest, including the 7.79-mile Cascade tunnel. In 1934, as president of the Burlington Railroad, he developed the famed "Zephyr," with a top speed of 112.5 miles per hour. He is considered a pioneer in the development of the diesel-electric locomotive. He served on Farm Foundation's Board from 1933 to 1949, and as chairman from 1947 to 1949.
- **Chris L. Christensen** was the executive secretary to the Federal Farm Board under Legge. He served as dean of the College of Agriculture at the University of Wisconsin from 1931 to 1944, and also as director of the university's agricultural experiment station and its state extension service. He left the university for a career with the Celotex Corporation. Christensen served on the Board from 1933 to 1964, as chairman of the executive committee from 1944 to 1953, and as chairman of the Board in 1944.
- **F.D. (Dave) Farrell** was president of Kansas State University from 1925 to 1943, and a member of the faculty until his retirement in 1953. "In those

pre-World War II days, Kansas State was admired as one of the half dozen most distinguished of this remarkable breed of learning centers and its presiding officer, Dr. Farrell, was hailed as a recognized national leader of the [Land Grant] system."[35] He served Farm Foundation's Board from 1933 to 1954.

- **Clifford V. Gregory** was the longtime editor of *Prairie Farmer*, the leading farm publication in Illinois and Indiana. He initiated the Prairie Farmer Protective Union and the Master Farmer Program in 1925, the nation's oldest award program for farmers. Gregory served on Farm Foundation's Board from 1933 to 1941.

- **Roy Johnson** was the farmer member representing the Northwest. A former county agent, he was once Speaker of the North Dakota House of Representatives and a candidate for lieutenant governor.[36] Johnson served on the North Dakota Board of Higher Education for sixteen years. He received the Master Farmer award from the Association of Standard Farm Papers in 1927. Johnson served on Farm Foundation's Board from 1933 to 1940 and from 1949 to 1959.

- **Robert E. Lambert** of Darlington, Alabama, was the farmer Trustee representing the South. His business, R.E. Lambert & Sons, grew seed, bred livestock and did general farming. He was awarded the Master Farmer award by Alabama Polytechnic Institute (Auburn University) in 1927. He was a member of Farm Foundation's Board from 1933 to 1941.

- **George MacDonald** was a New York construction and utilities magnate "...instrumental in developing the public utilities of Long Island, becoming a pioneer in the introduction of gas. He organized the Nassau & Suffolk Lighting Company, the Long Beach Gas Company and the Public Service Corporation of Long Island ..."[37] He served on the boards of many banks, corporations, charitable and religious organizations, and was a member of Farm Foundation's Board from 1933 to 1941.

- **Albert R. Mann's** career at Cornell University included positions as assistant professor of dairy industry, secretary-editor-registrar, professor of rural social organization, and director of the experiment station. He served as dean of the College of Agriculture from 1916 to 1931, dean of the College of Human Ecology from 1925 to 1931, and as Cornell's first provost from 1932 to 1937. "The Albert R. Mann Library is now internationally renowned for its collections, its preservation program, and its information technology developments."[38] He served on Farm Foundation's Board from 1933 to 1947.

- **Frank E. Mullen** was a pioneering farm broadcaster. He started the "National Farm and Home Hour" and later served as NBC's vice president and general manager. He served on the Board from 1933 to 1942.

- **Clarence Poe** was a North Carolina editor and publisher of *The Progressive Farmer*. He started as an editorial helper and within two years was made editor. Three years later, he purchased the magazine, which had 1.4 million subscribers. Poe received numerous awards and honors for his service to North Carolina and the South. He was a member of the Farm Foundation Board from 1933 to 1943.

- **William E. Riegel** of Tolono, Illinois, was the farmer member representing the Corn Belt. He managed the A.P. Meharry Farm in Champaign County. Meharry and Reigel were pioneers of the U.S. soybean industry. Riegel served on Farm Foundation's Board from 1933 to 1943.

- **Arch W. Shaw** was the founder of Shaw-Walker Business Machines. He is credited with designing the modern filing cabinet and using basic concepts of standardization and elimination of waste to increase efficiency in business and industry. He started the magazine which became *Business Week* and was instrumental in founding the Harvard Graduate School of Business. Shaw served on the Board from 1934 to 1944.

- **John Stuart** became president of Quaker Oats in 1922. "By the time he ascended to the board chairmanship in 1942, he had taken the company into such collateral lines as pet foods, chemicals, and ready-mixed pancake flours...the company would climb to a gross of $277 million on 200 different products by 1956, when he retired as chairman and chief executive officer."[39] He served on Farm Foundation's Board from 1933 to 1954, and as chairman from 1949 to 1954.

- **Charles C. Teague** was a Santa Paula, California, fruit grower and businessman. He was president of the Limoneira Company from 1917 to 1947, and president of Teague-Kevett Company from 1908 to his death in 1950. He was chairman of Sunkist and founded many organizations including Diamond Walnut. Teague was a member of Farm Foundation's Board from 1933 to 1938.

- **Melvin A. Traylor** became president of the First Union Trust and Savings Bank in 1928; by 1931, this was Chicago's largest bank. He received serious consideration as a Democratic presidential candidate in 1932. He was a member of the Board of Trustees from 1933 until his death in 1934.

- **Robert E. Wood** served as the Army's quartermaster general during World War I. He was president of Sears from 1929 to 1939 and its chairman from 1939 to 1954. "Almost single-handedly, Robert E. Wood transformed the way Americans did their shopping and built Sears Roebuck into a merchandising giant. In the early 1930s, Wood's innovations made Sears the leading catalog mail order supplier for American homes."[40] He was a member of the Board of Trustees from 1933 to 1954.

- **Owen D. Young** was a New York lawyer, businessman and public official. In 1919, he organized and chaired the board of the Radio Corporation of America (RCA) and helped establish America's commercial lead in the burgeoning radio technology. He became chairman of the board of General

Electric in 1922 and helped found the National Broadcasting Company (NBC) in the mid 1920s. Forced by the federal courts to choose between GE or RCA, he chose GE (1933). Teamed with Gerald Swope as president, he directed GE in making progress in public and labor relations while focusing on manufacturing electrical equipment, particularly consumer goods.[41] As a diplomat, he worked on reparations issues with Germany in the 1920s. He was voted *Time* magazine's "Man of the Year" for 1929. Young was a member of Farm Foundation's Board from 1933 to 1937.

*　　*　　*　　*

Farm Foundation's Sponsors. In a 1945 history of Farm Foundation,[42] the following individuals were identified, along with William Elliott and Arch Shaw, as taking part in the formation of Farm Foundation, either as members of the organizing group or through financial support:

- **William L. Clayton** served for many years as president of Anderson, Clayton and Company, a Texas-based cotton trading company. He was the first U.S. Under Secretary of State for Economic Affairs, during the Franklin D. Roosevelt administration. In 1963, when Clayton was in his eighties, President Kennedy asked him to work on the national export expansion program and nuclear test ban treaty.[43]
- **Paul A. Draper** of Canton, Massachusetts, was a partner in Draper Brothers Company, a textile mill, and owned half interest in the Stockton Wool Company. He was a member of the Alexander Legge Memorial Committee.
- **Arthur M. Hyde** served as governor of Missouri, 1921-1925, and as Secretary of Agriculture under President Herbert Hoover, 1929-1933.
- **Cyrus H. McCormick, Jr.** was president of the McCormick Harvesting Machine Company after his father's death in 1884 until the 1902 merger forming International Harvester. He was president of Harvester until 1918, when his brother Harold assumed the position. He was chairman of the board of Harvester from 1918 to 1935.
- **Harold F. McCormick** helped to spearhead the 1902 merger with Deering Harvester Company; Warder, Bushnell, Glessner and Company; the Milwaukee Harvester Company; and the Plano Harvester Company to form the International Harvester Corporation. He served as the company's vice president until 1918, president from 1918 to 1922, chairman of the executive committee from 1922 to 1935, and finally chairman of the board of directors from 1935 until his death in 1941.[44]
- **Samuel R. McKelvie** was a long-time public servant in Nebraska who served two terms as governor from 1919 to 1923. After retiring from office, he published *The Nebraska Farmer*. McKelvie declined appointment as

Secretary of Agriculture in the Hoover administration, but later served on the Federal Farm Board. McKelvie was a Farm Foundation sponsor in 1933. He served as chairman of the Alexander Legge Memorial Committee and as a member of the Board of Trustees from 1941 to 1951.

- **Henry M. Robinson** was a California lawyer and financier. He served four U.S. Presidents in various boards and missions, but declined offers from President Wilson to be Secretary of the Interior and from Presidents Harding and Hoover to become Secretary of the Treasury. Besides law, his business interests included newspapers, banking and manufacturing.

Chapter 4

Hiring Henry C. Taylor

"Henry C. Taylor (1873-1969) was the dean of agricultural economists worldwide; probably no other person influenced the shape of the agricultural economics profession as much as he did."[1]
—Kenneth H. Parsons, professor emeritus, University of Wisconsin-Madison

In Farm Foundation's formative years, its leaders faced a dilemma. It was nearly impossible to find additional funding without a program and it was difficult to develop a program without additional funding. Since the Board believed additional funding was paramount for the long-term viability of the Foundation, they sought programming advice from a wide variety of sources. The challenge was compounded because staff would have to be hired to implement the program. This was a critical decision, with literally every discipline in the fields of agriculture and conservation under consideration. This decision would set the character of Farm Foundation to this day.

After the second Board meeting, Charles Burlingham issued three additional reports to Farm Foundation. In the first, he described 45 files he had developed concerning activities of institutions and individuals conducting agricultural work. He also sought the opinions of many prominent individuals for Farm Foundation activities:

- Secretary of Agriculture Henry A. Wallace recommended "promotion of community co-operatives with special consideration to the human aspects."[2]
- M.L. Wilson, assistant secretary of agriculture, and H.R. Tolley, USDA planning section chief, suggested "adoption of a land use program broad enough to cover the whole field but attacking one carefully defined project at a time."[3]
- William Meyer, governor of the Farm Credit Administration believed Farm Foundation should, "(1) conduct educational work on cooperation and (2) establish a uniform auditing and cost accounting system for cooperatives."[4]
- George Peek, special advisor to the President on foreign trade and Mary Harriman Rumsey, chairman of the Consumers' Advisory Board of the

National Recovery Administration, proposed Farm Foundation "foster the movements already under way in cooperative selling, cooperative buying, and cooperative credit unions."[5]

- C.W. Warburton, director of Extension Work, USDA, and his assistant, C.B. Smith, recommended Farm Foundation "set up an organization for rural youth from 15 to 25 years of age."[6]

Burlingham developed two additional reports to expand the recommendations. The first, on the cooperation recommendations, sought to expand beyond cooperative marketing of crops to "community cooperation" and "cooperative buying." Burlingham reported that Wallace, Peek and Rumsey suggested this area and the idea paralleled George Russell's "rural civilization."

The report noted that the Farm Credit Act of 1933 provided loans for cooperative buying, but the ramifications of this had not been adequately studied. Cooperative buying had been permitted in Illinois since 1927, and its advantages were discussed. "The largest success in farm living will be attained only when the commercial advantages gained through group effort are made the avenue by which better things, more needed even than increased income, are brought into farm homes," Burlingham wrote. "It is desired that the program shall be based on thoroughly practical, economic, cooperative enterprise but also that the goal sought is community consciousness that just as the greatest financial success is reached through joint effort, so are the finer relationships of community life gained by a pooling of resources."[7] The report suggested Farm Foundation assist the cooperative movement and help develop community cooperatives to "give to America a new richness of rural life."

Burlingham's second report advocated soil conservation as a program focus. "The Trustees of the Farm Foundation recognize that Land Use is the most fundamental piece of work in which the Foundation can direct its attention. A number of Trustees have already taken cognizance of this matter in their own work. Dean Chris L. Christensen has the most advanced state program which has been put underway. Frank Mullen has been actively at work on it, particularly the conservation features, and has made the Foundation sponsor for a well-organized series of radio presentations of the activities of various conservation agencies."[8] Burlingham proposed Farm Foundation coordinate and publicize the work already being done.

By the summer of 1934, 15 men had indicated interest in the post of director, including Charles Burlingham. Most candidates were university deans, department chairmen, or USDA bureau chiefs. Christensen and Lowden were not overly impressed with the candidates and began to investigate alternatives.

Prior to the third Board of Trustees meeting in June 1935, Edwin G. Nourse of the Brookings Institute and Aldo Leopold of the University of Wisconsin were approached to develop proposals for Farm Foundation activities. Nourse's report recommended Farm Foundation "...become a center of leadership and coordinated agency in helping rural America face the questions: (1) Just what conditions of living do we farmers have today? (2) What, precisely, are the standards of living which we cherish or conditions which we should like to see brought about for rural American life? (3) What are the impediments in social consciousness, economic institutions and practices, or legal structures which are keeping us from attaining these standards? (4) How can these impediments be removed or lessened?"[9] He suggested rural health, rural education, rural communications, and rural policing and safety regulations as program subject areas to be considered.

Leopold's report began: "It seems necessary to plant in the public mind a new concept of agriculture. The public must see the farmer not only as a food grower who competes with other industries for his share of the national income, but also as the custodian of a public interest, for the safekeeping of which he has given bond, and the public has signed as his surety. The public must realize that for every farm wrecked by destructive land use, a farmer is evicted and foisted upon industry, and a tax-payer accepts the obligation sooner or later to pay for the public purchase, repair or administration of the wreckage."[10] Leopold offered two possible projects, the first a study of conservation economics. He asked, "Is

---

Edwin G. Nourse and Aldo Leopold

The Farm Foundation Board could not have chosen better consultants than Edwin G. Nourse and Aldo Leopold.

Nourse was one of the country's first agricultural economists. In 1924, he joined the Institute for Economics in Washington, D.C., later to become the Brookings Institute. According to *Progressive Farmer*, "When the farm economy weakened in the 1920s, Nourse became a vocal proponent of co-ops, although he warned they would not 'make everyone prosperous all the time.' His analysis of farm economics was realistic and often flew in the face of conventional wisdom. He had little faith in the government's ability to solve farm problems, believing farmers needed to look toward exports."[20] Nourse later served as the first chairman of the Council of Economic Advisers from 1946 to 1949.

After nearly 20 years with the U.S. Forest Service, Aldo Leopold became a professor of game management in the agricultural economics department at the University of Wisconsin. *Progressive Farmer* reported: "Long before ecology was recognized as a discipline, Aldo Leopold became an ecologist. He also was a naturalist, a conservationist and a forester, a professor, a philosopher, and a writer."[21] A founder of the Wilderness Society, Leopold is best known for his collection of essays, *A Sand County Almanac*. The Leopold Center for Sustainable Agriculture at Iowa State University was named in his honor.

Nourse and Leopold were selected by *Progressive Farmer* as two of agriculture's most influential leaders of the 20th Century.

it cheaper for the public to prevent destructive land use than to cure it *ex post facto?*"[11] No work on this topic had been done at this point. Leopold's second proposal dealt with educating extension service personnel in conservation procedures.

William Elliott presented a third proposal, which had been offered by Guy Noble, national director of the 4-H Clubs. It called for Farm Foundation to sponsor a 4-H soil saving prize[12] in which club members would receive awards for the best conservation work done during the year. Alexander Legge had been very active with the 4-H movement and many of the Trustees believed that, until a course of work was decided on, this would be an appropriate vehicle for sponsorship.

Ultimately, the Nourse, Leopold and Noble proposals were deferred due to "...a rather unexpected decision to employ a permanent Director of the Foundation next November, and the feeling of the Board that it would be inappropriate to determine a program of activities in advance of consideration by the Director."[13] One candidate already held broad support:

> "There was a general agreement that if the Farm Foundation was to become an effective organization for the purposes for which created, it should have a full time director of capability and recognized standing. It was also agreed that the securing of a satisfactory director should properly precede the determination of the field or activities to which the Foundation could best devote its efforts. Governor Lowden and Dean Christensen spoke of Dr. Henry C. Taylor as a man well qualified for the position and this opinion was confirmed by a number of the other Trustees who knew Dr. Taylor. Governor Lowden and Dean Christensen were requested to take the matter up with Dr. Taylor and ascertain whether he would be interested, and the Executive Committee was authorized to close an arrangement for the appointment of Dr. Taylor as Director if it should develop that he was available upon a mutually agreeable basis. If Dr. Taylor should not be available, the Executive Committee was requested to consider other possibilities and make further suggestions."[14]

Career of Henry C. Taylor.[15] Henry Charles Taylor was born to a farming family in Van Buren County, Iowa, in 1873. He studied at Drake University in Des Moines, Iowa, for two years, then at Iowa State College, where he graduated in 1896. He entered graduate study at the University of Wisconsin with the goal of a career as a farmer and politician. However, he found the study of economics much more interesting than he expected and decided to become a professional economist.

Taylor studied for two years in Germany, Switzerland and Great Britain as part of his Ph.D. program, collecting data for his thesis on tenancy, *The Decline of Land Owning Farmers in England after 1815.* After receiving his Ph.D. in 1901, he joined the University of Wisconsin's economics faculty. In 1909, Taylor moved to the College of Agriculture and established the first Department of Agricultural Economics in the United States. He persuaded Benjamin Hibbard, a long-time friend, to leave Iowa State College where he was head of the Department of Economics, and become the second professor in the new department in 1913. The Wisconsin department flourished, attracting graduate students in substantial numbers and producing knowledge useful to farmers.

In 1919, Taylor accepted an offer to move to Washington, D.C., to develop agricultural economics within the USDA. The opportunity to consolidate USDA's scattered economics work into the Bureau of Agricultural Economics (BAE) appealed to him, even though it meant a considerable cut in salary. He reported directly to the Secretary of Agriculture. Under Taylor's leadership, BAE became a premier economic research and service organization, as well as the largest economic agency in the federal government and one of the most influential agencies in USDA. The new agency covered many areas of work that would be carried out in the future by such USDA agencies as the Economic Research Service, National Agricultural Statistics Service, Agricultural Cooperative Service, Foreign Agricultural Service and Agricultural Marketing Service.

Herbert Hoover was appointed Secretary of Commerce in 1921 and quickly proposed a program which set the stage for clashes between USDA and the Department of Commerce over which agency was to have primary responsibility for securing agricultural data and information worldwide. Secretary of Agriculture Henry C. Wallace supported Taylor's position that USDA should have the lead, and it became a contentious issue between Hoover and Wallace. When Wallace died unexpectedly in 1924, Taylor lost his staunchest supporter. Howard M. Gore, interim Secretary of Agriculture, did not involve himself in the controversy.

W.M. Jardine was appointed Secretary of Agriculture by President Coolidge in March 1925. One of the conditions of Jardine's appointment was that he replace Henry Taylor. Jardine offered to find Taylor a position in government of equal stature to the BAE and pleaded with him to resign. However, Taylor simply ignored the request and continued his work. Finally, while he was out of town, Taylor received a note from Secretary Jardine that his appointment was terminated as of August 15, 1925.

Embittered by his experiences in Washington, Taylor joined the Land Economics Research Institute at Northwestern University. He then accepted the directorship of a Country Life Commission for Vermont in 1927 and oversaw a comprehensive survey of rural Vermont from 1928 to 1931. He also served on a committee reviewing the work of missionaries on rural problems in Japan, Korea, China and India. In 1933, President Roosevelt appointed him United

States member of the Permanent Committee of the International Institute of Agriculture in Rome.

The Decision to Hire Taylor. On May 2, 1935, when Governor Lowden was in Germany, he telephoned Taylor in Rome about Farm Foundation's interest. In his response written two days later, Taylor expressed interest in the position: "I have read the statement of objectives of the Foundation and find myself in complete harmony with the objectives stated in the Trust agreement creating the Farm Foundation."[16]

After the Board approved Taylor's hiring, Christensen wrote Taylor: "... your selection as Director of the Farm Foundation received the *unanimous* approval of the Board of Trustees. Governor Lowden gave each member of the Trustees an opportunity to express himself personally before the vote was taken and those individual expressions were all heartily favorable and in the case of several men who knew you personally they were enthusiastic."[17]

Taylor accepted Farm Foundation's offer and returned to the United States. He met Lowden at the Pullman summer estate in Alexandria Bay, New York, where "Mrs. Lowden recorded that [Taylor] and her husband talked without letup for two days...They had known each other for several years, but this marathon conversation deepened their friendship and convinced Lowden of the wisdom of Farm Foundation's choice."[18]

Taylor became managing director effective November 1, 1935. An undated press release noted: "Governor Lowden, speaking for the Board, said 'We consider ourselves fortunate in securing the services of Dr. Taylor...Dr. Taylor seems exceptionally qualified to head this work as his whole life has been spent in activities for improving farm life and his accomplishments and influence have been widely recognized.'"[19]

The appointment of Taylor as managing director came after much study, discussion and debate over the program direction of Farm Foundation. The choice represented a decisive rejection of more narrow subject matter such as conservation, youth programs and cooperatives, in favor of a broader economics and policy-based agenda.

Chapter 5

The Taylor Years

"Farm Foundation's program is designed to improve conditions of country life and the general welfare of the rural population of the United States. Especial attention is being given to the tenure of farm land, the problems of rural youth, and to national policies affecting agriculture and rural people. The Foundation is not a research institution; it hopes to take a hand at the point where research leaves off and stimulate the appropriate action."[1]

—Henry C. Taylor, Managing Director, Farm Foundation, 1938

Henry C. Taylor was Farm Foundation's first managing director, serving from November 1, 1935 to September 30, 1945. This chapter is based extensively on a 1945 history, *The Farm Foundation: 1933-45.*[2]

Taylor faced enormous challenges in developing a plan of activities. The U.S. economy was only just beginning to recover from the October 29, 1929, stock market collapse. After contracting by more than 25 percent, U.S. gross domestic product would not equal the economic output of 1929 until 1936. Unemployment was above 20 percent from 1932 to 1935 and would not dip below 14 percent until World War II. For agriculture, compounding the economic conditions was a pervasive drought in the Great Plains, which lasted from 1931 to 1939. At its height, the Dust Bowl covered an area of 300 miles by 500 miles. Close to 100 million acres lost all or most of its topsoil. Thousands of farmers were forced from the land. Agriculture would not return to prosperity until World War II.

Taylor's first activities. Taylor's first task was to study the opportunities for service by Farm Foundation. He was asked to investigate the activities of other organizations with similar objectives and to bring the Board suggestions of activities Farm Foundation might undertake. His 12-page report to the Board on June 24, 1936,[3] identified four areas for the Foundation to devote attention:

- land ownership and tenancy;
- land utilization and conservation;
- cooperation in marketing and providing services; and

- national and international policies affecting agricultural production, marketing and income.

After hearing Taylor's report, the Board agreed that, while all of the areas identified by Taylor had merit, "The problem of better land tenure as a fundamental basis for improving rural life was selected as the objective to which the Foundation should give major attention."[4]

In 1937, Farm Foundation hired Dr. Howard J. Stover as Taylor's assistant and Robert Wilson as secretary. A temporary office was established on the third floor of the Harvester Building, 600 South Michigan Avenue, in Chicago. In his report to the Board of Trustees, Taylor related that he had spent the year studying the work being done by USDA, the various colleges of agriculture, and other foundations to determine which fields of action deserved the attention of Farm Foundation.[5]

In June 1938, Taylor's report to the Board indicated that "Farm Foundation is still housed in temporary quarters in the old Harvester Building at 600 South Michigan Avenue. Permanent quarters consisting of four rooms have been contracted for on the ninth floor of the same building, which will be ready for occupancy within a few weeks."[6]

Taylor then reported that during the last year, he had studied "government activities intended to stimulate land ownership, and the state and private undertakings looking toward the improvement of the relation between landlord and tenant"[7] and policies affecting rural welfare. Taylor described his participation in national committees studying rural education and rural youth. He recommended the Foundation initiate graduate fellowships at the University of Chicago for advanced study in agricultural economics. Additionally, he sug-

---

Farm Foundation and the University of Chicago

During the Henry Taylor years, Farm Foundation had a close association with the private University of Chicago at a time when most of Farm Foundation's other university partners were public institutions. The University of Chicago was familiar to Farm Foundation's founders. In the 1920s, Alexander Legge had approached the University of Chicago for assistance in setting up Farm Foundation. Frank Lowden served as a trustee of the University of Chicago and later chose the University of Chicago as the repository of his papers. Much of the surviving documentation on the founding of the Foundation is preserved in the University of Chicago Archives.

Robert M. Hutchins, the president of the University of Chicago at that time, was a reformer who "...articulated a vision of American democracy and higher education's place in it that emphasized a citizen's responsibility to be an informed participant in public affairs."[17] Farm Foundation's ideals corresponded with Hutchins' vision of increasing educational opportunities for average Americans.

gested the Foundation do "something to stimulate better medical facilities for rural people."[8]

Considerable time at the meeting was given to discussing the general policy of Farm Foundation. The Board and Taylor agreed that the Foundation could be most effective by encouraging coordination of the work of existing organizations and by stimulating them to initiate new lines of work. A general principle was adopted that projects should not be undertaken independently where other organizations could be effective and had reason to be involved. Farm Foundation would devote its resources primarily to supplementing the work of others endeavoring to improve the quality of life of rural people.

The problems in agriculture and rural America were being addressed by agencies of the United States Department of Agriculture. These agencies were conducting such undertakings as agricultural experimentation, extension education in agriculture and home economics, training in scientific and vocational agriculture and home economics, elementary and secondary teaching, and the public health services. USDA had vastly greater resources than those available to Farm Foundation.

The Board desired that Farm Foundation's work serve as yeast—stimulating thought which would result in action that would be self-supporting and self-multiplying. In working with other organizations, the methods to be used were group conferences to encourage regional cooperation on projects, offers of grants-in-aid for new activities, and assistance in organization and supervision of regional projects. The result of Taylor's recommendations was that land tenure, health and medical care of rural people, rural education, and national policies affecting agriculture were the first subjects to receive consideration.

Land Tenure. The first major project of Farm Foundation concerned land tenure issues. The focus was on the improvement of farm land tenure, including the various problems of rural land ownership, tenancy, credit, land valuation, soil conservation, and other land problems affecting the social and economic status of the farming population. As an illustration of the importance of this issue to Farm Foundation, Taylor told the Board of Trustees in 1936:

"Land tenure presents one of the most serious and long-standing problems in agriculture as well as one of very great interest today. While the South is at the present time the center of greater agitation on this subject, the problem is equally important in the North. In Iowa and Illinois the farmers' equity is less than 30 percent of the value of the farms. This is important from two points of view—from the point of view of improving living conditions in farm homes and in rural communities and from the standpoint of making the best use of the soil when the welfare of both the present and the future generations is considered. As a general rule, low living standards and soil depletion go hand in hand on tenant farms. It is when a given piece of land becomes the permanent abode of a family that the soil will be conserved and the family and community life will attain the highest culture. It would seem important, therefore, that Farm Foundation give especial attention to the problem of tenancy and land ownership. An analysis of tenancy in the United States shows that in the North tenancy was once looked upon as a stepping stone toward ownership. In the black belts of the South, tenancy, including the cropper system, has been a mode of farming substituted for the ante-bellum plantation system. Tenancy may have a proper place in an agricultural system, but too much tenancy and the wrong kinds of tenancy are bad. The proper place of tenancy, the forces which facilitate and the conditions which retard the acquisition of land ownership by farmers should be studied with a view to finding rational means of promoting land ownership."[9]

Taylor's recommendation was based on his nearly four decades of intense interest and research in land tenure problems and policies, beginning with the doctoral research he had done in England.

Land tenure concerns re-emerged as one of the unforeseen outcomes of the New Deal agriculture legislation. With the goals of reducing production and raising commodity prices, federal agricultural policies unintentionally led to the mass eviction of tenants and sharecroppers and accelerated structural change.

Another important factor in centering the interest of Farm Foundation on land tenure was Frank Lowden's will, under which certain farm property became available to the Foundation for use in improving the land tenure system (see Chapter 12). Taylor discussed the need for tenure research with economists from various parts of the United States, as well as with representatives of several insurance companies. He also interacted with economists from other countries at the International Conference of Agricultural Economists and the General Assembly of the International Institute of Agriculture at Rome.

After a preliminary study, Taylor decided to secure a specialist to work in this field. Dr. Joseph Ackerman from the University of Illinois was chosen for this position on February 11, 1939. His work resulted in the development of several cooperative undertakings.

Joseph Ackerman

Farm Foundation Land Tenure Specialist, 1939-1942; Farm Foundation
Associate Managing Director, 1942-1954; Farm Foundation Managing
Director, 1955-1969

Joseph A. Ackerman was born July 20, 1904, near Morton, Illinois. He attended the University of Illinois, where he received his bachelor of science degree in 1929, masters of science in 1930, and a Ph.D. in 1938. He attended Harvard in 1931-32 on a social science research fellowship in agricultural economics. Between 1930 and 1939, he worked as a professional farm manager in Decatur, Illinois, and did extension work in farm management at the University of Illinois. He joined the staff of Farm Foundation in 1939, becoming associate managing director in 1942 and managing director in 1955.

While at Farm Foundation, he served the American Farm Economic Association as vice president in 1949-50 and as president in 1954-55. As secretary-treasurer of the International Association of Agricultural Economists, 1955-1973, he played a key role in organizing and conducting its triennial conferences and helping to insure its continuing effectiveness. He provided leadership in revitalizing the American Country Life Association in the postwar years, serving as its president in 1947-1948. He served as national president of the Farm House Fraternity from 1948-1952. He was secretary-treasurer of The American Society of Farm Management and Rural Appraisers from 1939-1944. He participated actively in school affairs as a board member and officer at the local, state and national levels. He served as president of the National School Board Association from 1966-67. He was named a Fellow of the American Agricultural Economics Association in 1964.

His efforts in expanding leadership training opportunities for extension personnel and in strengthening extension work in agricultural economics led to recognition in 1959 by Epsilon Sigma Phi, national honorary extension fraternity, for outstanding service to extension. After retirement from Farm Foundation, he spent three years with the Ford Foundation in New Delhi, India. Joe Ackerman died May 3, 1976.

The first was the organization, in 1939, of the North Central Regional Land Tenure Committee, through which staff of agricultural colleges in the North Central states working on the subject of land tenure collectively planned and organized the work in their respective institutions. Farm managers, agricultural agents of insurance companies, landlords and tenants participated in the development of the program. The committee's objective was to develop cooperation with and between the state agricultural colleges to:

- Coordinate and develop their tenure research programs;
- Coordinate and develop educational programs to promote a fuller understanding of farm tenancy;
- Serve as a clearinghouse for research and extension activities relating to land tenure; and
- Organize conferences for the North Central States and subdivisions of the region.

The organization of the committee was informal during its first two years, after which it was decided the committee could be more effective if organized as an official agency of the experiment stations in the region. This organization was formally established in March 1941, with H.C.M. Case, head of the Department of Agricultural Economics of the University of Illinois, as chairman, Joseph Ackerman of Farm Foundation as secretary, and Noble Clark, assistant director of the Wisconsin Agricultural Experiment Station, representing the North Central Directors of Agricultural Experiment Stations. Each of the North Central States was represented on the committee by one member selected by the director of the Experiment Station and the head of the Department of Agricultural Economics. The plan of the committee was to:

- Establish contacts between research workers in the various states, to keep everyone informed of the tenure work throughout the region, problems under study, methods employed, and results obtained;
- Call an annual meeting to review completed work, critique current studies, and outline new projects;
- Recommend to experiment station directors projects to be studied on a regional basis, and those to be studied by land economists in the respective states;
- Cooperate with Farm Foundation, USDA and other organizations interested in land tenure problems; and
- Consider publishing the results of tenure studies completed by the states or the committee.

Through the interchange of points of view and ideas, the committee stimulated interest in many new studies and in the development of various new and enlarged extension programs to improve farm tenure. In 1942 the committee outlined a regional study that resulted in publication of two reports: *Improving Farm Tenure in the Midwest: Problems and Recommended Policies*, printed in June 1944, by the University of Illinois Agricultural Experiment Station; and *Preventing Farm Land Price Inflation in the Midwest*, printed in March 1945, by the Iowa State College Agricultural Experiment Station and Agricultural Extension Service. The colleges of agriculture of the cooperating states, USDA and Farm Foundation shared the cost of printing and distributing these bulletins. In March 1945, Harold Howe, from the Department of Economics and Sociology, Kansas State College, was elected to succeed H.C.M. Case as chairman of the North Central Regional Land Tenure Committee.

A second land tenure project under the leadership of Farm Foundation was organization in 1939 of the Southwestern Land Tenure Research Committee for Louisiana, Texas, Oklahoma, Arkansas and Mississippi. This committee developed plans for and a central office to coordinate the work of the five Land Grant

Colleges. It secured the cooperation of USDA and the General Education Board.[10] The latter appropriated $150,000 to the three years' work commencing July 1, 1942. USDA contributed approximately $80,000 in the services and traveling expenses of members of the staff of the Bureau of Agricultural Economics; the five Land Grant colleges contributed a total of $107,000; and Farm Foundation contributed approximately $12,000 a year for three years in the services of Howard J. Stover, part of Joseph Ackerman's time, and the expenses of the general committee meetings. While the committee made good progress, it was slower than was anticipated due to circumstances arising from the war effort.

A third group encouraged by Farm Foundation was the Committee on Tenure, Land Values and Credit of the Northern Great Plains Agricultural Advisory Council, which included representatives from Colorado, Kansas, Montana, Nebraska, North Dakota, South Dakota and Wyoming, and from the regional offices of USDA, Bureau of Agricultural Economics, Farm Credit Administration and Farm Security Administration. When this committee began work in March 1945, its first task was to appraise the tenure situation. It soon produced a bulletin on improving farm tenure in the Northern Plains. In 1945, a land tenure committee was organized in the Southeastern States. In the years ahead, tenure issues would be major program focus of Farm Foundation.

Health and Medical Care of Rural People. In the 1930s and 1940s, rural people were not securing the full benefits from modern medical care for many reasons:

- The character of rural occupations set people apart on farms or in small trading centers remote from the larger centers of population where modern medical services were available;
- The lack of awareness by rural people of the value of preventive and curative medicine;
- Failure to budget for health protection;
- The higher cost of rural medical care;
- Inadequate public health services in rural areas; and
- The medical profession's failure to develop methods to make services more available to rural people.

The Trustees of Farm Foundation sought to cooperate with the medical profession and rural educators to make rural people aware of the importance and possibilities of modern medical care. In 1936, Taylor learned from rural women at a meeting in Lincoln, Nebraska, that they would like help in developing a program of better medical care for their state. After reviewing the work on medical care and health for rural people in various places in the United States, Farm Foundation concluded there was real need for an educational program to stimulate rural people to understand and solve for themselves the problems peculiar to each area.

The University of Nebraska, with financial aid furnished by the Foundation, undertook the Medical Care and Health of Rural People project. The work began in July 1939 under the auspices of the university's Extension Service in Agriculture and Home Economics, and led by Dr. Elín L. Anderson. Started in Dawson County, Nebraska, the project was designed to get farm people and their doctors to confer together on the best method of securing a more adequate health and medical program. As a result of these conferences, the people of Dawson County became interested in developing prepayment plans for preventive as well as curative medical services. In the community of Farnam, a medical cooperative was formed, with families paying $36 a year for general medical, surgical and hospital care. When developments of the same character in other parts of the county were blocked by leaders of the County Medical Society, the rural people expressed the need for stronger support from their College of Agriculture and the State Medical Society.

In the project's second year, the educational program was extended to the entire state of Nebraska. A circular, *Do We Want Health?*, prepared by Anderson, was studied in the state's 1,700 home demonstration clubs and stimulated such interest that many conferences on medical care took place throughout Nebraska. Action programs were developed in a number of counties, but little progress was made in solving the economic problems of medical care.

The turning point came in August 1941 with establishment of a State Health Planning Committee comprised of representatives of the medical and

Elín L. Anderson
Farm Foundation Rural Health and Medical Services Project, 1940-1947

Elín Lilja Anderson was born in Winnipeg, Manitoba, in 1900. She received her bachelor of arts degree from the University of Manitoba in 1920 and taught for five years in Canadian high schools. She attended the New York School of Social Work and received her M.A. from Columbia University in 1929. She served as a scholarship counselor in the Vocational Service for Juniors in New York City from 1928-1929 and was assistant director, Eugenics Survey, University of Vermont, from 1929-1936. She was executive director of the Family Bureau of Winnipeg from 1936-1938. Her Ph.D. thesis won the John Anisfield Award in 1937 and was published as *We Americans: A Study of Cleavage in An American City* by Harvard University Press.

While working with Farm Foundation, Anderson initiated and developed projects, published several bulletins and assisted state extension services in educational programs to improve organization and distribution of rural health and medical services. She died January 4, 1951, in Winnipeg. *Rural Health and Social Policy*[18] is a collection of some of her writings, published by friends in her memory.

dental professions, the University of Nebraska and rural organizations. This state committee focused on providing adequate health services to people in sparsely settled areas. By June 1942, the people of Thomas County had set up a cooperative health association. For $30 a year, families received the services of a physician and a public health nurse, who made regular weekly visits to the five small communities in the county, covering an area of 1,000 square miles. Media attention to the project included articles in the January 1943 issues of *Country Gentleman*, *Farm Journal* and *Farmer's Wife*. Later, the Thomas County cooperative health association, known as the "Sandhills Region Health Association," established a diagnostic center and a small community hospital. To meet the cost of additional medical facilities, the charges for care were increased.

The State Health Planning Committee also gave attention to legislation establishing local public health departments. Members of the committee prepared the legislative proposal, planned hearings before the Nebraska Legislature's Public Health Committee, and prepared educational bulletins. The Nebraska Extension Service in Agriculture and Home Economics continued with a broad educational program on medical care and health services for rural people. Two circulars, *Health on the Home Front*, and *L. B. 295 Gives the Green Light to Local Health Departments*, prepared by Anderson, were an impetus to establish local health councils. In July 1944, the Extension Service employed a full-time health specialist to develop an educational program with these councils and other groups, as well as to act as secretary of the Nebraska Health Planning Committee.

The Nebraska health project drew interest in other states. In the spring of 1942, Ohio asked Farm Foundation for help in improving its rural health and medical services. In 1943, the Ohio State University Extension Service, in cooperation with Ohio Farm Bureau and Farm Foundation employed a full-time health specialist to work with the Ohio Rural Health Committee in developing a statewide educational program. The first undertaking was to aid the people of Logan County set up a prepayment plan for medical care to test the usefulness of the Ohio Enabling Act of 1941. The attempt failed because of inability to secure support from 51 percent of the physicians in the county, a requirement of the enabling law to set up prepayment plans. This experience highlighted the need for a broad educational program on medical care and health services for rural people. Ohio State University and Ohio Farm Bureau cooperated closely in its development.

In April 1944, the Northern Great Plains Agricultural Advisory Council asked Farm Foundation for assistance in developing a research and educational program on medical care and health services in the states of that region. The Foundation assigned field worker Marguerite L. Ingram to work with the regional health committee of the Council. Ingram's first project was in North Dakota, where in August 1944 the governor set up an official State Health Planning Committee.

The committee's first work, *Medical Care and Health Facilities in North Dakota*, was a survey published in March 1945. The State Health Planning Committee studied hospital needs to develop a constructive statewide plan for hospitals, diagnostic and health centers after the war. Ingram served as executive secretary of the committee. The extension service of the North Dakota Agricultural College assigned one of its state specialists full time, commencing in July 1945, to develop an educational program on medical care and health services.

In May 1945, the Health Committee of the Great Plains Council had its first conference of rural representatives and technical specialists in Lincoln, Nebraska. This drew attention to the special characteristics of the Great Plains that affect planning for health and medical services and encouraged the cooperating states to develop research and education programs on medical care and health services. The first states to do so were South Dakota and Wyoming, both of which set up state health planning committees in June 1945.

A significant outcome of Farm Foundation's work was the growing interest of the extension services of colleges of agriculture of many states in an educational program on medical care and health services. For example, the Southern Great Plains Agricultural Advisory Council and the Western States Postwar Planning Group asked H.G. Gould, chairman of the Nebraska Health Planning Committee, to explain the group's work and the role of the extension service in the development of better medical services for rural people. The Federal Extension Service set up a special committee to help states interested in developing educational programs on rural health and medical services.

A conference on Medical Care and Health Services for Rural People, sponsored by Farm Foundation in April 1944, provided an opportunity for representatives of the national farm organizations to meet with medical and technical specialists to study the problems rural people face in obtaining medical care and health services, and to consider ways of improving these services. Proceedings of that conference were published, *Medical Care and Health Services for Rural People.*

The conference recommended Farm Foundation establish a national committee on rural health, providing technical services and information and inviting national farm organizations to name representatives to that committee. The Conference Committee on Rural Health Services had its first meeting in January 1945. Its objective was to stimulate farm organizations to bring about a coordinated rural health program. Joseph W. Fichter, Master of the Ohio State Grange, was elected chairman, and Elín Anderson of Farm Foundation, executive secretary. The committee was an opportunity for farm organizations to inform each other of their work in the health field, to pool information, to analyze legislation, and to provide study materials and other information to assist rural leaders work toward more effective health services.

In response to the increasing number of requests for help from organizations and states, the Trustees of Farm Foundation expanded the budget for work in this field and, in September 1945, hired Leland B. Tate (Ph.D., Cornell University), who had specialized in this field at the Virginia Polytechnic Institute. It was hoped that rural people and the medical profession, through joint study and experimentation, would understand and solve problems in a manner suitable to each community. Because Farm Foundation maintained that permanent improvement results from local initiative, it did not urge the adoption of any specific plan or program. It held that its function was to stimulate local interest in studying local needs and to help in the investigation of ways and means suited to the given community. Farm Foundation confined its efforts to educational methods.

Rural Education. Increasingly during the 1930s and 1940s, education was viewed as being of primary importance in improving the living conditions of rural people. In 1938, the Board of Trustees of Farm Foundation employed Iman E. Schatzmann to study experiments in improving rural education in various parts of the United States. Schatzmann had made previous studies in Denmark, Sweden, Switzerland, England, Iceland and Italy. Funding was also given to the board of directors of the American Country Life Association to set up a Committee on Rural Education to study conditions and problems of rural education, and to recommend ways to improve rural education and rural life in America. Concluding that the major problems concerned the quality of teaching and making education relevant to the local community, the committee initiated four projects. Three were demonstrations in rural elementary education, headquartered at Western Illinois State Teachers College, Macomb, Illinois; Northeast Missouri State Teachers College, Kirksville, Missouri; and the School of Education of Oklahoma Agricultural and Mechanical College, Stillwater, Oklahoma. While not identical in character, the three experiments had the common objective of identifying the best

Iman E. Schatzmann
Executive Secretary of the Committee on Rural Education

Iman Elsie Schatzmann, born in Switzerland, received her undergraduate education at the University of Geneva and earned a master's degree in education from Columbia University. In 1937, under the auspices of Farm Foundation, Schatzmann studied U.S. efforts to improve the quality of rural education. She combined this research with her studies of rural schools and rural life in Switzerland, Denmark, Sweden, Iceland, England and Italy, in her book, *The Country School at Home and Abroad* (University of Chicago Press, 1942). From March 1939 to the early 1940s, Schatzmann was executive secretary to the Committee on Rural Education of the American Country Life Association, which was supported financially by Farm Foundation.

procedures to improve the quality of teaching in rural schools and to apply teaching to the life of the community.

The fourth project involved helping the State of Wisconsin Committee on Rural Community High Schools assist seven high schools reshape the curriculum to suit the needs of the rural student body and better serve the whole community. A report on the work of this committee was published June 1944 in the *Journal of Experimental Education* as "Adventures in Rural Education—A Three Year Report."

In July 1942, American Country Life Association's Committee on Rural Education, in cooperation with the American Council on Education, had a conference, "The Rural Child in the War Emergency," which drew national attention to the fact that war conditions threatened to deprive many rural children of their educational opportunities. Fifty thousand copies of the conference report were distributed throughout the United States, and considerable radio time was provided free of charge over the national networks to draw attention to this problem.

In June 1943, the Committee on Rural Education issued its final report, *Still Sits the Schoolhouse by the Road,* which outlined a program of action to improve educational opportunities for rural people.

Although the Committee on Rural Education ended in June 1943, Farm Foundation's interest in this field continued. A grant-in-aid of $10,000 per year for three years was made to the University of Chicago, beginning October 1, 1943, with the condition the University would contribute an equal amount. The university appointed a faculty committee to organize a project on rural education, under the leadership of Dr. Floyd W. Reeves. Among the rural education needs identified were:

- Application of research findings to the problems of rural education;
- Improvement of the whole program of rural education, its instructional content and its teaching techniques;
- Improvement of the administration, supervision and organizational structure of the schools and colleges serving rural communities;
- Development of greater interest and participation of rural people in their educational programs; and
- Encouragement of a greater degree of cooperation between public and private organizations and associations engaged in educating children, youth and adults in rural areas.

Workshops in various aspects of rural education were conducted by the University of Chicago in 20 states, with participation by Land Grant colleges, state universities, teachers' colleges, state departments of education and state libraries. Papers presented at the Conference on Education in Rural

Communities at the University of Chicago in the summer of 1944 were published by the University of Chicago Press as *Education for Rural America*.

This project on rural education provided consulting services to educational institutions, organizations and lay associations. The work consisted primarily of assisting state agencies develop techniques to analyze rural education needs, develop study projects, and organize educational and lay leaders to study rural problems and devise improved educational programs. Groups receiving consulting services included:

- Director and research staff of the Cooperative Study of Rural Life and Education in Missouri;
- Director and research staff in charge of the studies of school district organization, educational administration, and school finance for the Kansas Legislative Council;
- Educational Policies Commission and the research staff of the Kansas Educational Association;
- Kansas State Chamber of Commerce;
- Committee on Rural Life and Education in Minnesota;
- Michigan State College;
- Research staff for the Committee on Services of the Illinois Post-War Planning Commission; and
- Public School Study Commission of the Illinois Association of School Boards.

In developing cooperative relationships with these organizations, the Rural Education Project believed the University of Chicago could be of greatest assistance by supplementing rather than duplicating services available within the states. This project stimulated instructional activities, publications and plans for research on rural education by the University of Chicago faculty. The University introduced new courses and placed increased emphasis on rural education in existing courses. From its inception, the purpose of the work on rural education sponsored by Farm Foundation was to develop a better understanding of the educational problems faced by rural people and to devise methods to help address those problems.

Public Policies Affecting Agriculture. A 1945 history of Farm Foundation noted that Taylor "has given such time as was available to the public policies affecting agriculture."[11] In 1937-1938, with the assistance of Howard J. Stover, Taylor studied the distribution of incomes in the United States. His 1938 paper, "Immediate Backgrounds of Present Agricultural Policies and Programs," was subsequently published in modified form in 1940 as "The Farmer in the Groupistic Regime." The paper not only dealt with the question of national polices affecting agriculture, but also with the idea of developing a better understanding of the basic economic interrelations of farmers, businessmen and laborers. Taylor participated in the organization and development of the National Farm Institute at Des Moines, Iowa (1938-1942), which gave special attention to land tenure, the farmer's stake in foreign trade, and the common interests of agriculture, labor and industry.

Taylor participated in a project, started in 1934, on world trade policy. It was supported by a Rockefeller Foundation grant and financial aid from the International Institute of Agriculture in Rome. This work resulted in a 1940 publication[12] by the International Institute of Agriculture. In 1942-1943, a summary volume, *World Trade in Agricultural Products*[13] was prepared by Taylor and his wife, Anne Dewees Taylor.

Rural Youth. Farm Foundation made two grants totaling $7,000 to youth activities of the American Country Life Association, and $1,000 to the Commission on Rural Life of the Illinois State Council of Churches. Both organizations assisted rural youth groups organized to work for the improvement of rural life.

Taylor also participated in the work of two national committees concerned with the problems of youth—the President's Advisory Committee on Education and the American Youth Commission. He gave special attention to work highlighted in three chapters, "Youth Unemployment," "The Problem of Full Employment," and "Occupational Adjustment" in the final report of the Youth Commission, *Youth and the Future*; and two special volumes entitled *Barriers to Youth Employment* and *Working with Rural Youth*.

Taylor also gave attention to the issue of providing vocational guidance for rural youth. The President's Advisory Committee on Education recommended organizing an Occupational Outlook Service, and was instrumental in securing appropriations to enable the Bureau of Statistics of the Department of Labor to plan a vocational training service for youth. However, World War II diverted this appropriation to other problems.

The Rural Church and the Rural Pastor. Various phases of the Foundation's work led to the conclusion that many problems of rural life arose from qualities in people which religion is intended to improve. For example, in relations between landlords and tenants, the economic and the legal issues may be comparatively simple once understood, yet trouble may develop unless landlords and tenants share a sense of justice and the will to do the right thing. Farm Foundation encouraged agricultural economists to ask rural ministers to help promote good landlord and tenant relations.

Farm Foundation, the Town and Country Committee of the Home Missions Council, the Federal Council of Churches of Christ in America, and the North Central Regional Land Tenure Committee cooperated in a 1940 conference attended by members of the sponsoring organizations, rural sociologists, agricultural economists, rural ministers, and representative landlords and tenants. A similar conference for the southern area was organized by Farm Foundation and the Town and Country Committee at Nashville, Tennessee, in 1941, and attended by representatives of departments of agricultural economics and rural sociology and by landlords, tenants, and rural ministers from the Southern States. The proceedings of both conferences were widely distributed.

In February 1943, representatives of Farm Foundation and the Town and Country Committee met with rural ministers, landlords, tenants, agricultural economists, and rural sociologists at Salt Lake City, Utah; Pullman, Washington; Corvallis, Oregon; and Berkeley, California. The principal ideas presented in these conferences were distributed to interested church and lay people.

As an outgrowth of the Chicago and Nashville meetings, the Home Missions Council of North America, with the cooperation of Farm Foundation, sponsored four one-week training schools for rural pastors during the spring and summer of 1941. These training schools clarified the significance of social and economic improvements needed in local communities. Emphasis was given to better relations between landlords and tenants, the importance of acquiring home ownership, improved production of food and feed, and the benefits of collaboration between rural pastors and agricultural organizations to improve the quality of rural life. The Home Missions Council employed nine extension workers for training programs in Alabama, Arkansas, Georgia, Mississippi, North Carolina, South Carolina and Texas. After 1943, the program was centered in sharecropper areas.

Fifty-two institutes for rural ministers were planned for 1945. The program was designed to give rural ministers a larger vision of their task and an understanding of land ownership, agricultural improvement, farm and home planning, and improved health and sanitation. Farm Foundation funded the involvement of agricultural economists in these conferences.

Teaching agricultural economics and rural sociology in summer schools for rural ministers was another effort. Many agricultural colleges offered short courses for rural ministers for two decades or more. The theological seminaries became interested in presenting the economic and social setting of the rural pastor to make religious work more effective in the lives of parishioners. In 1945, for the sixth year, Farm Foundation provided funds for the Garrett Biblical Institute, Evanston, Illinois, to employ professors of agricultural economics and rural sociology to teach classes for ministers and other rural leaders attending the Interdenominational Summer School for rural leaders. After 1941, agricultural economics and rural sociology were taught in the summer schools conducted by the National Catholic Rural Life Conference. In 1944 and 1945, financial assistance was given to the Pacific School of Religion for agricultural economics courses for rural ministers attending summer sessions.

Farm Foundation Fellowships. Farm Foundation used fellowships in agricultural economics and extension to increase the leadership capacity of individuals and organizations serving agriculture and rural people. The purpose was to broaden the outlook of Land Grant faculty trained in farm management, marketing and land tenure to better deal with emerging complex economic problems confronting farmers.

From September 1938 to June 1947, Farm Foundation made substantial contributions to the University of Chicago for scholarships to two groups of professional educators. The first group targeted agricultural economists with permanent appointments at universities, with the goal of providing additional training in agricultural economics, rather than credit for advanced academic degrees (Table 5.1).

Over nine years, 22 scholarships totaling $18,500 were granted by the University under Farm Foundation sponsorship. The grants were made to representatives of 10 Land Grant colleges and one from USDA. Fellowships of $1,000 each were offered annually on condition that the University of Chicago grant free tuition, amounting to $300 per year, to those receiving the Farm Foundation awards.

The scholarship program included an agricultural round table involving members of the social sciences faculties, graduate students interested in agricultural economics and Chicago businessmen interested in agricultural problems. Nobel Laureate T.W. Schultz,[14] noted to R.J. Hildreth that establishment of research and Ph.D. programs in agricultural economics at the University of Chicago owed much to Taylor and the Farm Foundation's graduate fellowships.[15]

The second group of scholarships was granted from an annual contribution to the Department of Education of the University of Chicago to improve the quality of rural teaching at the elementary and secondary levels (Table 5.2). Aside from summer school grants, amounting to $800, five six-to-nine month scholarships were awarded to leaders in rural education from four states.

In 1947, Farm Foundation adopted the policy of granting scholarships directly to applicants with an administrative level of responsibility in the state and federal agricultural extension services (Table 5.3). Priority was given to applicants studying social sciences, including educational administration, agricultural or applied economics, rural sociology and political science. The program continued for more than five decades. Recipients of the more than 300 fellowships given over the life of the program made important contributions to agriculture and rural society, serving as presidents of universities, directors of extension, chairs of agricultural economics departments, program leaders in extension, and extension specialists.

Taylor Retires. In January 1945, the 72-year-old Taylor asked Farm Foundation "...to consider, informally, the future development of the program of the Farm Foundation and specifically a plan to relieve Dr. Taylor from administrative duties in order that he might devote his energy to the writing of the

Table 5.1

Farm Foundation Scholarships Granted by the University of Chicago, 1941-1949

Name	Institution Represented	Position in 1949	Year
William Kyger Bing	South Carolina	Unknown	1941-42
Charles E. Bishop	Kentucky	Graduate student	1948-49
Oswald H. Brownlee	Iowa	Assistant professor of agricultural economics, University of Chicago	1941-42
Raymond T. Burdick	Colorado	Head of Department of Agricultural Economics, Colorado State University	1941-42
Charles M. Elkinton	Iowa	Head of Department of Agricultural Economics, State College of Washington	1938-39
Harold G. Halcrow	Montana	Assistant professor of agricultural economics, Montana State College	1941-42
Clifford H. Hardin	Wisconsin	Assistant director of experiment station, Michigan State College	1939-40
Irwin R. Hedges	Wisconsin	Farm Credit Administration, Cooperative Research and Service Division, Washington, D.C.	1940-41
Ernest Paul Heiby	Ohio	Unknown	1938-39
D. Gale Johnson	Iowa	Assistant professor of agricultural economics, University of Chicago	1940-41
Sherman C. Kessler	Purdue	Farmer, New Ross, Indiana	1940-41
Erven Long	Wisconsin	Assistant professor of agricultural economics, University of Wisconsin	1946-47
Arthur T. Mosher	Illinois	Director, Allahabad Agricultural Institute, India	1941-42
Wallace Ogg	Iowa	Assistant professor of agricultural economics, Iowa State College	1946-47
Franklin L. Parson	Kansas	Economist, Federal Reserve Bank, Minneapolis	1941-42
Everett Peterson	Bureau of Agricultural Economics, USDA	Assistant professor of farm management, Michigan State College	1946-47
Wilfred Harold Pine	Kansas	Assistant professor of agricultural economics, Kansas State College	1938-39
Lawrence Harry Simerl	Illinois	Associate professor of agricultural economics, University of Illinois	1940-41
Max Messick Tharp	Kentucky	Division of Land Economics, BAE, Washington, D.C.	1940-41
William Thompson	Illinois	Instructor in farm management, Department of Agricultural Economics, University of Illinois	1947-48
Lawrence W. Witt	Iowa	Associate professor of agricultural economics, Michigan State College	1939-40

Table 5.2
Farm Foundation Scholarships Granted by the University of Chicago for Rural Education Specialists, 1946-1947

Name	Institution Represented	Position in 1949	Year
Florence Davis	Alabama Polytechnic Institute	Associate professor of home economics	1946-47
Wendel Jones	Elizabeth City State Teachers College, North Carolina	Instructor in education	1946-47
L.J. Horlacher	University of Kentucky	Assistant dean, College of Agriculture	1946-47
John Paul Leagens	University of North Carolina	Extension program planning specialist	1946-47
Ole Sand	State Teachers College, Bemidji, Minnesota	Supervisor of rural education	1946-47

Table 5.3
Scholarships Granted by Farm Foundation, 1947-1949

Name	Position	Institution Represented	Institution Attended	Year
Eunice Kochheiser	Assistant home demonstration leader	Ohio	Cornell	1947-48
W.E. Skelton	Assistant club leader	Virginia	Cornell	1947-48
Mary E. Border	Assistant state club leader	Kansas	Cornell	1948-49
W.T. Kirk	Assistant director extension service	Wyoming	Minnesota	1948-49
Mabel C. Mack	Assistant state home demonstration leader	Oregon	Chicago	1948-49
Lucile Mallette	District home demonstration agent	Alabama	Minnesota	1948-49
John T. Mount	Assistant state leader	Ohio	Wisconsin	1948-49
Helen Turner	Home adviser at large	Illinois	Illinois	1948-49

history of agricultural economics in the United States."[16] Board members Francis D. Farrell, Arnold B. Keller, Allan B. Kline, and Frank W. Peck were appointed to recommend a successor. On July 30, 1945, Peck was named to succeed Taylor, at an annual salary of $14,000.

Taylor remained active after his retirement as Farm Foundation managing director. His first retirement project was writing a book, *The Story of Agricultural Economics in the United States, 1840-1932*, with his wife, Anne Dewees Taylor. The Taylors relocated from Chicago to Washington, D.C., and worked out of a carrel at the Library of Congress. Taylor remained a consultant to Farm Foundation until 1949 and received project support from the Foundation. *The Story of Agricultural Economics* took seven years to write and was 1,121 pages long. Its reception was only lukewarm. When the publisher remaindered the unsold stock, Taylor was livid and encouraged Farm Foundation to purchase the unsold copies. The book was reprinted in 1974. Today, copies are rare and fetch as much as $225 at online booksellers.

In 1966, Taylor attended his 70th class reunion at Iowa State and visited the farm where he was born. He soon began a new project documenting the history of that farm, *Tarpleywick: A Century of Iowa Farming*. While working on his new project, Taylor was diagnosed with bone cancer, but he continued work on the book even while hospitalized for 46 days in 1967. Before he died on April 28, 1969, at age 96, Taylor completed the manuscript for *Tarpleywick: A Century of Iowa Farming*. It was published by Iowa State Press in 1970 and reprinted in 1990.

Noted Board Members. During the Taylor years, the Farm Foundation Board included some of the nation's most prominent agricultural leaders:

- **Oscar Johnson** was known as "Mr. Cotton." Although his early career was in law and banking, Johnson became president of the Delta and Pine Land Company in 1927. He supervised 50,000 acres of farmland in the Mississippi Delta, the largest cotton enterprise in the world. Franklin Roosevelt appointed him director of finance of the Agricultural Adjustment Administration in June 1933; vice president of the Commodity Credit Corporation in October 1933; and manager of the Government Cotton Pool in January 1934. In 1937, he organized the National Cotton Council, serving as president until 1947. Johnson was a member of Farm Foundation's Board from 1941 to 1951.

- **Beardsley Ruml** served as a dean at the University of Chicago; chairman of the board of Macy's; chairman of the board of the Federal Reserve Bank of New York; and director of the National Bureau of Economic Research. He conceived of the domestic allotment plan in the Agricultural Adjustment Act of 1933 and the present-day payroll deduction system for income tax. He played a prominent role in the Bretton Woods Conference which led to the International Monetary Fund and the World Bank. Ruml served on Farm Foundation's Board from 1936 to 1945.

- **William W. Waymack** was a long-time editor of the *Des Moines Register and Tribune*. He received the Pulitzer Prize for distinguished editorial writing in 1938. In 1946 he became a founding member of the Atomic Energy

Commission. He served on Farm Foundation's Board of Trustees from 1939 to 1949.

- **Thomas E. Wilson** was president of Wilson & Company, developing such value-added beef and pork products as Wilson Certified Hams, Wilson's Continental Deli and Wilson's Corn King. He also worked to establish the National Committee on Boys and Girls Clubs and was chairman of the board for the 4-H Clubs. He served on Farm Foundation's Board from 1937 to 1947.

Chapter 6

The Birth and Growth of Committees

"Farm Foundation does not represent any special group, organization, movement, or pressure activity. Its independence is one of its major assets and is safeguarded with painstaking care. The Foundation has no axe to grind on its own account and will not turn the grindstone for those who have."[1]

—Farm Foundation promotional booklet, 1952

Frank Peck as Managing Director. In 1945, Joseph Ackerman was 41 years old with a Ph.D. from the University of Illinois and had been working for Farm Foundation for seven years. His work in land tenure included supervising the Lowden plantation and developing greater cooperation among universities through regional committees. While Henry Taylor worked on writing one book, *World Trade in Agricultural Products*, and researching a second, *The Story of Agricultural Economics*, Ackerman, as associate managing director, was largely responsible for the day-to-day activities of Farm Foundation.

Ackerman was fairly autonomous. His secretary in 1944-1945, Rita Dohrmann MacMeekin, noted Taylor and Ackerman "didn't meet together very much."[2] She added, "Dr. Ackerman seemed more concerned with the plantation in Arkansas and with speeches and meetings with professors than did Dr. Taylor. Dr. Ackerman worked hard and patiently at his job."[3]

Ackerman was well liked by the staff, and they were surprised he did not succeed to the managing director's position. Mae Ramclow Tappendorf, secretary to Henry Taylor and later Frank Peck, described Ackerman as "nice and easy going."[4] Staff members felt free to express their opinions or make suggestions to him.

MacMeekin commented: "If I were to speculate why he was not given the position, I would say it was because he lacked a certain polish, and I say that reluctantly, because I liked him very much. You must remember that we had been in The Great Depression from 1929 on, and it did not actually end and prosperity did not filter down to the common folk until after World War II. Dr.

Ackerman had grown up on a farm, far from the opportunities for 'culture' that the big city offered."[5] While Ackerman was hurt by the selection of Frank Peck as managing director, there was no animosity between them.

Frank Peck served as director of the Minnesota Agricultural Extension Service from 1921-1933. That year, he participated in organization of the Farm Credit Administration (FCA). He was appointed the first cooperative bank commissioner in the FCA and served in that capacity for three years, returning to Minnesota in 1936 as director of the Agricultural Extension Service. From 1938 to 1945, Peck was president of the Federal Land Bank of St. Paul. He also served on the Board of Trustees of Farm Foundation from 1942-1945.

Peck was 60 years old when he accepted the position. Tappendorf believed he viewed the position as a transitional job before retirement. He and his wife rented an apartment in Chicago, but still maintained a home in Minnesota. Peck was respected in the office, but was a change of pace from the scholarly Taylor. Tappendorf described him as "more of a businessman" or an "organizer or administrator."

The focus of Farm Foundation had changed in the later Taylor years. Less emphasis was placed on Farm Foundation-directed research and more emphasis was placed on coordinating the work of others. By 1945, when Peck took the helm, this transformation was almost complete. Peck and Ackerman began working to expand the committee system and within a few years, it was almost the total focus of the organization.

Frank W. Peck

Farm Foundation Board of Trustees, 1942-1945; Farm Foundation Managing Director, 1945-1954

Peck received his bachelor of science degree in 1912 and his master of science degree in 1917, both from the University of Minnesota. He started his professional career on the agricultural economics staff at the University of Minnesota from 1912-1919. He was elected vice president of the American Farm Economics Association in 1917 and secretary-treasurer 1918-1919. In 1919, he was called to Washington, D.C., to head the Office of Farm Management in the Bureau of Agricultural Economics, USDA.

He returned to the University of Minnesota to serve as director of the Minnesota Agricultural Extension Service from 1921-1933. During this period he also served five years as vice director of the Minnesota Agricultural Experiment Station. In 1933 he participated in the organization of the Farm Credit Administration (FCA). He was appointed the first cooperative bank commissioner of the FCA and served in this capacity for three years, returning to Minnesota as director of the Agricultural Extension Service in 1936. He became president of the Federal Land Bank of St. Paul in 1938. He served on the Board of Trustees of the Farm Foundation from 1942-1945. In 1945 he was appointed managing director of Farm Foundation and served until his retirement in 1954.

The Committee System. In cooperation with the Land Grant university system and USDA, Farm Foundation began supporting regional and national research and extension committees in the 1940s and 1950s. The committees were topical in eight general areas within the social sciences (Table 6.1). Committees on land economics, farm management, agricultural marketing, rural sociology, rural development, research strategy and administration are the focus of this chapter. The public policy area is addressed in Chapter 7.

The committees were envisioned as a two-way street—a way for Land Grant universities and USDA research and education agencies to propose ideas for Farm Foundation funding, and a way for Farm Foundation to assist and influence Land Grant university and USDA research and extension agendas. The committees were formed and supported at the expressed interest of participants, regional Land Grant university leaders and USDA administrators, as well as the judgment of Foundation staff that the committee would lead to improvement of "rural life and rural living."

The committees were an opportunity to bring together individuals interested in a topic, as well as to achieve cooperation and coordination on regional and/or national problems and opportunities in agriculture and rural life. The formation and support of committees changed Farm Foundation's operating style. The Foundation moved away from hiring staff to pursue its own agenda and began harnessing the expertise of Land Grant universities by paying travel expenses for them to cooperate in responding to critical national or regional issues.

Farm Foundation staff had substantial input to the agenda and content of the committee work. Staff brought the perspectives of the Farm Foundation Board of Trustees and the segments of agriculture and agribusiness they represented. This enriched the dialogue and ultimately, the research and extension agenda addressed by the committees.

A Changing Agriculture. The committee approach was a response to great changes in U.S. agriculture resulting from a technological and demographic revolution in the 1930s-1950s. From 1930 to 1935, economic conditions resulted in more than two million people returning to the farm. War mobilization in the 1940s, increased prosperity and the rise of technology resulted in more than five million people leaving farming from 1940 to 1945, never to return. The farm population has declined ever since.

At the same time, agriculture experienced a technological revolution. Robert and Don Paarlberg relate this perspective: "If a farmer from Old Testament times had come to visit an American farm 100 years ago, he would have been able to recognize—and use—virtually all of the implements he saw: the hoe, the plow, the rake, the harrow, all powered by human or animal energy."[6] Beginning in the 1940s, use of new mechanical, chemical, biological and management technologies expanded rapidly. Research by Land Grant scientists resulted

Table 6.1
Farm Foundation Sponsored Committees, 1939-1999

LAND ECONOMICS	Duration
North Central	1939-1970
Southwest‡	1940-1961
Great Plains	1945-1986
Southeast‡	1946-1961
Western Range Resources †	1951-1968
Western Water Resources †	1951-1968
Western Natural Resource Development †	1969-1975
Interregional	1955-1975
Southern‡	1962-1976
Northeast	1964-1975

FARM MANAGEMENT	
North Central Extension	1946-1999*
North Central Research	1946-1970
Southern Extension	1949-1999*
Southern Research	1949-1975
Northeast Extension	1951-1999*
Northeast Research	1951-1971
Western Extension	1953-1999*
Western Research †	1955-1968
Western Commercial Agriculture Committee †	1969-1975

AGRICULTURAL POLICY	
National	1949-2007
North Central	1964-1999*
Northeast	1964-1999*
Southern	1964-1999*
Western	1964-1999*

AGRICULTURAL MARKETING	
Western Research †	1956-1968
North Central Extension	1957-1995
North Central Research	1959-1970
Western Extension	1962-1999*
Southern Extension	1963-1999*
Northeast Extension	1964-1999*

RURAL SOCIOLOGY	
North Central	1951-1984
Northeast	1956-1976
Western Research	1964-1976
Southern	1968-1976

RURAL DEVELOPMENT
    Western Community and Resource Development †   1969-1975
    Western Extension   1970-1999*
    North Central Extension   1970-1977
    Southern Extension   1971-1994

RESEARCH STRATEGY
    North Central Research Strategy Committee
    on Commercial Agriculture   1970-1977
    North Central Research Strategy Committee
    on National Resource Development   1970-1978
    North Central Research Strategy Committee
    on Rural Community and Human Resource Development   1970-1977

ADMINISTRATIVE
    North Central Extension Program Leaders Committee   1968-1990
    North Central Council of Administrative Heads   1978-1999*

NOTES:
*   Farm Foundation discontinued line item support for research committees in the 1970s, with support for extension committees ending in the 1998-99 fiscal year. Some committees continue to receive Farm Foundation support on a project-by-project basis.
†   Grant administered by the Western Agricultural Economics Research Council.
‡   The Southwest and Southeast Land Economics Committees were dissolved and the Southern Committee was established in 1962.

in rapid technological changes in plant and animal production. Advances in land economics, farm management, public policy, rural sociology or agricultural marketing did not necessarily accompany those in the physical sciences.

Rural communities prospered by changing their economic base from supplying small farms with basic products and household needs, to supplying farmers the products of technological change while adding complementary manufacturing, trade, services and government jobs. This provided farm families opportunities for off-farm employment and increased interest in fostering community development. Committees supported by Farm Foundation served the economic and management needs of both farmers and community leaders during this period of rapid change and adjustment.

Besides the great demographic and technological changes which occurred, agricultural policy was re-evaluated after World War II. The New Deal legislation of 1933, originally envisioned as temporary emergency policy, had a goal of supporting farm prices while limiting the accumulation of surplus production. During World War II, the agricultural policy goal changed abruptly to encourage production. After the war, there was the problem of ensuring a smooth transition into the post-war economy. The post-war period brought intense debate over a wide range of innovative agricultural policy prescriptions. This debate over the degree of agricultural reliance on government versus markets continued through the 1960s and, arguably, continues even today.

Political Environment. In 1949, Farm Foundation initiated the National Public Policy Education Committee, which organized the first National Public Policy Education Conference in 1950 (see Chapter 7). At the 1953 National Public Policy Education Conference, Ernest A. Engelbert, a political scientist at the University of California-Los Angeles, outlined some unique political conditions which applied to agriculture.[7] While changing over time, these conditions provide insight into the reality of agriculture and the political process at the time and, to some degree, today:

- The unique social and economic problems of agriculture have led to a tendency to treat agriculture as a unique political problem.
- Historically, farmers and their organizations maintained an agrarian ideology. This concept was foreign to the rest of American society, which measured progress in terms of technological advancement and urbanization.
- It has been difficult to achieve unity in agricultural policies due to regional cleavages and differences in approach among farm groups.
- Agricultural and farm groups have relied on Congress as the entity to protect their political interests more than other interest groups.
- Close relationships have been fostered between agricultural groups and government.

These conditions provide insight into the need for economic and policy research and education by farmers, farm leaders and their elected representatives as beneficiaries of USDA/Land Grant university efforts. This demand helped define issues and problems addressed by Farm Foundation-supported committees.

Land Economics Committees. As discussed in Chapter 5, the first committees established by Farm Foundation were in land economics. Many USDA and Corn Belt Land Grant college economists struggled to develop cooperative research and extension programs that maximized output from available resources. Taylor and the Board of Trustees concluded Farm Foundation could be most effective by encouraging coordination of the work of existing agencies and stimulating new lines of work. In June 1939, the Foundation organized a meeting of land tenure specialists at Davenport, Iowa, that resulted in formation of the North Central Land Tenure Research Committee (see box, Conference Planning 1939, page 96). The meeting included representatives from Illinois, Indiana, Iowa, Kansas, Michigan, Minnesota, Missouri, Nebraska, North Dakota, Ohio, South Dakota and Wisconsin.

The committee provided "...an opportunity to develop ways and means by which the resources of the various agencies interested in land tenure in [the North

Central] region might be more effectively employed."[8] The committee emphasized dissemination of information to increase awareness of research findings. World War II aggravated the problems of travel and manpower. To enhance timely output, the committee changed emphasis from comprehensive research studies to short reports based on past research, readily available data and limited current research.

Much of the work of the North Central Land Tenure Research Committee was conducted through subcommittees working in 10 areas:

- Setting the objectives and focus of full committee activities.
- Content and methods of land tenure research.
- Farm tenancy.
- Attaining ownership in farming.
- Farm land prices, credit and taxes.
- Conservation of resources.
- Water resources.
- Marginal analysis compared to institutional analysis.
- Roadside development and highways.
- Miscellaneous activities, such as world land tenure; farm labor; USDA *Yearbook of Agriculture*; town and country church work; council of state governments; and family farm conference.

The committee worked with other regional land economics and land tenure committees, as well as with the Interregional Land Tenure Committee and the North Central Farm Management Research and Extension Committees. Many publications resulted from the work of the Land Economics Committee, including journal articles, agricultural experiment station and regional extension bulletins, and USDA publications. These publications were used to develop education programs for farmers, farm leaders and policy makers.

Staff working in land economics at the 13 North Central region experiment stations and a representative of the USDA planned the initial regional research programs to address:

- Better land use and conservation.
- How to obtain and maintain family-type farms, basic to a satisfactory rural economy.
- Leases and agreements between landlords and tenants.
- Getting established in farming.
- How farmers acquire ownership and tenancy.
- Farm land prices and tenancy.

In 1939, a similar group was organized in the South, including the states of Arkansas, Louisiana, Mississippi, Oklahoma and Texas. A third group, the

Conference Planning in 1939

The first meeting of the North Central Regional Land Tenure Committee was organized by Joe Ackerman in 1939 at the Hotel Blackhawk in Davenport, Iowa. This was Farm Foundation's first sponsored conference. The following correspondence offers insight into how conference planning and prices have since changed.

Hotel Blackhawk
April 19, 1939

Mr. Jos. Ackerman,
Farm Foundation,
600 South Michigan Ave.,
Chicago, Ill.

Dear Mr. Ackerman:

Received your letter of April 19th, and we have the facilities and accommodations to take care of your meetings on June 2d and 3d. We can guarantee your group single rooms with bath at our minimum rate of $2.50 per day, and on single rooms without bath, but having lavatory and toilet, at the rate of $2.00 per day.

We have a number of private rooms large enough for your meeting, which we will be glad to put at your disposal without any charge. I am enclosing sample menus at 75¢, 85¢, and $1.00 for your luncheon at noon on June 2d, and $1.00 $1.25 and $1.50 for your dinner on the night of June 3d, the lowest price meal being the minimum we serve in private room.

We are also mailing you, under separate cover, sample menus for breakfast, lunch and dinner in our Coffee Shop, and I am sure you will find our prices quite moderate. Our Coffee Shop is artificially cooled, also a number of our private dining rooms.

We have free fans for our sleeping rooms so that in case of the weather being warm during the period of your meeting, I am sure you will be quite comfortable in our hotel.

Thanking you for your inquiry, and hoping we may have the pleasure of serving you, I am

Cordially yours,
HOTEL BLACKHAWK

J.C. Kennedy, Manager.[11]

Joe Ackerman replied:

Farm Foundation
600 South Michigan Ave.,
Chicago, Ill.
May 2, 1939

Mr. J.C. Kennedy, Manager
Hotel Blackhawk
Davenport, Iowa

Dear Mr. Kennedy:

We have definitely decided to hold our meeting at Davenport, Iowa, on June 2 and 3, 1939. We do not know exactly how many will be in our group, but it will probably be somewhere between 30 and 40. We are tentatively planning to hold a luncheon meeting on June 2 and also a dinner meeting that evening, and then a luncheon and also a dinner meeting on Saturday, June 3. For our meetings we would like to have a room where we could have the entire group around a table so that we could have round table discussions. We want the discussions to be as informal as possible. Most people are more free to state their points of view if seated around a table.

We will limit our luncheons to the 75¢ meal and our dinners to the $1.00 meal. We would like the rooms with bath.

I have sent the invitation to the group and will let you know the exact number who will attend as soon as possible. Should you desire any more information, I will be glad to have you write me.

Yours very truly,

Joseph Ackerman[12]

Committee on Tenure, Land Values and Credit of the Northern Great Plains Agricultural Advisory Council, began work in 1945. It included Colorado, Kansas, Montana, Nebraska, North Dakota, South Dakota and Wyoming. In 1946, a similar regional committee was formed with representatives from Alabama, Florida, Georgia, North Carolina, South Carolina, Tennessee and Virginia.

The Western Range Resources and Western Water Resources Committees formed in 1951 under the direction of the Western Agricultural Economics Council. These committees developed and coordinated research on range, water and land resources issues and problems of the Western States.

An Interregional Land Economics Committee was established in 1955 with representatives from the regional committees and USDA. One of it first activities was publication of an evaluation of land tenure research, *Agricultural Land Tenure Research: Scope and Nature: Reappraisal* (Farm Foundation, 1955). This committee also conducted national land tenure research workshops, and organized the Land Economics Institute at the University of Illinois, June 17 to August 8, 1958. Attendance totaled 156, including representatives from 26 states, the District of Columbia, and eight foreign countries. Participants included representatives of USDA, the Department of Commerce, the Department of the Interior and the State Department.

The name of the committee was changed to the Interregional Land Economics Research Committee in 1964, and to the Interregional Resource Economics Committee in 1969. The committee had significant impact on USDA and state research and education on land tenure, economics and resource issues.

The Southwest and Southeast Land Economics Committees combined to form the Southern Land Economics Committee in 1964. With the formation of the Northeast Land Economics Committee in 1964, all of the regions in the United States had a committee in land economics.

Reflecting the evolution of priority agricultural issues, the research efforts of land economics committees were redirected to problems associated with alternative uses of land and water, the efficiency of these uses, and control of these resources. Problems varied with the geographic nature, climatic conditions, and resource use patterns of each region. Regional problems studied included: resource use for outdoor recreation; legal-economic aspects of agricultural resource use and development; regional development and interregional competition; competition among urban, industrial and agricultural uses of land; and the role of land taxes in financing local government services. Problems of the individual farmer studied included: farm land prices and acquiring farm ownership; equitable farm leases; agricultural credit needs; farm transfers; and legal aspects of the farm business.

These committees produced a large number of publications widely used with farm groups by extension workers. Many publications were the direct result of the interaction and collaboration of committee members. The result was higher-quality educational materials available for use with much larger audiences than would have been possible if each state produced its own materials.

The issues of land economics changed over time, with many in the late 1960s and early 1970s taken up by resource policy economists, business analysts, the legal profession and farm management economists. This resulted in the Foundation's decision in the mid-1970s to decrease support of research committees and focus support on workshops and seminars.

Farm Management. The rapid pace of technological change in agriculture following World War II led to larger and more complex farming operations that demanded more managerial expertise. In April 1946, Farm Foundation sponsored an exploratory conference of individuals interested in farm management. Participants represented departments of agricultural economics at the

University of Minnesota, University of Wisconsin, University of Illinois, Farm Credit Administration and USDA Bureau of Agricultural Economics. The problems discussed included: farm size and economies of scale; human factors in farming; helping young people start farming; work simplification; farm buildings; equitable rental rates; supervised farming; maintaining capital; farm management methodology; and closer relation between research and extension.

That meeting resulted in a second meeting later the same year of representatives of research and extension in farm management from all 13 North Central states. Also in attendance were representatives of USDA's Bureau of Agricultural Economics and Extension Service, Cornell University and Farm Foundation. Participants were asked to determine the value of initiating regional programs dealing with management factors that significantly affect net incomes from farming. The group recommended organizing working committees in research and extension to address problems such as: economics of soil conservation; impacts of technological changes in farm practices; use of farm records in improving farm decisions and lowering farm costs; farm and home planning techniques; effective allocation and use of capital and credit; and farmers' income tax problems.

A request was made to the Association of Land-Grant Colleges and Universities (that later became the National Association of State Universities and Land-Grant Colleges) to organize regional research and extension committees. The North Central Farm Management Committee first met early in 1947. It included representatives from Land Grant colleges, USDA Bureau of Agricultural Economics and the Federal Extension Service. The directors of an experiment station and an extension service served as liaisons. The committee exists to this day, meeting semi-annually to discuss common problems and create or share educational materials for use in all the states involved.

In 1949, similar committees in farm management research and extension were formed in 12 Southern states to develop recommendations for farmers on organization, choice of enterprises, types of farm and home practices, reduction in costs of production, and income tax problems. This committee continues to function today.

In 1951, Farm Foundation sponsored formation of research and extension regional farm management committees in the 12 Northeastern states. The problem areas included: getting started in farming; needed adjustments in Northeastern farming; economics of grassland farming; methods of doing farm management research work; labor use and management; and farmers' income tax problems. This committee no longer exists.

In 1953, the Foundation sponsored formation of an extension committee of the 11 Western states to develop a regional approach to farm and home planning as a basic part of the extension program. The committee also developed educational programs in planning farm adjustments and reducing costs of farm production. A Western research committee was established by the Western Agricultural Economics Research Council and supported by the Foundation in 1955. The Western Extension Farm Management Committee continues to thrive and meet annually.

The committees played a catalytic role in the development of new ideas and projects to help farmers and farm managers successfully manage their enterprises. For example, the application of economic logic and statistical methods to the problems of farm management was enhanced by committee workshops, seminars, and resulting research and extension projects. Extension publications, both state and multi-state were produced. Professional journal publications, as well as state experiment station bulletins from research committees, led the direction of methodology and progress in farm management research. The focus was not only on the microeconomics of the farm but the macroeconomics of the agricultural and rural sector of the U.S. economy and its role in the world economy.

These regional committees fostered application of computers to management problems for farm production and marketing. Growth in use of personal computers by farmers has been aided by computer programs developed from committee activities. Extension farm management committee members contribute each year to the *Farmer's Tax Guide*, published and distributed by the U.S. Internal Revenue Service.

In 1983, Gayle S. Willett, economist with Washington State University Cooperative Extension, noted: "As a result of the professional benefits I have gained from the regional meetings sponsored by the Farm Foundation, I have been able to more effectively conduct an extension farm management educational program in the state of Washington. Such increased effectiveness, in turn, improves the ability of our clientele (e.g., farmers, ranchers, and agricultural lenders) to more effectively allocate scarce resources among competing uses, thereby improving income and living standards."[9]

Support for the farm management research committees was discontinued in the late 1960s, as it was for research committees in other areas. Support for extension farm management committees continued until 1999, when a Foundation policy change discontinued support for most committees. The focus changed to workshops and seminars on specific priority farm management problems, research and extension needs. Some extension committees continue to seek periodic Farm Foundation support for projects or conferences they organize.

Agricultural Marketing. In surveys of farmers' needs in the early 1950s, marketing consistently surfaced as a primary concern. In December 1956, the Western Agricultural Economics Research Council (WAERC), comprised of organizational economics department heads, with the support of Farm Foundation, brought together marketing researchers from the Western states and

USDA to explore formation of a regional group to: discuss broad marketing problems and areas; make a critical review of regional marketing research projects; and establish priority areas of research and specific projects. The group recommended the committee function to: coordinate and develop subject matter and research methodology in marketing research; appraise marketing research in progress or completed in the Western region; and suggest means to resolve possible difficulties in administrative procedure of regional marketing projects.

At the 1957 meeting, the committee recommended that WAERC establish Western Regional Marketing Projects on procurement, organization and practices of large-scale food retailers, and on economic analysis of direct buying of livestock in the West. In 1959, there was a joint meeting of the Western Marketing and Farm Management Research Committees.

The North Central Agricultural Marketing Extension Committee was established in 1957 to expand and activate marketing work. Four areas were selected for study and possible regional extension programs:

- Improve the pricing efficiency in marketing hogs, and the significance of the lean hog and lean pork;
- Prepare and exchange between states basic information on marketing;
- Determine and extend the most effective business management tools for individual firms; and
- Determine the needed extension program in egg and poultry marketing.

Information was developed on marketing hogs and pork products, as well as poultry and eggs; the preparation and exchange of marketing information among states; and development of business management principles in marketing extension programs.

The North Central Marketing Research Committee was established in 1959 to set priorities for regional research on pricing systems, market structure, market organization, marketing risk and management. Extension marketing committees were formed in the South, West and Northeast in 1962-1964. These committees defined emerging problems, and developed and conducted educational programs to assist farmers, marketing firm managers, and consumers with marketing decisions.

Some of these committees continue to stimulate research and education on important issues. Extension committees continue to receive Farm Foundation support on a project-by-project basis.

Rural Sociology. In 1949-1950, Farm Foundation initiated a comprehensive study of research and extension activities, applying the principles of sociology to the economic and social problems of farm families. Foundation Trustees were concerned about problems in human relations and farm families caused by changes in farming and rural areas. Following a survey of all the Land Grant colleges, personal interviews were done with 915 Land Grant college administrators, USDA administrators and representatives of farm organizations. The report of the study, *Human Relations in Agriculture and Rural Life*,[10] was widely distributed to sociologists, farm organizations and colleges.

This study led to the Foundation's sponsorship of a regional group of rural sociology research, teaching and extension specialists from the North Central states in 1951. The committee was responsible for developing research findings and improving education techniques to advance human relations in rural areas. Lines of inquiry included:

- impacts of population change and migration on agriculture in the North Central states;
- methods of stimulating acceptance of new technology by farmers;
- changing social relations as a result of new technology; and
- improving extension in rural sociology.

The committee had research and extension members from each state until the late 1960s when support for research committees was discontinued.

A Northeast Rural Sociology Committee was established in 1956. A Western committee was formed in 1964 and a Southern committee in 1968. These committees dealt with a wide range of problems in agriculture, rural life and rural communities. Social action leading to rural development was an early emphasis and led to concern for development activities in rural communities, universities and government. Other topics included the impacts of population change and migration, sociological implications of vertical integration, farm labor issues, including assimilation of Mexican-American farm workers, farmers' organizations and movements, and rural poverty. The committees stimulated new research and extension projects in the areas of health, education, local government and rural employment opportunities. After Foundation support for research committees was terminated in the 1970s, some seminars and workshops supported by the Foundation had a sociological content.

Rural Development. The Foundation established rural development as one of its main program areas in 1970, based on its goal to stem the decline in rural communities and improve the quality of rural life. Rural development extension committees were established in the Western, North Central and Southern regions in 1970-71. The committees were composed of representatives of several of the social science disciplines, with the goal of increasing the scope and effectiveness of extension education efforts in community resource development. Objectives were to:

- Identify problems of a regional or sub-regional nature, on which educational programs could be effectively conducted;

- Recommend priorities for community resource development educational programs;
- Recommend community resource development extension training programs (state, regional, or national) and/or conduct training sessions;
- Develop, evaluate and exchange alternative methods of conducting educational programs on community resource development problems; and
- Combine staff resources to prepare educational materials.

The Western Agricultural Economics Research Council formed a committee for community and human resource development in 1969. The committee had four substantive meetings where papers were presented on development problems and methods of research. Topics included: migration in the West; rural development and the quality of rural life; the rural poor; social and economic problems faced by Mexican-Americans; information needs of state welfare and health agencies; and research methods to deal with community and human resource development problems.

Many of the rural development activities were concerned with strengthening the research and extension activities of Land Grant universities and USDA to deal with the nonagricultural problems of rural communities. These activities led to useful perspectives on rural development, educational materials for citizens, and training programs for university professionals. Publications were developed on such topics as: health education and rural health care; human relations resources; non-metropolitan community services; power structures, community leadership and social action; coping with growth; incoming population to rural communities; and policy issues and dilemmas in rural development.

Research Strategy. In 1970, the North Central Experiment Station Directors reorganized their research committees, replacing the land economics, farm management, marketing and rural sociology research committees with

Howard Diesslin
Farm Foundation Associate Managing Director, 1954-1962

A native of LaPorte County, Indiana, Howard Diesslin received most of his undergraduate and graduate training at Purdue University. Prior to his service with Farm Foundation, he was an associate professor of agricultural economics at Purdue where he focused on research and teaching in agricultural finance and farm management. Diesslin was associate managing director of Farm Foundation 1954-1962. He returned to Purdue as professor of agricultural economics and director of the Indiana Cooperative Extension Service in 1962. In 1983, Diesslin accepted a position with the National Association of State Universities and Land Grant Colleges as the first executive director for extension. He retired from Purdue in 1988 as professor emeritus of agricultural economics.

three new research strategy committees: commercial agriculture; natural resource development; and community and human resource development. The goal was to pool knowledge from all appropriate sources in major problem-solving efforts. The committees were effective in focusing on problems from a wider range of perspectives. They continued until the 1970s when the Foundation switched to support of seminars and workshops.

Administrative. Fostering institutional change in the Land Grant university system became an important focus of Farm Foundation in the late 1960s and early 1970s, reflecting increasing concern over the need to address national issues and maximize limited resources. The Foundation assisted in the formation of the North Central Extension Program Leaders Committee in 1968. Its goal was to improve program leadership through the study of program direction and development. The committee aided coordination and cooperation of multistate extension programs.

Formed in 1978, the North Central Council of Administrative Heads, Agriculture was comprised of deans of agriculture at the Land Grant universities. It provided an opportunity to exchange ideas on problems, operations and programs. The council has now become inactive.

Summary. Regional committees provided a means of pooling experiences and expertise beyond state borders. They reduced duplication of effort and saved resources for state research stations and extension services. Coordination broadened concepts, aided long-term planning, and gave more direction to priority research and extension activities. Discussions helped identify emerging priority problems, produced new research and extension approaches, and resulted in professional improvement of researchers and educators to better serve society. However, as agricultural problems became more focused and national in scope, Farm Foundation support shifted to the national focus that continues today.

From 1940 to 1970, Farm Foundation used Land Grant university regional committees as a vehicle to leverage and direct Foundation programs. This strategy initially reflected the overwhelming need for travel money that prevented all but a limited number of research and extension staff from sharing their expertise and experience. These regional efforts, which included USDA support, were highly productive.

By the 1960s, there was a shift from resource scarcity to a focus on specific complex problem areas, such as the evolution of world markets, increased risk, vertical integration, environmental issues, and the decline of rural communities. These were national problems that could best be addressed on a problem-specific basis. In the 1970s, Farm Foundation staff and Board adjusted to this change by discontinuing support for regional research committees, and focusing on problem-specific activities.

Noted Board Members

- **Ezra T. Benson** was U.S. Secretary of Agriculture 1953-1961 in the administration of Dwight D. Eisenhower. In 1985, he became president of the Church of Jesus Christ of Latter-day Saints. He died in 1994. Benson was a member of Farm Foundation's Board from 1946-1949.
- **Porter Jarvis** started as a trainee in the pork department of Swift & Company in 1926. By 1955, he had risen to be president of what was then the world's largest meat packer. Jarvis served on Farm Foundation's Board of Trustees from 1952-1962.
- **Allan B. Kline** rose through the ranks of the Iowa Farm Bureau, serving as president from 1943-1947. He led the American Farm Bureau Federation from 1947-1954. Kline was a consultant to the Eisenhower administration on agricultural policy and a vocal critic of fixed price supports on farm commodities. He was a member of Farm Foundation's Board of Trustees from 1940-1950, 1951-1961, and 1962-1968. He served two terms as chairman of the board, 1954-1961 and 1964-1968.
- **James L. Kraft** worked odd jobs until he became a cheese merchant. First distributing and later making cheese, Kraft sought to give cheese longer-lasting qualities. After years of research, he developed pasteurized process cheese in 1916. Since his cheese could be shipped long distances, the U.S. government purchased 6 million tons of Kraft cheese to feed soldiers during World War I. The company he founded became a household name. Kraft served on Farm Foundation's Board from 1947-1952.

Chapter 7

The National Public Policy Education Committee

"Work in public policy education presents special problems. Controversial issues are often involved. Our task is not to suggest the solution of such issues, but to present all of the circumstances, options and consequences to be taken into consideration in reaching decisions thereon."[1]

—Report of June 1949 meeting which developed the National Public Policy Education Committee

The role of public policy in agriculture and rural America interested both Farm Foundation's founders and staff. Under Henry Taylor's direction, the topic was treated as a research interest rather than a programming focus. In the late 1940s, Managing Director Frank Peck recognized an increasing need to inform the public of the consequences of public policy decisions. Peck, along with a far-sighted group of Land Grant university and USDA professionals, realized that the key for increasing public understanding of complex issues was an effective analysis of the policy options and consequences. They began work on a series of activities that would lead to formation of the National Public Policy Education Committee (NPPEC) and regional policy committees.[2]

Throughout the 1940s and 1950s, citizens in farming and rural areas sought more education about policy options and consequences. Their opinions differed widely on the extent to which government should be involved in issues and their organizations took specific positions on the option they preferred. Extension educators and administrators from Land Grant universities and USDA saw the need for developing methods for public policy education. In June 1949, the USDA Federal Extension Service convened a conference, "Educational Work on Public Problems and Their Relationship to Agriculture," "...to review what is being done, consider problems that are being encountered, and work together on suggestions that would be helpful in a further development of the work."[3] The 44 conference participants included Peck and representatives from 18 state extension services, the Bureau of Agricultural Economics, Federal Extension and university professionals.

During the conference, it became apparent that programming and emphasis varied widely across the United States. There was opportunity for coordination and cooperation among the various state, federal and university entities. Further development was needed in scope and objectives, educational methods and source material.

Farm Foundation staff realized that the Foundation was a perfect organization to serve in the coordinating role. In July 1949, Peck convened a meeting at the Union League Club in Chicago to "explore ways and means of increasing the knowledge and stimulating the interest of rural groups in public policy subjects important to rural life and public well-being."[4] Participants included: Joseph Ackerman, Farm Foundation; F.V. Beck, Rutgers University; J. Carroll Bottum, Purdue University; H.C.M. Case, University of Illinois; F.F. Elliott, Bureau of Agricultural Economics, USDA; G.W. Forster, North Carolina State University; Charles M. Hardin, University of Chicago; F.F. Hill, Cornell University; G.E. Lord, Agricultural Extension Service, Maine; J.H. McLeod, University of Tennessee; P.E. Miller, University of Minnesota; Tyrus R. Timm, Texas A&M College; H.R. Stucky, Montana State College; and Lawrence M. Vaughan, Federal Extension Service, USDA.

Here is how Peck summarized the meeting discussion and Farm Foundation's interest in the field of public policy education:

"For the past twenty years significant public policy in agriculture has profoundly affected the economic, social, and political destiny of this country. National experience with programs designed to promote the economic status of the agricultural industry has focused peculiar national attention upon relationships between agriculture and the balance of the economy.

"Presently, there is mounting interest in the fashioning of such a policy and program development as will achieve a common objective of farm welfare in line with the advancement of the general welfare. It is time that all segments of our intelligent population better understand all phases of existing and of proposed policies that bear so directly upon the levels of living that will prevail in our economy over at least the next quarter of a century.

"There is being manifested an experienced need, that constitutes almost a demand, that educational institutions, essentially those with extension resources, assume the leadership required to stimulate consideration and discussion of important public questions. This does not mean in any sense embarking upon a program of supporting, advocating, condemning, or advising what points of view or what judgments participants in discussions may embrace—the teaching function clearly is one of stimulating and leading consideration of all sides and angles of any given policy or hypothesis.

"In keeping with its objective of promoting better understanding by rural people of those forces and influences that bear upon their economic, social, and spiritual welfare, the Farm Foundation proposes to explore ways and means of increasing the knowledge and of stimulating the interest of rural groups in public policy subjects important to rural life and to public well-being.

"A project in this field falls into three major lines of emphasis:
(1) The <u>subject</u> matter that is basic as resource material for discussion.
(2) The <u>methods</u> of organizing group discussion and leading participants into orderly reasoning and logical analysis.
(3) The <u>training</u> of competent personnel to lead this field.

"It would appear that while researchers in this field are important and that urgent needs exist for attempting to measure the experiences of national farm programs of the past fifteen years, there is available a substantial amount of resource material as background for discussion purposes. Therefore, Farm Foundation at this time proposes to build a project involving relations with the land-grant [sic] colleges around the second and third major needs, namely the improvement of methodology and the training of personnel as the two principal limiting elements in this field."[5]

The meeting resulted in a motion to organize a national committee on agricultural public policy "to stimulate successful methods of presenting various issues in the field of public policy to agricultural people."[6] The newly formed committee elected H.C.M. Case as chairman, and Joseph Ackerman as secretary, beginning a tradition—the associate managing director (and later vice president) of Farm Foundation, has been elected secretary each term since.

The newly formed committee passed a resolution "that a three or four day training school be sponsored by the committee and Farm Foundation, sometime after January 1, 1950."[7] Carroll Bottum was appointed chairman of a committee that also included Ackerman, F.F. Hill and Paul Miller to plan the training school program. "Education and Methods Conference in Public Policy"[8] took place in Chicago, January 19-21, 1950. It brought together 68 individuals from 38 states to discuss extension's responsibility in public policy education. Peck explained Farm Foundation's role as "...merely to stimulate the organization and operation of the project...The Foundation had no proposed plan to offer, nor does it seek to establish viewpoints or attitudes concerning public policy questions. It is not concerned with formulating new policies or stimulating such action by others. It is seeking to advance public understanding, and because of the general objectives of the Foundation, we emphasize the rural field rather than the general public."[9]

Later in 1950, Farm Foundation sponsored regional conferences[10] in Boise, Idaho,[11] Petersham, Massachusetts,[12] Madison, Wisconsin,[13] and Atlanta, Georgia,[14] to further promote the project and share methodologies for dealing with complex public policy issues. In early 1951, a subcommittee of Bottum (chairman), Cagle, Hill and McLeod reviewed reports from the conferences and found strong support among the extension personnel who had attended.

At the March 2, 1951, NPPEC meeting, it was decided to sponsor a national agricultural policy conference in fall 1951 for those actively working in the field of public policy.[15] The National Agricultural Policy Conference (later National Public Policy Education Conference) was born. From a poll of committee members, the following topics were selected for the first conference: inflation; the growing interrelationship of agriculture and other segments of the national economy; how agricultural laws are made; international relationships; and economics of production.

Establishing a Focus. The first National Agricultural Policy Conference was at Allerton Park, Monticello, Illinois, on September 12-13, 1951. Almost immediately, it was decided that a two-day conference did not allow sufficient time for discussion. A majority of the members favored a four-day conference with a half-day devoted to discussion of methodology. Thus, a general format for the conference was established.

The educational philosophy of the conference was also defined early. At the January 25, 1952, NPPEC meeting, it was decided the conference's responsibility was the "presentation of alternatives and their economic implications to enable people to make a decision regarding what policy they would like to have."[16]

Public Policy Education Methodology

1. Identify and define the issue.
2. Develop relevant background facts on the issue.
3. Identify the full range of policy options for dealing with the issue, including the status quo (current policy) as the baseline.
4. Analyze the consequences for each option using the best neutral experts available.
5. Carefully evaluate the results for objectivity and neutrality.
6. Without advocating any one solution, present the results to policy leaders and let them decide which option is preferred.
7. If educators are asked for their preferred option, make it clear that such declarations are not part of their educational role.

That remains the guiding principle of the conference and of the individual participants in their state programs. The primary methodology of the conference—"the problem definition, policy options and consequences methodology"—was closely identified with J. Carroll Bottum and J.B. Kohlmeyer, both of Purdue University and long associated with the National Public Policy Education Conference. It is the standard for public policy education in agriculture, rural development, family life and environmental policy as delivered by extension educators.

Farm Foundation's commitment to public policy education has been a centerpiece of its programming. While the basic methodology of public policy education has been constant, the delivery system has been constantly refined. Typically, National Public Policy Education Conferences have brought together leaders from government, academia and the private sector, including advocates of particular positions, to set the stage for discussion of the issues, options and consequences. The 50th National Public Policy Education Conference was September 17-20, 2000, in Albany, New York. The half century saw many aspects of the conference change, yet the need, format and goal of the conference remained the same.

Over the years, topics explored at National Public Policy Education Conferences have mirrored national issues, anticipated new concerns, and explored education methods to increase understanding of policy issues (Table 7.1).

Agricultural policy issues have been consistent themes, especially in years leading up to new federal legislation, such as the 1988 session, "Priority Issues for a New Farm Bill" and the 2005 session, "Issues for the 2007 Farm Bill." After legislation was enacted, sessions over the years have covered the provisions of specific farm bills. The consequences of past policies have been evaluated in the discussion of new policy options. After the September 11, 2001 terrorist attacks canceled the 2001 meeting, the 2002 meeting addressed "Agrosecurity: The Challenge for Public Policy Education."

In the early years of the conference, when each commodity tended to have its own unique program, specific commodities policies were addressed, such as the 1953 session on "Wheat Price Policy in the United States." In the 1970s, food policy was integrated into farm policy as evidenced in the 1976 session, "Food and Agricultural Policy."

Trade policy and issues have also been consistent themes, such as the "International Affairs" session in the original 1951 conference. Trade was anticipated as an issue in the 1960s, years before U.S. agriculture became dependent on world markets and remained a consistent theme at conferences throughout the 1980s and 1990s.

Resource and environmental issues began to receive prominence in the 1970s and have continued since. "The Environment and Quality of Life" was a 1970 session, followed by "Energy Policy" in 1974 and 1977 sessions. In the 1980s and 1990s, sessions such as 1988's "Emerging Resource Issues" and 1997's "Administering Environmental Law: Impacts on Private Landowners and Public Uses" focused on the evolution of environmental policy from national concern to local impact.

The National Public Policy Education Conference often examined the implications for agriculture and rural areas of the political process and overall economic policy issues. The 1951 "Inflation" session and the 1953 "How the Political Process Works" session illustrate interest in these topics from the start. This interest continued with examples such as the 1985 session on "Tax Policy Revision" and the 1996 session on "Changing Federalism."

Issues concerning the changing nature of structure and industrialization in agriculture and the food system have been anticipated and addressed since the 1970s. Sessions have included 1971's "Struggle for Control of the Food System"; 1972's "Who Will Control Agriculture?"; 1978's "Policy Options for Small Farms"; 1980's "Dispersed vs. Concentrated Agriculture"; 1990's "Structural Changes in Food Industries and Public Policy Issues"; and 1997's "Industrialization of Agriculture."

Since NPPEC designed the conference primarily for those actively working in the field of public policy education, conference notices initially were sent to the Land Grant extension directors. In the early years Farm Foundation provided transportation expenses for one individual from each Land Grant, selected by the extension directors. As the conference's value was recognized, attendance increased with many of the attendees being members of the regional public policy committees. Federal extension service, other USDA agencies, non-profit organizations and non-Land Grant universities also sent participants. In 1998, Farm Foundation discontinued travel support for participants from each state, but continued to provide the funding for the program itself.

Evaluating Results. A mail survey of participants in the 1995-97 conferences indicated participants "highly value the National Public Policy Education Conference. One hundred and eight of 136 respondents agreed with the statement that the benefits they obtained by attending their most recent Conference exceeded the costs. Moreover, respondents were pessimistic, in general, that they could find a conference that would substitute for the National Public Policy Education Conference. Greenhorns, midlifers, old timers, state people and others, and extension educators across all program specialties value the conference without significant differences...the conference, thus, is satisfying a diverse set of extension educators."[17]

Proceedings. From 1951-1998, proceedings of the national conferences were published under the title, *Increasing Understanding of Public Problems and Policies.*[18] Copies were sent to each state extension director for distribution to every county office and public policy education specialist. Copies were also distributed to members of Foundation-supported research committees starting in the early

1970s. The publication was widely regarded as a resource for extension programming. In 1988, an evaluation questionnaire generated more than 500 responses. About 60 percent found *Increasing Understanding* very to moderately useful as an education resource and for background information.[19]

Several efforts were made to enhance the usefulness of *Increasing Understanding*, such as the decision in 1990 to include abstracts with the articles. From 1996-1998, an executive summary was published and more widely distributed "to stimulate interest in public policy issues, to provide educators and other interested parties with a quick review of the major presentations given at [the conference] and to serve as a resource for policy education programs."[20]

In the 1990s, it became apparent that *Increasing Understanding* was not as widely used as an extension education resource as in earlier years. In 1997, Farm Foundation limited the distribution of free copies to individuals and discontinued unlimited free bulk shipments to state extension offices. Additional copies were made available at a modest fee; unfortunately, no additional copies were requested. As the conference began using an increasing number of non-academic program speakers, it was difficult to obtain publishable manuscripts. With the emergence and ease of online publishing through Farm Foundation's Web site (*http://www.farmfoundation.org*), publication of *Increasing Understanding* was discontinued in 1998.

A "highlights" publication of the conference was begun as *Emerging Issues in Public Policy*[21] in 1999. *Emerging Issues* captured the essence of the conference, offering less material than a full proceedings but more material than the executive summaries. It complemented conference papers and presentation materials posted on Farm Foundation's Web site. *Emerging Issues* was discontinued in 2000. All issues of *Increasing Understanding* and *Emerging Issues* were electronically scanned and are available through the Internet at AgEcon Search (*http://agecon.lib.umn.edu/*).

In the early years, the NPPEC appointed a program committee to identify possible topics for the next year. Later, planning the upcoming conference became one of the major duties of the national committee, which generally met in December in Chicago to plan the fall conference program. Beginning in 1993, the national committee met to plan the upcoming conference the day following the current conference. It has drawn on conference participant surveys, rating speakers and sessions, and suggesting topics for the next conference.

Membership of NPPEC. The NPPEC membership categories have varied, but have served the committee's goals. Land Grant members of NPPEC have been selected by the regional committees. Before 1975, NPPEC membership was drawn from the following categories:

- Land Grant extension specialists, usually one from each region;
- Research economists, generally one from each region;
- Extension directors, usually one from each region;

- A representative of the USDA Federal Extension Service;
- Managing director and associate managing director of Farm Foundation;
- Representatives of USDA Economic Research Service; and
- Consultants were also a significant part of the membership of the committee in the early years. For example, Charles M. Harden, Department of Political Science, University of Chicago, participated in the meeting leading to the formation of the committee and served as a consultant for a number of years.

Until 1975, NPPEC operated without by-laws. The minutes of the 1974 meeting reflect a feeling that more transparency was needed "...pertaining to selection of Committee members and conference participants, and the election of officers."[22] On September 9, 1975, by-laws for NPPEC were approved at a special meeting of all participants at the 1975 National Public Policy Education Conference. The by-laws established the membership of the committee to be:

(a) Two representatives each from the North Central, Northeast, Southern and Western public policy extension education committees, as selected by those committees.

(b) The managing director and associate managing director of the Farm Foundation.

(c) One representative designated by the Cooperative Extension Service, USDA.

(d) The cooperative extension director serving as administrative advisor to each regional policy committee."[23]

Starting in 1985, two representatives each from home economics extension (now family and consumer sciences) and the 1890 Land Grant colleges were added to NPPEC to recognize the growing public policy education work by these groups. In 1996, the by-laws were revised to codify changes made since the 1975 by-laws were approved, and to provide more formalized direction of how NPPEC members are selected from the regional committees and other institutions represented.

Prior to 1996, NPPEC elected a chair from its ranks. The chair initially served a two-year term, but since the mid-1970s, served a one-year term. The 1996 by-law revision created a three-year officer term rotation through the positions of chair-elect, chair and past chair. NPPEC members select the chair-elect by ballot from a list submitted by the nominating committee. Such an arrangement permits for chair-elects who are not members of NPPEC at the time of election. It also allows officers to continue on the committee beyond their scheduled rotation off.

NPPEC chairs and their election dates are listed in Table 7.2. They have been predominately policy educators, researchers or administrators with strong extension programs in their state, and highly regarded by policy educators in other states. Ira Ellis, Maine's representative for many years, was the first county-level educator elected as NPPEC chairman. Judy Burridge of Oregon was also a county agent. The regional distribution of the chairs has been relatively even over time.

Public Policy Education Awards. In 1996, Farm Foundation and NPPEC inaugurated the R.J. Hildreth Award for Career Achievement in Public Policy Education "to encourage scholarship and leadership within the policy education professional community. It recognizes individuals who have demonstrated excellence in scholarship and public service through public policy education programs over their career, mentoring and support of colleagues working on public issues, and consistently high ethical standards."[24] Up to four outstanding policy educators have received awards each year, including:

James Christenson, (2006)	Ronald D. Knutson (1998)
Keith Collins (2006)	J. Paxton Marshall (1996)
Leon Danielson (2002)	Jeri P. Marxman (2003)
Ira L. Ellis (1996)	Neil Meyer (2001)
Ronald C. Faas (1999)	James L. Novak (2005)
Philip Favero (1999)	David B. Patton (2006)
Barry L. Flinchbaugh (1998)	Irvin W. Skelton (1997)
A.L. "Roy" Frederick (2000)	Georgia L. Stevens (2003)
Harold D. Guither (1996)	Barry Stryker (2000)
Alan J. Hahn (1997)	Warren L. Trock (2000)
Harold M. Harris, Jr. (1999)	Katey Walker (2001)
Lynn R. Harvey (2004)	L. Tim Wallace (1996)
Verne W. House (2002)	W. Fred Woods (1997)

In 1997, the Outstanding Public Issues Education Program Award was established to "encourage scholarship and leadership within the policy education professional community by recognizing education programs that have demonstrated excellence in scholarship, provided important public service, and demonstrated innovativeness."[25] Recipients include:

- *Responding Knowledgeably: From Welfare Reform to Well Being* (1997) Jean W. Bauer and Bonnie Braun.
- *Iowa's Pork Industry Dollars and Scents* (1998) Bruce Babcock, C. Phillip Baumel, Mike Duffy, Mark Edelman, Neil Harl, Marvin Hayenga, Dermot Hayes, Joe Herriges, Wallace Huffman, James Kliebenstein, Cathy Kling, John Lawrence, Kelvin Leibold, John Miranowski, Peter Orazem, Dan Otto, John Schroeter, Susan Thompson and Erda Wang.
- *The Natural Resources Leadership Institute: Using Conflict Resolution in Public Issues Education on Controversial Environmental Issues* (1998) Mary Lou Addor,

Leon E. Danielson, Simon K. Garber, Edwin J. Jones, Michael P. Levi, L. Steven Smutko, Donald H. Graves, Craig L. Infanger and Jennifer A. Thompson.

- *Collaboration to Achieve Agreement on Natural Resource Decisions: Different Approaches to Natural Resource Education in Eastern Nevada* (1999) Robert E. Wilson, Sherman Swanson, Hudson Glimp, Don Holloway, Alice Crites, Michael Havercamp, Bill Evans, Marlene Reborri, Dan Weigel, Gene Kolkman, Brent Eldridge, Ray Flake, Richard Carver, Joel Twitchell and Gerald Miller.
- *County Based Multidisciplinary Public Policy Education Program for Hillsborough County (Tampa) Florida* (1999) Michael F. McKinney.
- *Local Taxes in Our Community: Understanding Tax Reform in Pennsylvania* (2000) Timothy W. Kelsey, Pennsylvania State University.
- *National Survey of State Animal Confinement Policies* (2000) Andrew F. Seidl, Colorado State University; Mark A. Edelman, Iowa State University; Mellie Warner, Clemson University; Hal Harris, Clemson University; Nelson Bills, Cornell University; Charles Abdalla, Pennsylvania State University.
- *Copin County U.S.A.: A Citizen Involvement Workshop* (2001) Jeri Marxman, University of Illinois; Robin Orr, University of Illinois; Jeanne Warning, Iowa State University; Katey Walker, Kansas State University.
- *Land Use Conflict: When City and Country Clash* (2001) Mark A. Edelman, Iowa State University; David Patton, Ohio State University; Charles W. Abdalla, Pennsylvania State University; Del Marks, Iowa State University; Farm Foundation; Kettering Foundation; National Land Use Task Force.
- *What the Public Values about Farmland* (2005) Mary Ahearn, USDA Economic Research Service; Charles Abdalla, Pennsylvania State University; John Bergstrom, University of Georgia; Kevin Boyle, Virgina Tech University; Tom Daniels, University of Pennsylvania; Julia Freedgood, American Farmland Trust; Stephan Goetz, Pennsylvania State University; Fen Hunt, USDA, CSREES; Doug Lawrence, USDA, Natural Resources Conservation Service; Larry Libby, Ohio State University; and Andrew Seidl, Colorado State University.

Developing Methods for Public Policy Education. A significant outcome of the National Public Policy Education Conference has been development of public policy education methodology. Public policy education in extension family and consumer sciences (formerly extension home economics) began to receive attention in the 1970s and 1980s. A task force on public policy education in home economics was organized through the Extension Committee on Organization and Policy (ECOP) and received support from Farm Foundation. The task force's report, issued in 1984, concluded: "If democracy is to serve as well in the future as it has in the past, families need to be involved. Many policy decisions have implications for families, yet often there is no advocate to represent their interests. Therefore, the major goal of public policy education in home economics is to help people effectively represent their families' interests in the formation of public policy."[26] The report also stated that families need to understand the public decision-making process, have access to information on issues and the skills to interact effectively in the policy process.

Accepting the challenge of public policy education helped extension consumer and family economists broaden the scope of their profession and its contributions. There has been an increase in the participation of extension consumer and family economists in the National Public Policy Education Conference, as well as an increase in public policy educations programs at state and local levels.

Farm Foundation, in collaboration with the W.K. Kellogg Foundation, funded 11 innovative public policy education projects between 1988 and 1992 "to strengthen or develop ongoing public policy education programs and involve more people and institutions in discussions of agricultural and rural issues." A key stipulation for selection was that the project proposal come from a coalition of two or more organizations. The publication, *Educating About Public Issues: Lessons from Eleven Innovative Public Policy Education Programs*, reported an evaluation of the projects, lessons learned and how each project fit into the ongoing process of public policy education.[27] This publication has become a valuable resource for public policy educators.

In 1994, a NPPEC task force prepared *Public Issues Education: Increasing Competence in Resolving Public Issues*.[28] The publication was a guide for elected officials, advocacy groups, private citizens and extension educators wishing to start a process of exploring public issues. It provided a framework for enhancing the efforts of individuals and organizations to increase understanding of issues and the process of dealing with them. Updated in 2002, it remains a valuable resource for public issues education.

These publications are tools to help educators move toward dispute resolution at various levels, e.g. local and state levels, rather than only doing issue definition, alternative solutions, and consequences education. They enhance the way extension professionals help society deal with controversial issues and public choices.

Cooperation with Other Policy Education Groups. NPPEC has long worked with other organizations concerned with increasing knowledge of policy alternatives and consequences by farmers, agricultural business people and citizens.

The Center for Agricultural Adjustment—later called the Center for Agricultural and Economic Development—at Iowa State University was formed in the late 1950s to emphasize the need for "adjustments," i.e., policies, practices and ways of doing business in agriculture. The Center received research funding from the state legislature. A grant from the Kellogg Foundation in 1959 expanded educational work throughout the country. The Center and NPPEC developed a number of joint activities.

An Agricultural Policy Institute was established at North Carolina State College in 1960. A joint steering committee reviewed current and prospective programs at the Iowa State Center, the Institute and NPPEC to avoid duplication. Publications were one resulting joint activity. A major workshop examined the relevancy of research and educational programs in the social sciences in serving a changing society. Changes brought about through research findings coming from the colleges of agriculture were explored, and priorities were identified concerning problems for future consideration.

The steering committee continued until the early 1970s when grant funds for the Institute expired. In 1971, the Iowa State Center became the Center for Agricultural and Rural Development (CARD) and took on more of a research focus. Cooperation between CARD and NPPEC has continued, but the relationship has become less formal and more sporadic.

In 1984, at the request of the Agriculture Committees of the United States Congress, the Food and Agricultural Policy Research Institute (FAPRI) was formed as a consortium of policy analysts, led by the University of Missouri and CARD, to evaluate the quantitative impacts of changes in farm policy proposals. In times of crises and farm bill development, these analyses, as well as FAPRI's annual baseline projections of agricultural prices, costs and financial status, were presented at NPPEC's annual conference. Since 1983, the Agricultural and Food Policy Center at Texas A&M has been a focal point for analyzing farm-level impacts of policy changes within the FAPRI framework.

With the exception of *Increasing Understanding of Public Problems and Policies*, NPPEC publications were frequently co-sponsored with other policy education groups. (Table 7.3.) The Center for Agricultural and Economic Adjustment at Iowa State University and the Agricultural Policy Institute at North Carolina State College were co-sponsors for most of the publications in the 1960s. The Federal Extension Service/USDA was a co-sponsor for many publications. USDA's Economic Research Service also co-sponsored one publication. State extension services, such as Illinois, Texas and Pennsylvania, also co-sponsored publications. These were widely distributed within and across states, and played a significant role in policy education work in the United States for 50 years.

Trade Policy Education. Expanded programs in foreign agricultural trade and policy began in 1958, with recognition that relatively little policy education attention had been given to this area. The foreign trade program under Public Law 480 was closely related to U.S. farm price and income programs, and many, especially agricultural people, sought a better understanding of it. In 1959, a proposal developed by NPPEC was approved by the Extension Committee on Organization and Policy of the Extension Directors, the Foreign Agricultural

Service, and the Federal Extension Service/USDA. A team of public affairs specialists was sent to European countries in May and June of 1959, and presented a detailed report to the cooperating agencies at the 1959 National Public Policy Education Conference. Teams of seven policy specialists sent to Asia and South America presented their findings at the 1960 policy conference. Six leaflets, "World Trade-What are the Issues?," published in 1962, were one outcome. In 1962, another set of teams was sent to Europe, Africa, the Middle East, Asia and the Caribbean.

An evaluation of the Extension Foreign Seminar Teams was presented to NPPEC in 1963. Extension educators found the seminars an excellent method of acquiring knowledge that enabled them to inform agricultural and business leaders about foreign markets and the implications for U.S. agriculture and the economy in general.

In 1969, NPPEC proposed that the Foreign Agricultural Service send three groups of extension specialists to foreign countries to hone educational programs dealing with market development and the promotion of U.S. agricultural products. One group went to Asia, one to the free trade area of Europe, and the third to Yugoslavia, Greece and Spain. The project produced six leaflets in a series, "Agricultural Trade Policies: What Are the Choices?" A total of 15,500 copies was distributed for use in extension education throughout the United States.

Policy Training for County-Level Educators. For several years, NPPEC gave attention to the problems/opportunities of involving and training county-level extension workers in public policy education. The minutes of the September 3, 1952, NPPEC meeting state: "Some consideration should be given to methods of working more specifically on the county level. How can county workers be involved in a conference? What type of program can be developed for these people separate from national meetings?"[29]

In 1953, Farm Foundation established three-week courses in agricultural policy for county extension educators as part of training schools at seven universities: Colorado State University, University of Wisconsin, University of Arkansas, Cornell University, University of Arizona, North Carolina State University and the University of Minnesota. The Foundation also provided scholarships for county extension educators to attend the courses. A total of 71 agents participated the first year. Initially, the Foundation paid two-thirds of the cost, not exceeding $100 to any one individual. The amount of the grant increased over the years. In 1955, 91 scholarships were provided to agents from 41 states. The number of agents participating ranged from 70 to 110 during the 1960s.

NPPEC coordinated course content, and many of the courses were taught by NPPEC members. Starting in the 1980s, scholarships were also provided for extension management courses. The extension schools were discontinued in the mid-1990s.

NPPEC Projects. NPPEC, in concert with the regional committees, developed a number of public policy related projects.

- **Who Will Control U.S. Agriculture?** This project illustrates the interaction of research and extension specialists in bringing national attention to an issue which continues to fester. Farm Foundation attention to this issue began with a 1960s seminar on policy issues related to industrialization of agriculture. This was followed by publication of *Who Will Control U.S. Agriculture?*, which included data on the increasing concentration of agriculture and agribusiness. It was subsequently used by extension public policy educators to develop a set of leaflets on options for control of agriculture, including corporate control, cooperative control, and decentralized control. Policy options and consequences were discussed for each control structure. The extension materials were used throughout the United States in national, regional, state and county meetings, all of which were well attended by diverse interests expressing a wide range of views. Discussion was often passionate on all sides of the issue. While it is difficult to tie specific legislative action to this activity, the level of awareness of the issue and the quality of the debate were increased.

- **Farm Bill Options and Consequences.** Beginning with the Iowa State University and North Carolina State University activities in the late 1950s, Farm Foundation and its Land Grant university committee structure became a focal point for farm policy education. Recognizing the widely divergent views on this issue, ranging from no program to production controls, with particular farm organizations advocating the extremes, Farm Foundation and its public policy education committees have explained the options and consequences for virtually every farm bill since the early 1960s. Within NPPEC, initial leadership centered in the North Central Policy Committee with the universities of Illinois, Minnesota, Missouri, Purdue and Kansas State being key contributors. In the late 1970s, leadership began to shift to the Southern Public Affairs Committee with Texas A&M, Clemson and Oklahoma State being prominent. Regardless of which region or university was in a leadership position, a concerted effort was made to seek the best expertise in all Land Grant universities and USDA as authors of leaflets. Farm Foundation leveraged support for authors' meetings from cooperative agreements with USDA, particularly Federal Extension and the Economic Research Service. Leaflets were initially printed by Farm Foundation; beginning in the 1970s, page proofs were provided to the state extension services, which reproduced them, often under their name with attribution to Farm Foundation. Project leaders often present the educational materials to Congressional staff, sometimes in Agriculture Committee hearings. Congressional Committee compliments were expressed when the policy options were presented for each of the major farm bill titles. Recognizing the need for objectivity, policy options were never written for the research and extension title of the farm bill.

- **Land Use Policy.** In 1999, Farm Foundation and the Kettering Foundation teamed with NPPEC under the leadership of Iowa State University to develop the policy education program, *Land Use Conflict: When City and Country Clash*. It was designed to explain the options for state and local governments confronting issues of rural-urban sprawl. Policy options analyzed ranged from the free market to redeveloping central cities as a means of reducing pressures on suburban and rural area development. This publication became a key introductory national educational guide for land use conflicts in both rural areas and on the rural-urban fringe, and is still in demand today.

Regional Public Policy Committees. In 1963, Farm Foundation received a $60,000 grant from the Ford Foundation to support education programs for public affairs specialists and administrators in the agricultural extension services. The project was developed by NPPEC in cooperation with the Center for Agricultural and Economic Development at Iowa State University, the Agricultural Policy Institute of North Carolina State University and the Federal Extension Service/USDA. Regional extension directors proposed creating four regional public affairs committees: North Central, Northeast, Southern and Western.[30]

A planning committee was organized in each region. The regions had been established as regional subcommittees of NPPEC in 1950. Farm Foundation staff participated in the meetings, which resulted in plans of action. The Southern, North Central and Western Committees met at the National Public Policy Education Conference in College Station, Texas, in September 1964. The Northeast Committee had its first meeting December 1965, in Hartford, Connecticut. Membership of each regional committee included a representative from each state, the Federal Extension Service, an administrative advisor appointed by the extension directors, and a Farm Foundation staff member.

These regional committees enhanced the previously ad hoc cooperation within the four regional subcommittees of NPPEC. Work began in earnest on developing extension public policy education programs in the states and regions. By 1966, the North Central Committee had developed a series of six leaflets, "Occupational Education and Training for Tomorrow's World of Work," published by Michigan State University. A conference at Purdue University addressed public policies related to water resources.

In 1965, the major activity of the Northeast Committee was organizing a land use seminar for extension educators. An indication of the impacts of this regional activity was that the Northeast Committee and its Land Grant university affiliates continued to be a focal point for land use and rural-urban conflict issues. With the demise of the Northeast Committee in the early 2000s, that role shifted to the Northeast Regional Center for Rural Development.

The Southern Committee, in cooperation with the Agricultural Policy Institute at North Carolina State University, developed a slide presentation on human resource development for local and state extension educators. It also developed educational materials on cotton policy and general agricultural policy development. Both areas of work continue to be an ongoing part of the Southern Committee's work. The Western Committee prepared educational materials on land and water policy, taxation, farm labor, finance and increasing educational opportunities of rural people. The Western Committee has remained a center of expertise on water and labor policy.

These early efforts had significant impact on extension public policy education at the state and local levels, and the committees have continued to be productive in their regions as well as at the national level. As needs in the regions have evolved, so have differences in the direction of the committees, reflecting the nature of regional problems and the expertise of extension staff. For instance, the Southern Committee has a greater interest in agricultural policy compared to the Northeast Committee's later focus on consumer, land use and community issues.

Farm Foundation shifted to a priority-area focus for its project activities in the early 1990s. After the 1998-99 fiscal year, Farm Foundation discontinued line item support for the regional Extension committees, but continues to sponsor regional activities on a project-by-project basis. Some of the regional Extension committees continue to function, although their activities have become more focused, as the number of extension public policy educators has

---

Move to the Electronic Age

At the 1983 National Committee meeting, "Ron Knutson [of Texas A&M University] presented a proposal to exchange policy information via the electronic mail system. After discussion, the NPPEC decided to establish a Subcommittee on Electronic Mail to work with federal extension to investigate the feasibility of the proposal, the types of services which could be provided, who would pay the costs involved, and how policy specialists would get access the material on the system."[31] The committee investigated the concept and concluded it was not feasible at that time due to the lack of access to electronic mail. The concept was re-examined in 1987-88. In discussing the continuing efforts in 1988, Fred Woods [of USDA/CSREES] related: "Technical problems should be cleared up by the first of the year and it would be possible to put up policy information on a bulletin board. ERS reports, abstracts, working papers, etc. might be put on the board."[32] In 1989, an electronic bulletin board was established, jointly supported by the Economic Research Service and Federal Extension Service. This system was the predecessor of the USDA's Internet presence.

declined and responsibility for public issues education has become more dispersed among a variety of extension educators.

Changing Times. As NPPEC evolved, the professional diversity of participants expanded. Proceedings publication became less academic, eventually migrating to the Internet. In the late 1990s, attendance at the National Public Policy Education Conference started to decline due to several factors. The number of positions in the Extension system devoted to policy education work declined over the years. The reorganization of USDA in the 1990s placed Extension in a less visible position, and USDA ceased to play a leadership role in NPPEC. The reduced number of policy education positions in the Extension system, particularly in the Northeast and Western regions, strained the regional committee system. It became obvious that some people attended the conference only because Farm Foundation paid their way to the event. In 1998, when Farm Foundation started phasing out travel support, attendance declined further.

At the 2006 National Public Policy Conference in Fayetteville, Arkansas, Farm Foundation and the NPPEC leadership decided to discontinue the National Public Policy Education Committee and the annual conference, and develop a new institutional framework for public policy education. While there is ample evidence that the need for objective public policy education remains great, the existing institutions and methods are not working.

In the beginning, NPPEC was a partnership of Farm Foundation, the Land Grant system and USDA. In recent years, only Farm Foundation was providing financial resources for the effort. Farm Foundation remains committed to public policy education because it lies at the root of the Foundation's mission. But this effort cannot succeed without partners. Farm Foundation is seeking ways to reinvent the partnership for the 21st century. Perhaps it is time for another meeting of the type when NPPEC began, involving leading university agriculture administrative heads, USDA extension and research leaders, and key public policy educators who know the historical context of this highly productive program. Together, they may be able to create a new partnership for public issues education.

Table 7.1

Locations and Subjects Discussed at the National Public Policy Education Conference, 1951-2006

Year	Location	Topics
1951	Allerton Park, Monticello, Illinois	International Affairs • Inflation • Agricultural Production Policy • Interrelations of Agriculture and Other Segments of Our National Economy
1952	Allerton Park, Monticello, Illinois	The Farmer's Stake in Foreign Trade • Taxes and the Federal Budget • Farm Price and Income Supports
1953	Allerton Park, Monticello, Illinois	Wheat Price Policy in the United States • A Price-Support Policy for Farm Commodities • Old-Age and Survivors Insurance • How the Political Process Works
1954	Allerton Park, Monticello, Illinois	Expanding Outlets for American Farm Products • Alternative Methods of Stabilizing Farm Income • Increasing the Effectiveness of Public Policy Education
1955	American Baptist Assembly, Green Lake, Wisconsin	Taxation in Relation to Changing Demand for Services • Water Problems and Policies • Economic Growth and Stability • Problems of Low-Income People in Rural Areas
1956	Montreat, North Carolina	The Nature of Education in Agricultural Policy • Agricultural Policy in a Changing Economy • Balancing Supply and Demand • Extension's Role in Rural Development
1957	Turkey Run State Park, Marshall, Indiana	Issues in Agricultural Policy • Appraisal of Agricultural Programs • Experiences in Public Policy Programs • Effective Public Policy Education
1958	Gull Lake Biological Station, Hickory Corners, Michigan	Approaches to Solving the Income Problem of Commercial Agriculture • Major Problems and Trends in Farm Policy • Research in Agricultural Policy • Extension Education in Farm Policy • Agricultural Programs Around the World
1959	YMCA Conference Grounds, Estes Park, Colorado	International Relations and Agricultural Trade • Farm Price and Income Policy Programs • Problems and Trends in Agricultural Policy • Local and State Financing • Land Use
1960	Lake Hope State Park, Zaleski, Ohio	Farm and Economic Policy • The Farm Problem-What Are the Choices? • Foreign Agricultural Trade Policy • The Land-Grant System and Public Affairs Education • Economic Growth
1961	Rock Eagle 4-H Club Center, Eaton, Georgia	Extension Education in Farm Policy • Economic Development • Marketing Agreements and Orders • International Trade and American Agriculture
1962	Gull Lake Biological Station, Hickory Corners, Michigan	Foreign Policy Alternatives • Agricultural Policy Issues • Educational Policies and Methods • State and Local Taxation Policies

Year	Location	Topics
1963	Nebraska Center for Continuing Education, Lincoln, Nebraska	Economic Development • Foreign Trade and Aid Issues • Evaluation of Agricultural Programs • Improving Policy Education Programs
1964	Texas A&M University, College Station, Texas	Education in a Democratic Society • Meeting Our International Obligations • Farm Policy Issues-1965 and Beyond • Extension Programs in Public Policy
1965	Allerton Park, Monticello, Illinois	Emerging Foreign Policy Issues • New Directions: Trade, Aid, Farm Policy • Politics and Agricultural Policy • Human Resource Development Issues
1966	Lake Hope State Park, Zaleski, Ohio	Meeting World Food Needs • The Food Marketing System • The Crisis in Cotton • Breaking the Poverty Cycle • Helping People Solve Public Problems
1967	Estes Park, Colorado	Southeast Asia Policy Alternatives • Response to World Food Outlook • Policies for Commercial Agriculture • Minimum Family Income Proposals • Community Development Policy
1968	Sequoyah State Park, Wagoner, Oklahoma	Extension Public Affairs Programs • United States' Role in World Affairs • Agricultural Policy Alternatives • Rural Poverty
1969	Williamsburg, Virginia	Successful Extensions Programs • Inflation and Economic Growth • Competitive Structure for Agriculture • Foreign Trade and Development • The Changing Structure of American Society
1970	Pokagon State Park, Indiana	The University's Role in Public Policy Education • Policy Issues for the Seventies • Income Maintenance Programs • Environment and Quality of Life
1971	Custer State Park, South Dakota	Who Makes National Policy? • Struggle for Control of the Food System • Where Will People Live and Work?
1972	New England Center, Durham, New Hampshire	Current Economic Policy • Who Will Control Agriculture? • Rural Development • Property Rights and Land Use • Policy Education
1973	Cragun's Resort, Gull Lake, Minnesota	Energy Policy Issues • Policy Education Methods • Land Use Policy • Agriculture and Foreign Trade • New Policy Perspectives and Dimensions
1974	Osage House, Lake of the Ozarks, Missouri	State of the Economy • Food Policy • Energy Issues • Land Use Policy and Planning • Improving the Performance of Government
1975	Inn-at-the-Park, Clymer, New York	The U.S. Economic System • Energy and Transportation • World Food Issues • Domestic Food and Farm Policy • Public Policy Education in Perspective

Year	Location	Topics
1976	Illinois Beach Lodge, Zion, Illinois	The U.S. Political Economy • Food and Agricultural Policy • Impacts of Judicial and Regulatory Decision Making • Energy Policy
1977	Inn at Otter Crest, Otter Rock, Oregon	Federal Policy Process • U.S. Energy Policy • World Food—U.S. Policy Choices • 1977 Food and Agricultural Legislation • Agent Training and Leadership Development
1978	Burr Oak State Park, Ohio	Food and Nutrition Policy • Policy Options for Small Farms • International Agricultural Trade • The Land-Grant System and Public Policy
1979	Provincetown, Massachusetts	Controlling Inflation: Alternative Approaches, Impacts, and Implications • Policy Legislative Process
1980	Crest Resort, Vail, Colorado	Dispersed vs. Concentrated Agriculture • Ethics of Public Policy • Productivity • Rural Transportation • Energy Policy Issues • Policy Issues and Educational Approaches
1981	Stone Mountain Inn, Stone Mountain, Georgia	Government Programs and Individual Decisions • Public Support of Research and Extension • Agriculture in the 1980s • Methodology of Public Policy Education
1982	Interlaken Lodge, Lake Geneva, Wisconsin	Domestic Economic Policy • Federal Government Role in Resource Management • Trade Policy • Financing Government Under Tight Budgets • Food Policy
1983	Illinois Beach Resort, Zion, Illinois	Economic Transition • Land Ownership Issues and Policy Education Approaches • The U.S. Food and Agricultural System in the International Setting • The Policy Education Process
1984	Airlie House, Airlie, Virginia	Federal Deficit • Providing Public Services in an Era of Declining Taxpayer Support • Water Policy • Distribution Issues in Food and Agricultural Policy • Methodology Workshops • Emerging Policies of Food and Agriculture
1985	Inn of the Hills, Kerrville, Texas	The Changing Face of America • The Changing Face of Agriculture • Status of 1985 Agricultural and Food Legislation • Tax Policy Revision • Developing Policy Education Programs on Controversial Issues
1986	Denver, Colorado	Balancing the Federal Budget Effects of Agriculture and Trade Policies on the Competitiveness of U.S. Agriculture • Human Stress and Adjustment in Agriculture • The Food Security Act of 1985 and Public Policy Education for the Future
1987	Kennebunkport, Maine	Socioeconomics of Rural America • Rural Revitalization • U.S. Agriculture in the International Arena • Role of Values, Beliefs and Myths in Establishing Policy • Policy Education and the Policy Process

Year	Location	Topics
1988	Cincinnati, Ohio	Policy Choices for Revitalizing Rural America • Priority Issues for a New Farm Bill • Opportunities for Joint Public Policy Education • Emerging Issues in Agricultural and Food Policy • Emerging Resource Issues • International Agricultural Relations
1989	New Orleans, Louisiana	The Global Environment for the U.S. Economy in the 1990s • Family Policy • Rural Development Policy • Public Policy Education • Water Quality Policy
1990	Park City, Utah	An Evolving Public Policy Education • Safe Food and Water: Risks and Tradeoffs • Balancing Environmental and Social Concerns with Economic Interests in Agriculture • Structural Change in Food Industries and Public Policy Issues • Toward a New Europe
1991	Omaha, Nebraska	Global Competitiveness, Productivity and Social Impacts • Public Policy Education Methods • Policy for Environment and Economic Development • Rural Resource Development and Work Force Productivity • Political Economy of the Dysfunctional Family
1992	Burlington, Vermont	Public Policy Education in the 1990s • Agriculture and Environmental Policymaking: Issues, Actors, Strategies • The Rural Social Infrastructure • Domestic Consequences of Evolving International Trade Policy
1993	Clearwater Beach, Florida	The Status of Agriculture and Rural America • An Evolving Public Policy Education • Health Care Reform • Public Issues Education and the NPPEC Environmental Policy: The Legislative and Regulatory Agenda
1994	Boise, Idaho	Ethical Perspectives in Public Policy Education • Transition of Food and Agricultural Policy • Building Human Capitol: Reforming Education • Environmental Policies • Local Impacts of Trade Policy • Financing K-12 Education • Sustainable Rural Policy
1995	Overland Park, Kansas	Citizen Involvement • Renegotiating the Social Contract • Environmental Policy Trends: Implication for Agriculture and Natural Resource Use • Food Safety Policy • 1995 Farm Bill Update • Sustainability and Industrialization: Conflicting or Complementary
1996	Providence, Rhode Island	Changing Federalism • Forces that Shape Our National Values: Implications for Policy Education • The 1996 Farm Bill: Implications for Farmers, Families, Consumers and Rural Communities • Societal Issues of Work and Family • Property Rights: Their Allocation and Distribution

Year	Location	Topics
1997	Charleston, South Carolina	The Future of Land-Grant Universities • Agricultural Policy at the End of the 20th Century • Industrialization of Agriculture • Administering Environmental Law: Impacts on Private Landowners and Public Uses • The Changing Nature of Rural Communities
1998	Portland, Oregon	Land Use Conflicts at the Rural-Urban Interface • Food Safety Policy and Issues • Agricultural International Trade Policy • Consequences of Devolution • Extension Accountability • Gaming
1999	St. Paul, Minnesota	The New Geography of World Trade • Developing Local Policy • The Impacts of the Food Quality Protection Act (FQPA) • Immigration and the Changing Face of Rural America • Regulation of Confined Animal Feeding Operations • Supporting Families by Strengthening Communities • Innovative Extension Land Use Policy Programs
2000	Albany, New York	Biotechnology, Food and the Environment • The Emerging Food Supply Chain • Land Use/Water Quality and Watershed Management • The Future of Rural America • Financing and Delivering Rural Health Care • The Graying of America • Small Farms • How FAIR 2002?
2001	San Antonio, Texas[33]	Evolving Agricultural and Rural Policy • Responding to the Challenges Facing Rural Governments • Evaluation and Accountability of Extension Public Issues Education Programs • Economic Issues of an Aging Population • Innovation and Creativity in Financing Growth Management: Beyond PACE and TDRs • Genetically Modified Foods: Whose Choice, Whose Responsibility? • Changing Rural Workforce • Food Security and Hunger • The Farm Bill: Evolution or Revolution?
2002	Reno, Nevada	Agrosecurity: The Challenge for Public Policy Education
2003	Salt Lake City, Utah	Biotechnology and the Food System • Impacts of an Aging Population on Rural Communities • Payment Limits and Other Agricultural Policy • Growth and Sprawl: Information, Tools and Approaches for Extension Educators • America's Bioenergy Potential: Options and Consequences for U.S. Agriculture
2004	St. Louis, Missouri	Community-based Food Systems • Competition for Water • Distributional Equity of Farm Programs • Rural Health Systems • Agricultural Trade • Rural Entrepreneurship and Economic Development
2005	Washington, D.C.	Issues for the 2007 Farm Bill • Environmental Conflict Resolution and Litigation • Nutrition, Obesity and Food Policy • Rural Governance
2006	Fayetteville, Arkansas	Consequences of the 21st Century Food System

Table 7.2
Chairs of the National Public Policy Education Committee

Chair	State	Date elected
H.C.M. Case	Illinois	July 26, 1949
F.F. Hill	New York	March 2, 1951
J. C. Bottum	Indiana	January 25, 1952
G. B. Wood	Oregon	September 8, 1953
T. R. Timm	Texas	October 5, 1955
Mervin Smith	Ohio	September 11, 1957
Frank V. Beck	New Jersey	September 18, 1959
Skuli Rutford	Minnesota	September 13, 1960
J.C. Bottum	Indiana	September 13, 1962
G.B. Wood	Oregon	September 16, 1964
C.E. Bishop	North Carolina	September 14, 1966
S. Avery Bice	Colorado	September 14, 1967
L.T. Wallace	California	September 11, 1968
Gene McMurtry	Virginia	September 24, 1970
S. Kenneth Oakleaf	Colorado	September 20, 1972
Wallace Barr	Ohio	September 24, 1974
J.B. Wycoff	Oregon	September 16, 1976
Fred Mangum	North Carolina	September 14, 1977
William Wood	California	September 19, 1978
Eugene Engel	Massachusetts	September 19, 1979
Warren Trock	Colorado	September 18, 1980
Otto Doering	Indiana	September 16, 1981
B.H. Robinson	South Carolina	September 21, 1982
B.F. Stanton	New York	September 12, 1983
Ronald D. Knutson	Texas	September 25, 1984
Dennis Henderson	Ohio	September 17, 1985
Barry Flinchbaugh	Kansas	September 16, 1986
Lavaughn Johnson	Alabama	September 15, 1987
Karen Behm	Louisiana	September 13, 1988
Roy Carriker	Florida	September 19, 1989
Barry Flinchbaugh	Kansas	September 18, 1990
Ira Ellis	Maine	September 15, 1991
Larry Sanders	Oklahoma	September 22, 1992
Charles Abdalla	Pennsylvania	September 14, 1993
Neil Meyer	Idaho	September 20, 1994
Carole Yoho	Minnesota	September 25, 1995
Harold M. Harris, Jr.	South Carolina	September 17, 1996
Judy Burridge	Oregon	September 23, 1997
Mark Edelman	Iowa	September 22, 1998
Robert Gorman	Alaska	September 21, 1999
Georgia Stevens	Nebraska	September 19, 2000
Leon Danielson	North Carolina	September 2001
Andy Seidl	Colorado	September 15, 2002
Joe Outlaw	Texas	September 23, 2003
Jeri Marxman	Illinois	September 20, 2004
Brad Lubben	Nebraska	September 19, 2005
Tom Johnson	Missouri	September 17, 2006

Table 7.3
National Public Policy Education Committee Project Publications

Title	Year	Co-Sponsorship
Agricultural Adjustment: A Challenge and Opportunity for Land-Grant Colleges	1960	Center for Agricultural and Economic Adjustment at Iowa State University
The Farm Problem: What Are the Choices? A series of 13 leaflets.	1960	Center for Agricultural and Economic Adjustment at Iowa State University
World Trade - What Are the Issues? A series of six leaflets.	1962	Agricultural Policy Institute at North Carolina State College and Center for Agricultural and Economic Adjustment at Iowa State University
Developing Human Resources for Economic Growth. A series of six leaflets.	1964	Federal Extension Service, USDA, Agricultural Policy Institute at North Carolina State College and Center for Agricultural and Economic Adjustment at Iowa State University
Your Part in Agricultural Policy Development	1964	Agricultural Policy Institute at North Carolina State College, Center for Agricultural and Economic Adjustment at Iowa State University and Federal Extension Service, USDA
People and Income in Rural America - What Are the Choices? A series of 10 leaflets.	1968	Agricultural Policy Institute at North Carolina State College and Center for Agricultural and Economic Adjustment at Iowa State University.
Agricultural Trade Policies - What Are the Choices? A series of six leaflets.	1969	USDA Foreign Agricultural Service, Agricultural Policy Institute at North Carolina State College and Center for Agricultural and Economic Adjustment at Iowa State University.
Our Poor Neighbors - What are we doing to help? What can we do?	1970	Agricultural Policy Institute at North Carolina State College and Center for Agricultural and Economic Adjustment at Iowa State University.
Financing State and Local Government - What Are the Choices? A series of three leaflets.	1973	Extension Committee on Policy of the National Association of State Universities and Land Grant Colleges.
Your Food	1975	USDA Extension Service and various State Extension Services
Who Will Control U.S. Agriculture? Series of six leaflets.	1975	North Central Public Policy Education Committee and USDA Extension Service

Title	Year	Co-Sponsorship
Marketing Alternatives for Agriculture - Is there a better way? A series of 13 leaflets.	1976	USDA Extension Service and various State Extension Services
Speaking of Trade: Its Effect on Agriculture	1978	Extension Service, USDA and various State Extension Services
Speaking of Trade: Key Issues for Agriculture. A series of six leaflets.	1979	Extension Service, USDA and various State Extension Services
Food and Agriculture Policy Issues for 1980	1980	Science and Education Administration - Extension, USDA and various State Extension Services
Federal Marketing Programs in Agriculture: Issues and Options.	1983	Farm Foundation, Federal Marketing Issues and Options. Programs in Agriculture Steering Committee
Federal Agricultural Marketing Programs A series of 10 leaflets.	1985	Texas Agricultural Extension Service and various State Extension Services
The Farm Credit Crisis: Policy Options and Consequences	1986	Texas Agricultural Extension Service and USDA Extension Service
The Farm and Food System in Transition A series of 50 leaflets.	1986	Michigan State University Cooperative Extension Service, Extension Committee on Policy, USDA Extension, and various State Extension Services
Agricultural Trade Between the United States and Canada	1987	USDA Extension Service, USDA Economic Research Service, and various State Extension Services
Policy Choices for a Changing Agriculture	1987	USDA Extension Service, and the North Central, Northeast, Southern and Western Rural Development Centers.
Policy Options and Consequences for the 1990 Farm Bill	1990	National Public Policy Education Committee, Southern Extension Public Affairs Committee, Farm Foundation, USDA Economic Research Service, and State Extension Services.
Public Issues Education - Increasing Competence in Resolving Public Issues	1994	University of Wisconsin-Extension and USDA Extension Service
1995 Farm Bill: Policy Options & Consequences	1995	National Public Policy Education Committee, USDA Extension Service, and State Extension Services.
Land Use at the Rural-Urban Fringe	1997	Land Use and Rural-Urban Interface Task Force, Farm Foundation

Title	Year	Co-Sponsorship
National Survey of State Animal Confinement Policies	1998	Animal Confinement Policy National Task Force, Farm Foundation, USDA/CREES and various State Extension Services
Land Use Conflict: When City and Country Clash	1999	Kettering Foundation Farm Foundation
The 2002 Farm Bill: Policy Options and Consequences	2001	Texas A&M University Farm Foundation
The 2002 Farm Bill: U.S. Producer Preferences for Agricultural, Food and Public Policy	2001	Kansas State University and Farm Foundation
The 2007 Farm Bill: U.S. Producer Preferences for Agricultural, Food and Public Policy	2006	Kansas State University and Farm Foundation
The 2007 Farm Bill: Policy Options and Consequences	2007	Texas A&M University Farm Foundation

Chapter 8

Farm Foundation Programming in the 1950s and 1960s

"...Important roles of the Foundation through the years [have] been that of coordinator... pooling experience and thinking in studying problems that extend beyond state borders and beyond rural boundaries... path breaker... to provide an environment that is conducive to creative thinking and innovation... educator... [supporting] conferences and training courses and publishing and distributing materials [to further] knowledge and understanding... [and] 'lookout'... to scan the horizon for emerging problems."[11]

—*Farm Foundation Annual Report 1968-1969*

Joseph Ackerman became managing director of Farm Foundation after Frank Peck's retirement in 1954. Ackerman had been with Farm Foundation since 1939, serving as associate managing director since 1942. He developed extensive contacts with extension workers in the Land Grant universities and USDA. During the later years of Taylor's tenure and throughout Peck's leadership, Ackerman encouraged the research and extension committee system. As managing director, Ackerman focused Farm Foundation on further developing partnerships between university and federal government agricultural social scientists, with the Foundation serving as a facilitator and catalyst.

Ackerman was well-respected by the university community. Howard Ottoson, who began attending committee meetings in 1952 when he was an assistant professor at the University of Nebraska, described Ackerman as "...a vigorous, enthusiastic man who could always be counted on to provide sage advice on any kind of a problem. He always had time to give a young professor counsel. He was very effective in making suggestions to committees with which he habitually sat, either in exploring new activities, in reacting to current developments, or in gently defining obstacles which the committee might confront. He was liked and appreciated by everyone. He had very good contacts with experiment station directors and extension directors in the region."[2]

Bernard F. Stanton, who began attending committee meetings as a representative from Cornell in the 1950s, described Ackerman "...as a kindly man who spoke well of nearly everyone and sought to help rather than hinder. He provided a fine image of supporting worthwhile projects where he was in the background, not out in front as the one seeking credit for his work or that of the Farm Foundation."[3]

Ackerman viewed Farm Foundation as the organization to provide cohesiveness in the nation's agricultural social science research and extension programs. He also saw it as a vehicle to recruit talent into the profession. Closer ties were established with extension professionals, university professors and university agricultural economics departments. Neil Harl was an undergraduate at a Farm Foundation-sponsored seminar at the University of Iowa in 1960 when he first met Ackerman. Harl recalls that Ackerman and Farm Foundation Associate Managing Director Jim Hildreth "...were highly instrumental in fostering close ties with university communities on a nationwide basis, but especially in the North Central Region. Both were well-known on university campuses and were frequent visitors at universities, including the 1890 institutions."[4]

Larry J. Conner, dean emeritus of the College of Agricultural and Life Sciences at Michigan State University, "...first met Joe Ackerman at the Honors House Fraternity at the University of Nebraska in 1954 or 1955. He was national president, and gave an outstanding talk on the importance of life-long education. What an outstanding individual!"[5]

Ackerman was also well-liked by the staff at Farm Foundation. Esther Olsen, who was secretary to Associate Managing Directors Howard Diesslin and Jim Hildreth from 1958 to 1970, recalls that "all of Dr. Ackerman's work was 'high priority', and was carried out vigorously and with enthusiasm. He was a dynamic leader."[6] "Working with him was a pleasure," noted Howard Diesslin, who served with Ackerman as associate managing director from 1954 to 1962. "We were a total and complete partnership on all matters pertaining to the Foundation. Joe was a unique person; he developed and personified the catalyst that the Farm Foundation ultimately became to agricultural economics nationally."[7]

Agriculture in the 1950s and 1960s. During the 1950s and 1960s, researchers began to note tremendous demographic and structural changes in rural areas. In 1950, 25 million people lived on farms; farmers comprised 12.2 percent of the U.S. labor force. There were 5.4 million farms averaging 303 acres. Twenty years later, the farm population had declined to 9.7 million, farmers were 4.6 percent of the labor force, and there were 2.8 million farms averaging 390 acres.[8] These trends continue to this day.

The transition from animal to mechanical power contributed to increasing farm size, but was not the only cause. Farmers adopted a package of agricultural technology, including new and better machines, improved (often hybrid) seeds and breeding stock, careful tillage, fertilizer, water management through irrigation and/or drainage, the application of weed control chemicals, and the widespread use of conservation practices. These and other innovations created an agricultural revolution.[9]

U.S. agricultural policy was also in transition. During World War II, the government encouraged production. These policies continued through 1948 to ensure agriculture's smooth transition into the post-war economy. With decreased demand after the war, surplus production was once again a problem. Many policy alternatives were explored, but surpluses continued to build. In the 1960s, USDA enacted production controls and increased international food aid to eliminate excess stocks, resulting in agricultural policy that was more market-oriented with an international focus.

Poverty in rural America also became an issue. In 1964, a report by President Johnson's National Advisory Commission on Rural Poverty, *The People Left Behind*, noted that 25 percent of the rural population was poor, compared to 15 percent of urban people.[10]

Farm Foundation's management and Board of Trustees recognized the changes affecting agriculture and rural people. They tailored Farm Foundation's programming to address areas in which its limited resources could make the greatest difference.

The Trustees wanted the Foundation's work to result in self-supporting and self-multiplying activities. The Foundation continued to cooperate with the Land Grant colleges and USDA research and extension elements in developing regional subject-matter-specific committees, with representation from all 50 states (Figure 8.1). This coordinated approach pooled experience and focused work on state, regional and national problems.

Collaborations with other organizations and foundations expanded the impact of this work. For example, in the mid-1960s, the regional Farm Management Extension Committees cooperated with the Agricultural Credit Committee of the American Bankers Association to develop four regional editions of an agricultural credit handbook. One result was educational credit programs, led by individual state banking associations and Land Grant universities, to improve credit procedures of commercial banks and wiser use of credit by farmers.

Farm Foundation organized a series of administrative workshops, financed by the Sears-Roebuck Foundation, for deans and directors of academic programs in agriculture. The published proceedings had significant impact on courses taught in Land Grant colleges of agriculture.

Farm Foundation focused its programming with the university committees in five areas: public policy, commercial agricultural management, environmental quality and natural resource development, leadership development, and rural development.

Figure 8.1

States Represented on Farm Foundation Sponsored Committees, 1965-1966

★ - Regional public affairs committee
● - Regional farm management research committee
○ - Regional farm management extension committee
✳ - Regional land economics research committee
■ - Regional agricultural marketing research committee
□ - Regional agricultural marketing extension committee
✱ - Regional rural sociology committee
▲ - Western water resources committee
◆ - Western range committee

Alaska- ● ✳
Hawaii- ● ○ ■ □ ✱ ★ ◆

Source: Farm Foundation. Farm Foundation Annual Report 1965-66. Chicago, IL: Farm Foundation, 1973. pp. 26-27.

Throughout the 1950s and 1960s, Foundation programming examined many policy issues, including: the farm bills, individual commodity policies, agricultural trade issues, small farm policy, and corporate farming issues. Other policy issues included: public land and water policy, rural poverty, human development in rural areas, transportation policy, rural taxation issues, rural development policy, natural resources policy, and collective bargaining in agriculture. The policy issues addressed illustrate the ability of the committee members and Foundation staff to identify emerging issues impacting agriculture. The 1960s saw expansion of public policy education methods to include not only agriculture, but resource and nutrition policy issues.

The Foundation had a catalytic role in developing new ideas and methods to assist farmers, farm managers and marketing firms manage their enterprises. The application of economic logic and statistical methods to the problems of farm and marketing management was enhanced by workshops and seminars sponsored by the Foundation and the committees it supported. Issues addressed included:

- How to raise incomes on individual farms.
- Farm and marketing firm analysis, planning and decision making.

- Using computers in farming, marketing, record keeping and decision making.
- Capital and credit needs in a changing agriculture.
- Development and annual revision of the *Farmer's Tax Guide* with the IRS.
- Regional supply responses for individual commodities.
- Farm management decisions.
- Effects of tenure on production adjustments in agriculture.
- Management and operating problems in agricultural marketing firms.
- Farm loans.
- Law and the market.
- Investigating the changing structure of commercial agriculture.
- Farm labor management and enterprise growth issues.
- Market structure and market performance issues.
- Farm leasing problems and custom farming.
- Food and fiber data systems for improving agricultural statistics and outlook information.
- Reaching low-income and small/part-time farmers.
- Opportunities and cost of roadside and direct marketing of farm products.
- Helping farmers cope with risk and uncertainty.

Farm Foundation also supported the study of the economic, legal and policy aspects of natural resources and environmental quality. The following issues, topics, and problems were addressed by Foundation workshops and seminars:

- Land use policy and planning.
- Land settlement patterns in United States.
- Role of rural institutions.
- Recreational development.
- Sociology of natural resources and environmental quality.
- Effects of investment in natural resources on regional income and employment.
- Legal and economic aspects of agricultural resource use and development.
- Economics of watershed planning.
- Natural resource use.
- Economic and social impact of limited energy on agriculture and rural communities.
- Role of property and property rights.

Leadership development issues supported by the Foundation included:

- Leadership training for county agents and extension supervisors.
- Evaluation of Land Grant university information services.
- Rural pastor training in economics and sociology.

- The sociology of leadership.
- Effective informational and educational support for social and economic development programs.
- Publication of *How to Create Coordination Among Organizations: An Orientation and Planning Guide*.
- American Medical Association rural health conferences.
- A home economics/community development workshop.

The population exodus from rural America in the 1960s, and the reverse migration from urban to rural areas which started in the 1970s, led to the need for research and extension in rural development. Rural development activities supported by the Foundation in this era included:

- Seminars on the sociology of community power structures, community development, rural manpower, and rural health care.
- Research workshop on migration theory.
- Publication of *Community Development Southern Style*.
- Seminar on coping with growth in rural areas.
- Research symposium for 1890 Land Grant institutions on the problems of community and human development.
- Workbook to help decision makers choose rural health care alternatives.
- National conference on non-metropolitan community services research.
- Research on the repopulation of rural areas.
- Publication of *Community Development and Human Relations*.
- Analysis of cost, quality and demand for selected community services.
- Catalyzed delivery and financing of rural public services.
- Community decision making and training of professional workers.
- Coordinated research on community services in rural areas.
- Seminar on "People Problems in the Plains."

Staff Roles. The managing director and associate managing director were responsible for the administration of Farm Foundation, dealing with financial, personnel and office issues. Budget and program plans were approved by the Board of Trustees. Staff had a major role in the activities of all the committees supported by the Foundation.

Staff advisory roles and special assignments complemented and contributed to Farm Foundation's goal of improving the well-being of rural people. Over the decades, Farm Foundation staff have had leadership roles in a number of professional organizations including:

- President, National School Boards Association;
- President, American Agricultural Economics Association;

- President, Chicago Farmers Club;
- Member of Joint Council on Food and Agricultural Sciences;
- Secretary-treasurer of the International Association of Agricultural Economists;
- Temporary chairman, National Agricultural Credit Committee;
- Member of Economic Advisory Panel, American Veterinary Medical Association;
- Board of Directors, National Center for Voluntary Action;
- Advisory Committee, Council on Rural Health, American Medical Association;
- Advisory Council on Consumer Affairs, American Bankers Association;
- National Council, Boy Scouts of America;
- Delegate to the White House Conference on Inflation;
- President, American Country Life Association;
- Citizens Advisory Committee, College of Physical Education, University of Illinois; and
- Chairman, USDA Economic Research Service Task Force on Farm Income Estimates.

Notable Board Members

Earl L. Butz was head of the agricultural economics department at Purdue University when President Eisenhower appointed him U.S. Assistant Secretary of Agriculture in 1954. He returned to Purdue in 1957 as dean of the school of agriculture. He was Secretary of Agriculture in the Nixon administration from 1971-1974. Butz was a Farm Foundation Trustee from 1960-1969.

Cason J. Callaway was the son of a prominent textile miller in LaGrange, Georgia. He became involved in the family business and was immensely successful. In 1938, at age 44, he retired to devote his efforts to running a demonstration farm in Harris County, Georgia. After a heart attack in 1948, he left farming and turned his undeveloped property into a public garden, Callaway Gardens. Callaway was a Farm Foundation Trustee from 1951-1956. His son, Cason J. Callaway, Jr., served on the Board from 1956-1966.

Ernest S. Marsh started at the Atchison, Topeka & Santa Fe Railroad in 1918, and became the company's president in 1957. Marsh's efforts modernized the Santa Fe, making it competitive with other railroads and the trucking industry. He served on Farm Foundation's Board of Trustees from 1962-1966.

Brooks McCormick, great grand nephew of Cyrus Hall McCormick, was CEO of International Harvester from1971-1978, the last McCormick to serve as a senior executive of International Harvester. McCormick served on Farm Foundation's Board from 1962-1972.

Wheeler McMillen led a distinguished career in journalism, serving as editor-in-chief of *Farm Journal* from 1939-1955. Author of 10 books, McMillen was also a pioneer in the chemurgic movement, serving as chairman of the National Farm Chemurgic Council from 1937-1962. He served on Farm Foundation's board of trustees from 1953-1963.

Carroll P. Streeter succeeded McMillen as editor of *Farm Journal,* serving from 1955-1968. Early in his career, Streeter's path crossed with Farm Foundation. In 1930, while a field editor for Dan Wallace's *The Farmer's Wife,* Streeter worked with Wallace on an agricultural foundation prospectus for Mary Harriman Rumsey. Streeter was a member of Farm Foundation's Board from 1963-1971.

Oliver S. Willham was vice dean of agriculture at Oklahoma State University from 1939-1950, and president of Oklahoma State 1952-1966. Willham served on Farm Foundation's Board from 1958-1967.

Chapter 9

The Farm Foundation
Round Table

"In 1984, when I returned from my first Round Table meeting in Fargo, my husband John wanted to know all about it. I was on cloud nine. I said, 'Everybody there was a wheel, except me. Everyone's a president or CEO. I even rode on a hay bale with Clayton Yeutter. On the way back to the hotel on the bus, I did sit with an ordinary farmer from Indiana. His name was Will Erwin.' John said, 'I know Will. I don't think he's 'an ordinary farmer.' Better ask him about his office in Washington.'"[1]
— Connie Greig, Little Acorn Ranch, Estherville, Iowa

One of Farm Foundation's unique programs is the Farm Foundation Round Table. It offers leaders in agriculture and agribusiness an opportunity to interact in off-the-record, semi-annual seminars on current and emerging issues. The Round Table was founded by Charles Dana Bennett, who spent his career on agriculture issues.

Bennett was born in Syracuse, New York, April 20, 1903, and spent his early life in Syracuse and New York City. His father was a plant manager and later the owner of a boiler manufacturing company. Bennett attended private schools and studied at Columbia University from 1921 to 1923. He was an accomplished outdoorsman, camper and canoeist, frequently contributing articles to sporting magazines about his adventures.

Bennett married Edith Thoman on September 20, 1924, and they worked as a team for more than 60 years. During the 1930s, they lived in Europe and traveled widely. They returned to the United States as World War II approached. In 1940, Bennett served as public relations director for Vermont Governor George Aiken, who introduced him to agriculture. In 1941, Aiken was elected to the U.S. Senate.

From 1942 to 1945, Bennett was public relations director for the National Grange and editor of the Grange's *Washington Farm Reporter*. During the same period, he assisted the National Cooperative Milk Producers' Federation and the National Council of Farmer Cooperatives.

On March 31, 1945, with the help of his farm organization and agribusiness friends, Bennett organized the Foundation for American Agriculture (FFAA). Although incorporated in Illinois, the organization's offices were in Washington, D.C. FFAA's purpose was "...to educate the public with reference to American agriculture and its importance to the national economy, through publication of articles and pamphlets on agricultural subjects and through lectures, meetings and other methods of dissemination of educational material relating to American agriculture."[2]

FFAA was governed by a 32-member board of directors—16 were representatives of agriculture and the remainder represented agribusiness and related industries. The directors met twice a year. The autumn meeting was in Chicago the week after Thanksgiving and concurrent with the International Livestock Exposition. The spring meeting was at a place determined by the directors. FFAA depended "primarily on annual contributions from members to cover its expenses (in addition to a substantial input by Dana and Edith Bennett themselves.)"[3]

Dana Bennett

Dana Bennett might have been the last person one would have expected to become one of agriculture's kingpins. Born into wealth, he was not a product of the land. Bennett dropped out of college, spent years living in European hotels and did not take his first job until he was 37. He was hardly the kind of person with whom most farmers could identify. Yet, in the last 43 years of his life, he built a lasting legacy in agriculture.

Foremost to Bennett's success was his charisma and networking ability. William Erwin recalls that "...Dana impressed me as being very bright, charming, knowledgeable and a man who knew more national leaders than anyone I had ever met. Someone said, 'When I first met him I thought he was a name dropper, but over the years I found out he was just talking about his friends.'"[25]

Bennett also swam against the prevailing political current. Ever since Franklin Roosevelt's New Deal, agricultural policy had been the domain of the Democrats. Bennett was a very vocal member of the opposition. Clayton Yeutter recalls "...how conservative the Bennetts were, not just in agricultural policy, but in the entire political sphere." Bennett would often rant about "how the Democrats were ruining agriculture, ruining the country and unknowingly ruining the world!"[26]

He sought out conservatives and helped develop their careers. During the Eisenhower administration, he helped shape freer market policies. In the Nixon, Ford and Reagan administrations, Bennett's cadre of Republican leaders in agriculture was in position to take leadership posts.

"Dana Bennett represented the quintessential flinty New Englander," relates attorney and Round Table member Gary Baise. "Even though Dana was not a farmer in any sense, he had Thomas Jefferson's unerring belief that agriculture and farmers are the bedrock of this American democracy. Dana not only spoke about this concern, but I think his instinct in picking leaders was to leave a legacy of leadership to protect our fragile democracy."[27]

FFAA collaborated with many educational and philanthropic groups. It was a member of the Advisory Council of the 4-H Foundation, the Rural Service Committee of the Boy Scouts of America, the Donors Committee of the Future Farmers of America Foundation, the board of trustees of the Intercollegiate Studies Institute, the Council on International Non-Theatrical Events, the American Association of Agricultural College Editors and the National Association of Farm Broadcasters.

FFAA formed the National Farm-City Council to sponsor Farm-City Week and the independent Farm Film Foundation, which distributed educational motion pictures to vocational agriculture departments and other farm groups. A number of awards and grants were offered, including a Professional Improvement Award from 1955 to 1971 to assist educational advancement in agricultural documentary films.

In 1955, FFAA "...in conjunction with the Moffett Foundation, the Whitehall Foundation and International Harvester Company underwrote the research done by Dr. John Davis, former Assistant Secretary of Agriculture, at the Harvard Graduate School of Business, which led to the publication of 'A Concept of Agribusiness' at Harvard and the publication of 'Farmer in a Business Suit' by Simon and Schuster."[4] This landmark work coined the word "agribusiness" and sold more than 30,000 copies.

In 1953, the Eisenhower administration advocated a change in agricultural policy from dependence on high support prices and acreage allotments to a more market-oriented approach. Secretary of Agriculture Ezra Taft Benson organized an Agricultural Advisory Committee of about 30 leaders from agricultural organizations, commodity groups, Land Grant universities and agribusiness to help develop the Agricultural Act of 1954. Lorenzo Hoopes, retired senior vice president and director of Safeway Stores, served as Benson's executive assistant.

"During and after this effort, many, if not most of the members of the Committee felt a need to retain some semblance of an Advisory Group to peri-odically discuss agricultural policy," said Hoopes. "Since many were acquainted with Dana Bennett (Dana had been a frequent visitor in the Secretary's Office during these deliberations), it is my recollection that it was decided to use Dana's organization as a 'home.' Thus the Foundation for American Agriculture evolved, as a vehicle for discussion of agriculture policy...up to that time [it had] been primarily interested in film distribution and matters pertaining to Farm/City subjects."[5] The original Advisory Group consisted of 15 to 30 members, all of whom were close friends of Dana and Edith Bennett.

After the mid-1950s, as these policy meetings became formally established, they were merged with FFAA board meetings. Bennett planned informative pro-grams and dinners for the participants. Program participants, current FFAA board members and members of FFAA's advisory council were able to become acquainted and interact in spirited discussions about timely topics.

William Erwin, Indiana farmer and former U.S. Assistant Secretary of Agriculture, joined the FFAA board in 1959. "The early Foundation for American Agriculture meetings were very fraternal. I was in my early thirties and managed to be treated as a peer by the CEOs of Agway, Ralson Purina, Quaker Oats...almost every member was a CEO, dean of agriculture or a board chairman. All were friends of Dana's. My most lasting impression is of warm and cordial people coming together to learn and share ideas. I learned a great deal from the presentations, but even more from the informal conversations."[6]

Clayton Yeutter began attending meetings in the 1970s, while CEO of the Chicago Mercantile Exchange. He noted, "In those early years this was a very intimate organization. The membership was small enough that everyone got to know everyone else very well and the same could have been said of the spouses. Many of those personal, family friendships have continued for a lifetime...With the group being relatively small, there was ample opportunity for everyone to comment on whatever subject was being discussed. That included commentary by spouses. Dana personally presided over much of the meeting and there was never any doubt about his view on an agricultural policy issue! As I recall we did not have much of an agenda for these meetings. If there was an agenda, Dana departed from it at will and frequently. Notwithstanding all the organizational shortcomings of many of these meetings, the camaraderie was splendid."[7]

Bennett thought of himself as a catalyst and planned programs accordingly. Donald Lerch, who first met Bennett while serving as director of agriculture for the CBS Network in 1949, started attending FFAA meetings in the 1960s and found the speakers "...limited to VIPs who Dana rounded up—some at the last minute. The meetings were very informal and off the record, which enabled discussion of key issues with government officials and CEOs of agribusinesses."[8] Program participants included not only prominent individuals in agriculture and agribusiness, but those outside of agriculture, such as David Rockefeller, Dean Rusk and Douglas MacArthur II.

In his 1987 tribute to Bennett, Round Table member Jim Roe said, "Dana knew literally everyone. The great entrepreneurs of the agricultural and food industries: the McCormicks of International Harvester, the Magowans of Safeway, the Victor Emanuels of Avco, the Funks of Funk's Hybrid Corn, the Stuarts of Quaker Oats, Tom Ware of International Minerals and Chemicals, Roy Utke of Sunkist, Cliff Cox of Armour, Ernest Marsh of the Santa Fe. He knew the national thought leaders and policy makers in agriculture: the farm organization heads, the economists, the agricultural school deans, the farm writers and broadcasters. He knew the Secretaries and Assistant Secretaries of Agriculture: Ezra Benson, Earl Butz, Bob Bergland, Jack Block, Dick Lyng, John Davis, Will Erwin, Clayton Yuetter. He knew them all *long before* they occupied their second-floor offices and *long after*. Dana's friendships were enduring."[9]

Entering Dana Bennett's orbit was not only a good career move, it had the potential to make a career. Roe continues, "Dana had an uncanny knack for recognizing and attracting the true achievers who really run the show. The men and women who make things happen. Today's young striver who felt the touch of Dana's sword on his shoulder had a way of becoming tomorrow's vice president, president, chairman. Indeed, it is not at all unlikely that the Bennett blessing often helped bring about this favorable succession of events."

FFAA was a Bennett enterprise. Donald Lerch noted that Bennett was "one of the first men to work with his wife on a daily basis. Edith had her desk next to his in the *same room*. She participated in all activities except *lunch*—that was his free time with the boys!"[10] Clayton Yeutter remembers that "without the Bennetts' personal financial support the FFAA clearly would never have become a reality. But, the Bennetts did far more than simply support the organization financially. In the early years of its existence they were a whirlwind, two person organizational/logistics committee. As I recall, they planned the meetings, selected the location, made the lodging arrangements, invited the members, hosted the social events and picked up the tab for most everything!"[11]

Merger with Farm Foundation. In 1969, the FFAA board commissioned a Long Range Planning Committee to examine FFAA and two associated organizations, Farm Film Foundation and Visual Education, Inc., "presupposing that at some time in the future, the Bennetts, for whatever reason, would not be available to carry on their day-by-day supervision of the activities of these organizations."[12]

For some time there had been considerable overlap between the members of the boards of FFAA and Farm Foundation. The Committee "...recommended that a small Committee be named to be composed of members of the Board of Directors of FFAA and Farm Foundation to see what, if any, working relationship might be developed which would take effect in a post-Bennett era..."[13]

In 1970, the Joint Committee of the Foundation for American Agriculture and Farm Foundation reported: "The managements of both organizations are in close communication and often cooperate, unofficially at least, on joint projects."[14] The report advocated continued and expanded cooperation. Dana Bennett's retirement was anticipated in three or more years, and it was proposed that efforts should be made to combine the two foundations at that time.

At the 1972 Farm Foundation annual meeting, the executive committee presented a plan, developed by Farm Foundation staff, whereby Farm Foundation would assume management of FFAA. It was agreed to give the proposal further thought, and the issue was slated for the 1973 annual meeting agenda.

By January 1973, Farm Foundation Managing Director Jim Hildreth had made several decisions concerning the merger. He believed there were "...few advantages and many disadvantages...with the assumption of the management of the Farm Film Foundation by the staff of Farm Foundation..."[15] Visual Education, Inc. was a commercial corporation and did not interest Farm Foundation. Concerning FFAA, Hildreth noted, "The time demands for the management of the Foundation for American Agriculture would not be as great as for the Farm Film Foundation."[16] The major activity of the FFAA—having two discussion meetings a year—would be of interest to the Farm Foundation Trustees and, since some Trustees were members of both boards, a merger would "'tidy up' the scene for some very busy people."[17] Finally, Hildreth stressed that the proposed merger should not "jeopardize Farm Foundation's status as a 'private operating' foundation" or result in "a significant use of Farm Foundation finances for the operation of the Foundation for American Agriculture."[18]

At the May 1973 Farm Foundation Board meeting, there was discussion of legal and management issues of a merger. The situation was slightly complicated due to Farm Foundation's status as a trust and FFAA's status as a corporation. Financially, FFAA was "...a relatively small organization with total assets of around $50,000 and annual receipts, in the form of contributions and interest, of $50,000 or less. Farm Foundation has total assets of approximately $5,000,000 and annual receipts of about $300,000."[19] The Trustees "...agreed the Executive Committee should continue the examination of alternative arrangements whereby the program of the Foundation for American Agriculture would be included under the management of the Farm Foundation, subject to the condition that the philosophy, style and program of the Farm Foundation not be impaired."[20] At its June 1973 annual meeting, the FFAA board approved the merger with Farm Foundation.

At the 1974 Farm Foundation annual meeting, the executive committee reported on initial steps for including FFAA under the management of Farm Foundation. Activities of FFAA would become a program of Farm Foundation. The meetings usually organized by FFAA would continue. The Farm Foundation Board meeting and the summer meeting of the FFAA would be combined. Bennett would become a special consultant to Farm Foundation for this new program, which later became the Edith and Dana Bennett Round Table.[21] Bennett was paid $25,000 per year until 1983, when he retired from active involvement. A program Advisory Council was established which included many of the FFAA board members. The Farm Film Foundation and Visual Education, Inc. would not be a part of Farm Foundation.

At its May 27, 1975, meeting, FFAA voted to dissolve, effective July 1, completing the merger. All funds were transferred by December 23, 1975. The Farm Film Foundation and Visual Education, Inc. continued to operate independently for several more years.

The merger with FFAA benefited Farm Foundation in two ways. First, it helped Farm Foundation meet the requirements to change its status from a private foundation to a public charity. This change, contingent on Farm Foundation receiving more than 10 percent of its income in the form of donations, exempted the Foundation from the private foundation excise tax. (See Chapter 12.) Second, it expanded linkages between Farm Foundation, industry and agribusiness.

By the mid-1970s, the Round Table meetings became more formalized with thematic topics (Table 9.1). The Round Table began to evolve in other ways, remembers Clayton Yeutter, who served as Secretary of Agriculture in the George H.W. Bush administration:

"I believe it was one of the old-timers who asked me to meet Dana and then to join the Round Table. As I recall, the pitch to me at that time was centered on the need to bring some younger agriculturalists with leadership potential into the organization and the need to enlarge the Round Table group. My recollection is that there were no more than 15 or so active Round Table members at that time and that essentially all of them were long time personal friends of the Bennetts. That meant, of course, that most of them were in approximately the same age range as the Bennetts. As the group added years, the leadership began to recognize the need for greater diversity in age among its membership.

"One of the thrusts of the [FFAA] in the 1970s was to prepare young, conservative agriculturalists like me for potential USDA positions at the sub-cabinet and cabinet level in later years. Earl Butz and Don Paarlberg got their first exposure to public service in the Eisenhower Administration, returned to academia thereafter and then came back to top leadership positions at USDA under President Nixon. The hope was that Round Table members like myself and others who then got our first public exposure in the Nixon/Ford years could be prepared for service when the next Republican President came to office. Whether we were then in academia or private business, the Round Table experience was expected to help ready us philosophically, through expansion of our knowledge base and through personal relationships. That objective was realized in a major way, as numerous Round Table members accepted high level positions in the government during the Reagan and Bush Administrations.

"The Round Table had a significant impact on my career. I had the privilege of returning to government as U.S. Trade Representative in 1985, continuing then as Secretary of Agriculture beginning in 1989. Not only did the Round Table influence what I sought to accomplish in those two Cabinet posts, but it provided lots of help via my being able to bring many of its members into government with me." [22]

Bennett's special talents continued at Farm Foundation. As Jim Roe noted, "Dana often referred to himself as a catalyst. He was the man who brought together—for discussions of their mutual interests—people who might not have known they needed to get together."[23] For example, the winter 1976 meeting concerned the world food crisis. The four individuals on the program were the U.S. Assistant Secretary of Agriculture, the presidents of the Chicago Board of Trade and the Chicago Mercantile Exchange, and the administrator of the U.S. Agency for International Development. Bennett's prescience was uncanny. The January 1980 meeting, "If Agricultural Exports Fade...?" took place the same week President Jimmy Carter announced the embargo on agricultural sales to the Soviet Union, derailing what had been a recent boom in agricultural exports.

In 1983, Bennett retired at age 80 and Farm Foundation assumed full management of the program. On January 26, 1984, at the USDA Administration Building in Washington, D.C., Farm Foundation honored Edith and Dana Bennett at a dinner. It was attended by 84 of their friends and associates. That year, the name of the program was changed to the Edith and Dana Bennett Agricultural Round Table. Dana Bennett died in Bethesda, Maryland, on February 15, 1987. Edith Bennett died July 16, 1989.

In 1983 and 1984, guidelines were established and registration fees instituted to cover meeting expenses, previously subsidized by Farm Foundation. Plans were made to expand the membership from 70 to 120. In 1984, a Round Table Steering Committee was organized to suggest to the Farm Foundation Board the location of meetings, plan the program and oversee membership management. To more accurately reflect its role and identity, the name of the Round Table was changed to Farm Foundation Agricultural Round Table in 2004, and in 2005 to the Farm Foundation Round Table.

The Round Table is an invitational group of agricultural and agribusiness leaders. Any Round Table member may invite guests, who may subsequently become members. Focus is on individuals having an influential leadership rank in their profession or organization. Currently, membership is limited to no more than 150 individuals. The present members represent a wide range of commodity and business interests from across the nation and food chain.

The Round Table Steering Committee Chair attends Farm Foundation Trustee meetings to report on Steering Committee deliberations on program plans, membership and suggested meeting locations.

The Round Table meets twice yearly, with the program topics determined by the Round Table Steering Committee. Attendance at Round Table meetings is limited to members and invited guests. Since 1992, an optional bus tour precedes the meeting, highlighting farming and agribusiness activities in the area of the meeting location. These tours have included stops as diverse as a Delaware biotechnology center, an Idaho plant producing French fries, the King Ranch, a California vineyard, and a Florida sugar mill.

Round Table programs examine such diverse topics as farm bills, trade, water policy, conservation, the environment, food safety and consumer demand. Speakers, often with views outside the mainstream, set the stage for open discussion. The Round Table today is bipartisan, with wide political diversity among the members, making for plentiful discussion filled with differing opinions. Clayton Yeutter noted, "As the Round Table evolved it inevitably lost some of its 'family' attributes, the trade-off being a richer experience overall for the members at their Round Table meetings."[24]

Round Table members are expected to support the Foundation through an annual contribution and to regularly attend meetings. They are also invited to participate in the Foundation's Strategic Planning Priority Area Advisory Committee process.

A number of Secretaries of Agriculture were Farm Foundation Trustees or Round Table members before their appointments. That list includes Ezra Taft Benson, Earl Butz, John Block, Richard Lyng, Clayton Yeutter and Ann Veneman. Former Secretaries of Agriculture Clifford Hardin and Bob Bergland were members after their government service. Butz, Block, Yeutter and Veneman rejoined the Round Table after their government service and are current Round Table members. Mike Espy and Dan Glickman are also current Round Table members.

Table 9.1
Farm Foundation Round Table Meetings, 1976-2007

Technology, Agriculture and the Environment
Chapel Hill, North Carolina, June 7-9, 2007

Trade Issues and the 2007 Farm Bill
Ponce, Puerto Rico, January 4-6, 2007

Energy from Agriculture–Exploring the Future
Wichita, Kansas, June 15-17, 2006

Setting the Stage for the 2007 Farm Bill
Phoenix, Arizona, January 5-7, 2006

Sustainable Agriculture, Land Use and Resources in Conflict.
Portland, Oregon, June 16-18, 2005

Consumer Power in the Food Chain
Coral Gables, Florida, January 6-8, 2005

Business Structures for the 21st Century Food System/Challenges of Cross Border Agricultural Trade,
Fargo, North Dakota, June 10-12, 2004

Taking the Pulse of Rural America
Tucson, Arizona, January 8-10, 2004

Agriculture's Effect on the Environment: Fact or Fiction?
Birmingham, Alabama, June 12-14, 2003

Agricultural Trade and the Pacific Rim
San Diego, California, January 10-11, 2003

The Future of Biotechnology and the Food System
Wilmington, Delaware, June 14-15, 2002

Food System Biosecurity, Cuban Trade and U.S. Agricultural Policy
Coral Gables, Florida, January 9-10, 2002

Local Impacts of National Policies
Sun Valley, Idaho, June 8-9, 2001

Farming in the Sight of the City: Challenges and Opportunities
Jupiter Beach, Florida, January 4-6, 2001

21st Century Food Systems to Serve the Consumer
Kohler, Wisconsin, June 8-10, 2000

The Environmental and Financial Challenges Facing U.S. Agriculture
Corpus Christi, Texas, January 6-8, 2000

Making U.S./Canada Free Trade a Reality
Banff, Alberta, Canada, June 11-12, 1999

The Asian Financial Crisis and U.S. Agriculture
Kailua-Kona, Hawaii, January 7-8, 1999

Industrialization and the Organization of Agriculture
Omaha, Nebraska, June 5-6, 1998

Immigration, Agricultural Labor and Rural Communities
Tucson, Arizona, January 9-10, 1998

Innovative Approaches to Environmental and Food Safety Issues in Agriculture
Monterey, California, June 20-21, 1997

U.S. and Mexico Trade
Mexico City, Mexico, January 9-11, 1997

Agricultural Markets and Rural Economies in the 21st Century
Little Rock, Arkansas, June 7-8, 1996

Progress Toward Global Markets
Orlando, Florida, January 5-6, 1996

The Environment for Northeast Agriculture
Burlington, Vermont, June 9-10, 1995

Agricultural Policy in a Changing Era
Palm Desert, California, January 6-7, 1995

Technology in Agriculture's Future
Bettendorf, Iowa, June 10-11, 1994

International Trade: 1994 and Beyond
Phoenix, Arizona, January 7-8, 1994

Rural Development
Atlanta, Georgia, June 11-12, 1993

Institutional Change for a Dynamic Agriculture
Phoenix, Arizona, January 8-9, 1993

The Agricultural, Food and Environmental Policy Interface
Sacramento, California, June 26-27, 1992

U.S. Food and Agricultural Competitiveness
Boca Raton, Florida, January 3-4, 1992

Global Agricultural Markets for the 21st Century
Washington, D.C., June 6-7, 1991

Agriculture and Public Perceptions
Phoenix, Arizona, January 4-5, 1991

Biotechnology and the Future of Agriculture
Rosemont, Illinois, June 7-8, 1990

European Community 1992
Phoenix, Arizona, January 4-5, 1990

Society's Contract with Production Agriculture
Rosemont, Illinois, June 8-9, 1989

Forces Shaping Policies Impacting Food & Agriculture
Phoenix, Arizona, January 5-6, 1989

The Rural Development Issue
Rosemont, Illinois, June 16-17, 1988

Issue Management: A New Challenge for Agriculture
Phoenix, Arizona, January 7-8, 1988

Will U.S. Agriculture Adjust to a Changing World?
Rosemont, Illinois, June 11-12, 1987

Multilateral Trade Negotiations: Implications and Prospects for U.S. Agriculture
Phoenix, Arizona, January 5-6, 1987

Agricultural Policy in 1986 and Beyond
Rosemont, Illinois, June 12-13, 1986

U.S. Agricultural Competitiveness
Phoenix, Arizona, January 6-7, 1986

Various Issues in Agriculture
Oak Brook, Illinois, June 13-14, 1985

Farm Legislation in 1985 and Beyond
Tucson, Arizona, January 10-11, 1985

Policy Alternatives for Improving Agricultural Trade
Fargo, North Dakota, June 14-15, 1984

New Government Forces Shaping Future Agricultural Policy
Washington, D.C., January 26-27, 1984

A Look Ahead
Oak Brook, Illinois, June 9-10, 1983

The Past Two Years—The Next Two Years
Washington, D.C., February 3-4, 1983

Financing Agriculture and Agribusiness
Oak Brook, Illinois, June 10-11, 1982

Positive Roles for Agriculture/Agribusiness in Fulfilling Our National Purposes
Marco Island, Florida, January 7-8, 1982

Transportation: Its Impact on Agriculture and Agribusiness
Delavan, Wisconsin, May 28-29, 1981

Protecting the Ability of American Agriculture and Agribusiness
to Produce and Market Products
Lake Buena Vista, Florida, January 15-16, 1981

New Approaches for Agriculture and Agribusiness in the 1980s
Oak Brook, Illinois, May 29-30, 1980

If Agricultural Exports Fade...?
Naples, Florida, January 10-11, 1980

China, Our New Relationship: Problems and Opportunities
Oak Brook, Illinois, May 31-June 1, 1979

The Tax Revolt — Its Effect on Agriculture/Agribusiness
Phoenix, Arizona, January 11-12, 1979

Financing the Future of American Agriculture — Sources of Capital
Saratoga Springs, New York, June 14-15, 1978

*Protecting our Power to Produce So That America May Eat

Agriculture/Agribusiness Under Changing Rules
Mackinac Island, Michigan, June 2-3, 1977

Which Direction Agriculture/Agribusiness 1977
Chicago, Illinois, December 1-2, 1976

How Can Agriculture and Business Participate More Effectively
in Political Education and Action?
Kansas, City, Missouri, May 19-20, 1976

NOTE: *Evidence exists that this meeting took place, but the location and date could not be determined.

Chapter 10

The Hildreth Legacy: Farm Foundation Programming in the 1970s and 1980s[1]

"Jim Hildreth possessed an uncommon ability to sense evolving problems, identify promising talent, and back risky but worthy projects. He could encourage intellectual productivity without stifling professional creativity. That might be through a casual visit in the hallway, an unexpected phone call, or offer of limited financial support."[2]
—Robert Spitze, University of Illinois at Urbana-Champaign

When Joe Ackerman retired in 1969 at the age of 65, Associate Managing Director Jim Hildreth was appointed managing director of Farm Foundation. The 44-year-old Hildreth was a member of the World War II generation of agricultural social scientists beginning to come to prominence.

Hildreth was an enthusiastic supporter of the university committees and the Land Grant system. At the time, Farm Foundation was sponsoring no fewer than 38 formal university committees. Projects were also sponsored on an ad hoc basis with university agricultural social scientists. Hildreth, who had been with Farm Foundation since 1962, was very active with the committees and well-known by the Foundation's university and USDA partners. The committees brought together professionals from different institutions and regions, who frequently had minor disagreements and arguments over methodology and focus. Hildreth fully embraced the challenge to help work out a meeting of the minds.

Joe Coffey, who served as head of the Agricultural Economics Department at Virginia Tech in the 1970s, remembers Hildreth as "...one of the wisest listeners and consensus builders I ever met. He did it with humor, grace and insight. He was most stimulating. I never heard anyone say a negative word about Jim."[3] Bernard F. Stanton, a professor emeritus at Cornell University who met Hildreth in the early 1960s, said: "He had a special role in meetings, seeking ways to think otherwise, telling a story to lighten tension, and making a pointed observation at the crucial moment. His was a special role in working with agricultural economists and rural sociologists. He helped them keep on track when discussing important issues. He sought to bring people together or find ways to bridge apparent differences."[4]

Hildreth rarely presided at the meetings, but his presence, unique wit and trademark tobacco pipe were felt. Larry Libby, a faculty member at Michigan State University, met Hildreth in the 1970s. He described him as "...the consummate provocateur. He could ask the probing question, expanding beyond the

---

R.J. "Jim" Hildreth

Farm Foundation Associate Managing Director, 1962-1969; Farm Foundation Managing Director, 1970-1991

R.J. "Jim" Hildreth was born November 26, 1926, in Des Moines, Iowa. He was reared on a farm near what he described as the "Norwegian Ghetto" of Huxley, Iowa. After military service in Europe in World War II, Hildreth did undergraduate work in economics at Iowa State University (1949), and specialized in labor economics for his master of science degree (1950). After teaching at Augsburg College in Minneapolis for two years, he received a Ph.D. in economics from Iowa State University in 1954.

He then joined the faculty of the Department of Agricultural Economics at Texas A&M University. He was appointed research coordinator for West Texas, Texas Agricultural Experiment Station and assistant director one year later. He joined Farm Foundation in 1962, serving as associate managing director until 1970. He was managing director until his retirement in 1991.

During his tenure, Hildreth was elected president of the American Agricultural Economics Association and secretary-treasurer of the International Association of Agricultural Economists. He served on committees and the Board of Trustees of the National Planning Association, as well as advisory committees of the American Medical Association, American Bankers Association, American Veterinary Medical Association and Boy Scouts of America.

He was elected a Fellow of the American Agricultural Economics Association, the American Association for the Advancement of Science and the Soil and Water Conservation Society. He also received the Distinguished Service to Rural Life Award from the Rural Sociological Society, and the Henry A. Wallace Award from Iowa State University.

In retirement, Jim retained his keen interest in Farm Foundation, visiting the office a few times each month and attending Round Table meetings from time to time. He gave the keynote address at the 50th National Public Policy Education Conference sponsored by Farm Foundation in September 2000. He was in the process of writing this book at the time of his death, May 22, 2002.

specific point at issue to the broader context. He pushed people to question their own position on things, and the underlying assumptions."[5]

Part of Hildreth's success was his unpretentiousness. "Jim knew how to plant ideas in another person's mind and make him feel that it was their idea,"[6] according to University of Nebraska professor Howard Ottoson.

Verne House of the University of Montana Extension Service said, "Jim bridged many chasms in our profession. He did not appear to worry over the chasms; he focused on good that could be done by working together. He was respected by researchers, teachers and extension specialists, by females as well as males, by sociologists as well as economists." Hildreth had the ability to be both a respected leader and good friend. "There were few people in our profession who did not consider Jim Hildreth their friend," said Stanton. "I think Jim would feel that statement to be a compliment, and might even admit that it was true."[7]

Hildreth's guidance was frequently requested. Lowell Hill, a professor at the University of Illinois, asked Hildreth to participate in several of his programs: "His greatest contribution in these programs was his ability to cut through all the rhetoric to the central issues, to clarify divergent opinions, and identify compromises and commonalities leading to conflict resolution...His objectivity and clarity of expression gained immediate respect, regardless of the topic, from all participants. I invited him to meetings when I knew there would be conflict, as one of the few people with the ability and perceptivity to function as mediator."[8]

Hildreth viewed his responsibilities beyond coordinating committee meetings. Larry Libby noted, "Jim was well known in all Land Grant agricultural economics departments and by all Deans and Directors."[9] He was, as Warren McCord, Extension Assistant Director at Auburn University recalled, "... the Land Grant's 'insider outsider.' Jim Hildreth knew as much about Land Grant as those of us who were employed by it. However, because he was not an employee of the Land Grant system he could provide a perspective that was bold and relevant."[10]

Larry J. Conner, dean emeritus of the College of Agricultural and Life Sciences at Michigan State University, saw Hildreth as someone who could get things done. "At the North Central Agricultural Economics Chairs meeting one year, I commented on the need for agricultural economics chairs to have a national meeting. Jim immediately responded by hosting the first agricultural economics chairs reception at the American Agricultural Economics Association meetings."[11] Countless stories exist of Hildreth providing a recommendation which got an important idea in motion or someone a promotion or job.

There was more to Farm Foundation programming than the university committees. Barry Flinchbaugh, Kansas Extension State Leader, noted, "Jim and Farm Foundation had a significant impact on higher education by providing 'seed money' for countless projects." Hildreth was well-known for his frugality. Flinchbaugh added, "No one could get more bang for the buck than Hildreth."[12]

Agricultural and Political Environment.[13] The 1970s and 1980s were a turbulent period for U.S. agriculture. A succession of events shaped U.S. agricultural policy and by association, Farm Foundation's program focus. During this period, Farm Foundation and U.S. agriculture realized that events previously viewed with cursory interest, such as government monetary policy decisions and foreign affairs, now had major implications for agriculture and rural communities.

The first occurrence would lead U.S. agriculture into one of its worst crises since the Great Depression. In the early 1970s, the United States experienced its first trade deficit since World War II. The Nixon administration responded by devaluing the dollar and moving from a fixed to a flexible exchange rate system. This change made U.S. commodities more attractive overseas and encouraged increased exports.

At about the same time, poor weather and crop disease in the United States drastically reduced U.S. feed grain production. These losses were exacerbated by adverse weather conditions in other parts of the world. Public concern soon developed about the world's ability to feed itself. Further, the potential for exports increased when the United States began normalizing relations with China in 1972 and exporting grain to the Soviet Union in 1973.

With favorable investment incentives in the U.S. tax code and government loans to producers at below-market interest rates, U.S. farmers responded to the call to "feed the world" and agricultural production skyrocketed. Between 1970 and 1973, U.S. exports of feed grain, wheat and related products doubled. During the same period, net farm income also doubled.

With the agricultural sector generating impressive returns and the optimism that these conditions would persist indefinitely, tremendous investment occurred in agriculture. Farm land began to be viewed speculatively as a hedge against inflation. Between 1969 and 1978, the value of farm land and buildings in the U.S. increased 73 percent. Since a large share of the increased investment was financed, farm mortgage debt increased 59 percent between 1970 and 1980.

The first crack in the boom occurred when agricultural prices and farm income leveled off. The 1977 farm bill sharply increased commodity target prices and loan rates, and tied future rates to temporary, inflation-driven increases in farm production costs. Many producers found they could no longer cover their debt payments from farming returns. Loans were frequently refinanced with the rising value of land as collateral.

Another crack occurred on January 4, 1980, when President Jimmy Carter announced a grain embargo in retaliation for the Soviet Union's invasion of Afghanistan. Rather than starving the Soviets out of Afghanistan, Australia, Argentina, Europe and Canada continued exporting wheat, corn and barley to the Soviet Union and captured the U.S. market share. Additionally, the 1981 farm bill assumed continued inflationary growth and provided for an additional 6 percent annual increase in commodity target prices.

W. Neill Schaller
Farm Foundation Associate Managing Director, 1969-1977

W. Neill Schaller was born in Stamford, Connecticut, and grew up on a farm near Lynchburg, Virginia. He obtained an A.B. degree from Princeton University in sociology and a Ph.D. in agricultural economics from the University of California-Berkeley in 1962.

Schaller served on the staff of the U.S. Department of Agriculture from 1957-1969. From 1957-1960, he worked for the Economic Research Service in Berkeley conducting economic research at the University of California. He served for one year as acting deputy assistant administrator for International Agricultural Development and for nine years as program leader in the farm production economics division of the Economic Research Service in Washington, D.C.

Beginning in 1969, Schaller served as associate managing director of Farm Foundation. After his service with Farm Foundation, Schaller was administrator of Extension Service, USDA. He later served as associate director of the Henry A. Wallace Institute for Alternative Agriculture. Schaller recalled some of the highlights during his tenure:

> "I don't think we ever had anything like a single or dominant focus. That just wasn't the Foundation's style. However, there were a number of special, timely projects in which we played an active role as a catalyst and participant. One was a national public policy extension education project entitled 'Who Will Control U.S. Agriculture.' It was a down-to-earth, substantive educational effort to help the public realize that there were different possible futures for American agriculture. It could consist of individual family-owned-and-operated farms, a corporate agriculture, or an agriculture in which cooperatives played a dominant role. And it went on to explain who might be affected by each kind, and how, and what people could do to encourage the kind of agriculture they believed to be the most desirable.

> "Another challenging educational project was entitled 'Your Food.' It too was an especially timely, well-organized effort to shed light on current and prospective food-related issues of growing public interest and concern. These were prime examples of fact-based educational projects that might never have come about—or gained public interest—without the convener-catalyst role of the Farm Foundation.

> "There were other subjects of interest and concern to us in those days. Issues such as rural community development and the provision of health care in rural areas were always calling for careful thought and attention. They too were public issues that might have been seriously neglected by agricultural research and extension folks if USDA and Land Grant people had not been encouraged by the Foundation to address them."[29]

The Reagan administration's fiscal policy resulted in higher interest rates, and the dollar appreciated relative to major trading partners. U.S. agricultural exports peaked in 1981 and by 1986 fell by more than 50 percent. U.S. commodity prices and farm income fell drastically.

During 1981-1986, U.S. agriculture experienced its worst depression since the 1930s. Many farm families lost their way of making a living, their lifestyles and their accumulated wealth. Farm population declined more than 50 percent to 4.6 million in 1990 from 9.7 million in 1970. Farmers made up 4.6 percent of the labor force in 1970 and 2.6 percent in 1990. The number of farms fell 25 percent to 2.1 million in 1990 from 2.8 million in 1970.[14] The impacts were felt throughout rural communities as well as by those sectors of the economy that support production agriculture, especially agricultural finance. As land values fell, both lenders and borrowers suffered. The U.S. Farm Credit System lost $2.7 billion in 1985 alone.

U.S. farm policy also fell into a crisis. When market prices fell to levels below newly legislated target prices, record government cash outlays occurred. Market prices fell to the loan rate level and farm products that would have been exported were put into USDA's Commodity Credit Corporation (CCC) storage at high government cost. The focus of the 1985 farm bill was reducing supply and increasing export competitiveness. While retaining target price and loan rate mechanisms, that legislation reintroduced land retirement programs, introduced export-enhancement programs, created marketing loans and paid dairy producers to slaughter entire herds.[15] Traditional agricultural policy approaches survived in the 1990 farm bill, though budgetary issues were front and center.

Farm Foundation Programming. At its 1970 annual meeting, the Board of Trustees endorsed regrouping Foundation activities into four main program areas: commercial agriculture, rural development, environmental quality and natural resource development, and leadership development. Recognizing that improvement in rural life required the participation of many people and agencies, the Board encouraged the staff to urge universities and USDA to develop new relationships with groups concerned with improvement of rural life.

The following excerpt from the Farm Foundation 1972-73 *Annual Report* provides perspective on the Foundation's style and approach in the 1970s:

"Nature of Our Public Responsibility

"Farm Foundation works far back in a means-end chain. We do not provide rural people with direct means to their well-being, such as income, a better environment, or enhanced opportunity; nor do we produce any thing that contributes to those means, such as employment and improved health care. Rather, we encourage the development and dissemination of knowledge in the belief that a better rural life will not result, or if attained that it will not endure, without a strong knowledge base for making decisions.

"But before useful knowledge is developed, the raw material—observations, ideas, and facts—must pass through many minds, where it is interpreted, tested, improved, and finally communicated to decision makers. In a sense, Farm Foundation's role is to help ensure not only that the raw material is converted into knowledge but that it is done well. We do this in two ways: by providing, or encouraging others to provide, a forum for this conversion process—for example, through our support of some thirty-two research and extension committees; and by becoming involved in the process through staff participation in committee activities and other advisory work.

"Like so many other organizations, Farm Foundation has found that the composition and needs of its ultimate clientele have change dramatically since its establishment. No longer are rural people mainly farmers, and no longer is a better income the only, or even the most important, means to their well-being. Through a recent change in our program we have increased our emphasis on human and community development, and on natural resource development and environmental issues."[16]

A decision was made in the 1970s to provide financial and staff support for research activities on an ad hoc basis, rather than through ongoing research committees. The Foundation subsequently brought together researchers and users of research to identify problems and needs, to develop research strategies, or to seek improvements in data and research methodology. The Foundation sought to expand its ability to serve as a catalyst by focusing on identified priority problems and needs—a philosophy of programming which continues in the 21st century.

Priorities and specific plans were established for multi-state or formal regional research projects. The number of requests for extension seminars and workshops grew. These events provided a basis for national and regional cooperation in developing educational materials and promoting research to improve the quality of information for extension education. The Foundation used its limited funds in areas it believed had the highest payoff potential. Private organ-

---

Farm Foundation's 50th Anniversary

Farm Foundation commemorated its 50th anniversary November 8, 1983, at the Kansas City Club, Kansas City, Missouri. The celebration was attended by 73 current and former Board members, staff and friends. The program included a presentation on Farm Foundation's past 50 years by Managing Director Jim Hildreth and remarks by Bob Bergland and Earl Butz on "U.S. Agriculture and Rural Life in the Next 50 Years." Hildreth noted, "The Farm Foundation staff over the last 50 years has been a small group. Only seven people have served as managing director or associate managing director. It is more important to think about what the Farm Foundation is going to do during the next 50 years than it is to remember the last 50 years."[30]

izations and firms with a concern for better knowledge and understanding supported Foundation activities.

Public Policy. In addition to its four program areas, Farm Foundation continued to emphasize policy education across program areas. Through the National Public Policy Education Committee (Chapter 7), Farm Foundation organized several major public policy education programs in the 1970s.

- "Who Will Control Agriculture?" was a multi-state educational effort consisting of a booklet (35,000 copies) and series of educational leaflets (43,000 copies) on organization and control alternatives for commercial agriculture. The project also included a series of briefings with producers, agribusiness, rural community leaders, state extension workers, and congressional committees.
- A major multi-state extension education project, "Your Food," included a publication, educational leaflets (100,000 copies) and briefing materials. Policy issues addressed included: Will there be enough food? Who will get it? Will you share it? Will it be safe and nutritious? Who will control the food system? What can you do about it?

Other public policy projects sponsored by Farm Foundation in the 1970s and 1980s included:

- Organized and participated in programs to brief House and Senate staffers on agricultural policy options in cooperation with the Congressional Research Service and other agencies.
- Co-sponsored a symposium on legal, economic and social issues concerning animal patents.
- Sponsored and published *Decoupling Farm Programs.*
- Studied the effect on agriculture of the Immigration Reform and Control Act of 1986.
- Sponsored a conference on federal policy options to develop and revitalize rural America.
- Published *Policy Choices for a Changing Agriculture.*
- Published *Outlook for U.S. Agriculture Under Alternative Macroeconomic Policy Scenarios.*
- Developed a policy agenda for increasing U.S. agriculture competitiveness and trade.
- Published *Agricultural Policy and its Impact on Agribusiness.*
- Sponsored public policy education programs on child and family issues.
- Supported research on ramifications of the national dairy herd buyout program.
- Published *The Farm Credit Crisis: Policy Options and Consequences.*

- Organized an agricultural policy workshop, "Policy Options for 1985."
- Published *Retention of Farmland*.
- Sponsored *Federal Marketing Programs in Agriculture: Issues and Options*, which was initially published by the Congressional Agriculture Committees and then by Farm Foundation to obtain a wider distribution.
- Co-sponsored a rangeland policy seminar.
- Published *Property Taxes – Reform, Relief, Repeal*.
- Conducted a natural resource use and environmental policy seminar.

Commercial Agricultural Management. Farm Foundation continued to support activities promoting research and distribution of knowledge about improving commercial agricultural management. Examples are:

- Sponsored a seminar to help extension workers assist small and low-income farmers.
- Supported scientific studies and reports on how agricultural commodities are priced.
- Funded an analysis of the competitive position of Southern agriculture in a world economy.
- Studied factors influencing farm size and structure in the North Central region of the United States.
- Supported the Food and Agriculture Committee of the National Planning Association.
- Sponsored a research seminar on the determinants of land prices.
- Convened a forum on market risk management for farmers.
- Organized a seminar on using computers for improved decision making on the farm.
- Co-sponsored an international conference on sustainable agricultural systems.
- Sponsored a research/extension symposium on farming systems.
- Organized a workshop on the interaction between climate and agriculture.
- Promoted a study to evaluate agricultural research and its effect on farm productivity.
- Co-sponsored a conference to assess the impacts of biotechnology in agriculture and the food system
- Studied women's roles on North American farms.
- Studied rents, rentals and renting in agriculture.
- Investigated the policy consequences of transportation deregulation.
- Worked with the U.S. Internal Revenue Service on annual revisions of the *Farmer's Tax Guide*.

Environmental Quality and Natural Resource Development. Projects included:

- Supported a Great Plains conservation tillage seminar.
- Promoted a conference on the theology of land.
- Published *Water Scarcity: Impacts on Western Agriculture.*
- Sponsored studies and reports on land use, the energy crisis and environmental concerns.
- Facilitated research on land use transitions in areas that are urbanizing.
- Studied the social, economic and environmental consequences of the Food Security Act of 1985.
- Studied the assessment and valuation of land for taxation.
- Studied economic issues in waste management.
- Conducted a workshop on policies for retention of farmland.
- Promoted a research methodology in natural resource economics.

Rural Development. Projects included:

- Co-sponsored a series of joint conferences and workshops with the American Medical Association on rural health care.
- Supported a workshop titled, "A New Agenda for Rural America."
- Conducted a forum on rural adult education.
- Sponsored a seminar on "Financing Rural Health."
- Studied community economic development by retention and expansion of existing business.
- Promoted research on rural financial markets and state and local government finances in the 1980s.

Leadership Development. Activities included:

- Support of the George Washington Carver Public Service Hall of Fame Award.
- Support of the 4-H Executive Development Institute Program.
- Promoted staff coordination among Land Grant university administrative groups.
- Studied the impact of vocational agricultural programs in secondary schools.
- Co-sponsored workshops of the Agricultural Economics Reference Organization.
- Supported rural pastor training in economics and rural sociology.
- Supported the Committee on Women in Agricultural Economics.
- Sponsored a workshop on the role of ethics and values in agricultural and natural resource curricula.

- Supported the Great Lakes Church Leadership School.
- Assisted development of the Higher Education in Agriculture Policy Statement by industry and university administrators.
- Co-sponsored seminars on "Ethics and Agricultural Research, Teaching and Extension."
- Helped organize the American Agricultural Law Association.
- Supported the Blacks in Agricultural Economics committee.
- Supported the North Central Council of Administrative Heads of Agriculture.

As one significant element of its leadership development program, Farm Foundation made significant contributions to rural life by helping rural pastors understand the economic and social realities of rural life.[17] Topics included efficient land use and conservation, farm and home planning, improved health and sanitation, and how to work effectively as leaders in rural communities. (See Chapter 5 for an earlier perspective on this program area.) A number of institutional interdenominational centers and colleges of agriculture cooperated with Farm Foundation in presenting this training, including:

- Agricultural Missions, Inc., New York, New York
- American Country Life Association, Chicago, Illinois
- Appalachian Ministries Education Resource Center, Berea, Kentucky
- Boston University School of Theology, Boston, Massachusetts
- Center for Parish Development, Naperville, Illinois
- Chicago Theological Seminary, Chicago, Illinois
- Christian Rural Fellowship, New York, New York
- Christian Theological Seminary, Indianapolis, Indiana
- Emory University Candler School of Theology, Emory, Georgia
- Garrett Biblical Institute, Evanston, Illinois
- Iliff School of Theology, Denver, Colorado
- Interseminary Commission for Training of Rural Ministers, Boston, Massachusetts
- Michigan State University, East Lansing, Michigan
- National Catholic Rural Life Conference, Des Moines, Iowa
- National Council of Churches of Christ, New York, New York
- National Lutheran Council, Chicago, Illinois
- National Town-Country Institute, Parksville, Missouri
- Northeastern Association for Church and Society, Boston, Massachusetts
- Oberlin College, Oberlin, Ohio
- Ohio State University, Columbus, Ohio
- Oregon State University, Corvallis, Oregon
- Rural Church Center, Green Lake, Wisconsin

- Tennessee State University, Nashville, Tennessee (Bi-Vocational Ministers Workshop)
- University of Arkansas, Fayetteville, Arkansas
- University of Minnesota, St. Paul, Minnesota
- University of Wisconsin, Madison, Wisconsin
- West Virginia University, Morgantown, West Virginia
- Westminster Theological Seminary, Westminster, Maryland

Formed in 1961, the National Committee of Continuing Education for Town and Country Pastors brought together church leaders and personnel from Land Grant universities. They explored contributions Land Grants could make to continuing education for pastors, and defined the role and responsibility of both the universities and the pastors. Farm Foundation Trustee Paul Johnson chaired the committee for a number of years.

In the 1990s, as church bodies turned their attention to growing memberships in suburban areas, the number of training courses for rural pastors decreased. During this time, the general rural population, and thus membership in congregations, declined and Farm Foundation's program moved from assisting church workers to more adequately ministering to the needs of rural people. It shifted to helping church leaders better understand the forces influencing and

American Agricultural Law Association

In December 1979 Farm Foundation sponsored a meeting in Rosemont, Illinois, to explore the idea of creating a national organization for professionals interested in agricultural law. Jim Hildreth organized that event with Neil Harl of Iowa State University, and Dale Dahl of the University of Minnesota. About a dozen academic agricultural lawyers, many being the only lawyer within an agricultural economics department, participated. At a second meeting in August 1980 at the University of Illinois, catalyzed by Farm Foundation, participants endorsed draft articles of incorporation and bylaws for what was to become the American Agricultural Law Association (AALA).

In December 1980, approximately 150 agricultural lawyers and other professionals participated in that First Annual Agricultural Law Symposium at the University of Minnesota. Farm Foundation provided financial support for that meeting, at which AALA was created by the adoption of articles of incorporation and bylaws. Harl was elected AALA's first president and a board of directors was named.

Today, AALA has more than 550 members, including agricultural lawyers, government representatives, academics and other professionals. The academic community plays a large role in organizing the annual program, which includes a broad range of practitioners as presenters. The annual symposiums draw more than 200 participants. Walt Armbruster served as AALA president in 1996 and Steve Halbrook served as AALA president 2006-2007. The Association is on sound financial footing and has great demand for its annual programs.

impacting rural communities and people, allowing them to better serve those needs. At the Rural Ministry Collegium in New Rochelle, New York, in 1990, an event supported by Farm Foundation, theologians, academics, sociologists and professional ministers reviewed demographic data, research and position papers on rural life, as well as values and conceptual frameworks.

More than 200 representatives from 22 denominations participated in a 1991 Consultation on Pastoral Leadership for the Appalachian Region. It provided an open forum for ideas and strategies to better enlist, equip and sustain effective church leadership in Appalachia. In 1994, a Tri-State Ministers Workshop, organized by Tennessee State University and supported by Farm Foundation, provided training and support to predominantly minority ministers working in poor rural communities.

Farm Foundation also supported efforts of the Rural Church Network for the United States and Canada (RCN). One project was to revive interest among selected seminaries in teaching courses related to rural ministry. The Association of Theological Schools cooperates with RCN.

David C. Ruesink, a retired extension sociologist at Texas A&M University and an active participant in the National Committee on Continuing Education for Rural Clergy at Land Grant Colleges and State

---

NEC-63

In April 1985, Farm Foundation and USDA agencies sponsored a conference entitled "Research on Effectiveness of Agricultural Commodity Promotion" in Arlington, Virginia. The conference convened under the co-leadership of then Farm Foundation Associate Managing Director Walt Armbruster and Les Meyers of USDA Economic Research Service, to assess the current state of research knowledge about and availability of research tools for further work on agricultural commodity promotion programs. This meeting was in response to growing interest among agricultural producers to establish generic advertising promotion programs to increase commodity sales, though the effectiveness of such programs had not been thoroughly researched. From that conference, the NEC-63 Commodity Promotion Research Committee was established as a research coordinating committee under the Northeast Experiment Station Directors of the Land Grant Universities. This national organization brings together the academic research community, government agencies administering commodity promotion programs, and the industries involved in those programs to assess the value of the programs and provide guidance on how to increase program impacts. At semi-annual meetings, researchers exchange recent findings and developments in methods to better refine estimates of program impacts. These meetings are also an opportunity to interact with government officials and industry leaders concerning economic and policy issues facing the programs. This institutional structure has retained a strong role and continues to bring improved analysis to federally authorized programs, a number of which require periodic evaluation of impacts.

Universities, provided a perspective: "Clergy and lay leaders in rural and small membership churches are becoming more informed about social, economic, and political changes affecting their community. A better understanding of how to serve the congregation and community results in improved interfacing between religious organizations and other agencies. This has come about because of Farm Foundation's interest in supporting meetings which encourage Land Grant universities to continue working with church leaders as a special category of community influence."[18]

Farm Foundation Staff. The activities of Foundation staff within other organizations and groups continued to increase in the 1970s and 1980s. They served in influential positions in organizations and activities working to improve the economic and social well-being of agriculture and rural people. They were also involved with national and international professional associations, such as the American Agricultural Economics Association, American Agricultural Law Association, National FFA Farm Business Management Contest, Council on Education of the American Veterinary Medical Association, National Planning Association and the International Association of Agricultural Economists.

They served regional needs through the Chicago Agricultural Economists Club, North Central Rural Development Center, Southern Rural Development Center, Joint Council on Food and Agricultural Sciences, and the Kettering Foundation Agribusiness Advisory Board.

They addressed topical issues through review teams to evaluate research, extension and instruction programs at departments of agricultural economics; work groups for the Office of Technology Assessment project on U.S. Food and Agriculture Research; and the International Association of Agricultural Economists Task Force on Professional Relations with the People's Republic of China; and as a workgroup leader at the 1976 World Food Conference at Iowa State University. Staff also presented numerous seminars at Land Grant universities, USDA agencies and other groups of agricultural economists and rural sociologists.

Notable Farm Foundation Board Members

Richard E. Albrecht, president of Farm Progress Publications, served on Farm Foundation's Board of Trustees from 1971-1981. Jim Hildreth recalled, "As a communicator with farm audiences, he provided useful perspectives on farm and rural problems as seen by readers and professional agricultural communicators. He had a wide range of contacts with agricultural organizations and agribusiness firms."[19]

Boyd C. Bartlett, president and CEO of Deere & Company, was a member of the Board from 1976-1986. "Bartlett's knowledge of the economic status of farmers was very large and useful as an officer of Deere & Company. He provided insight and perspective for the Foundation programming and activities, as well as business management suggestions for the operation of the Foundation," recalled Hildreth.[20]

Orville G. Bentley, dean of the College of Agriculture at the University of Illinois, was a Farm Foundation Trustee from 1968-1978, and chairman of the Board 1972-1978. Hildreth noted, "Bentley provided linkages with research, extension and instruction of the colleges of agriculture in the Land Grant system. He also provided perspective on Midwest farming and rural problems and opportunities for Foundation programming."[21]

C. E. Bishop, president of the University of Arkansas, served on the Board from 1969-1979. Hildreth wrote, "Bishop was trained as an agricultural economist and served many roles as an economist and administrator in higher education. These experiences provided useful insight and perspective on opportunities for Foundation projects and programs. His knowledge and contacts in the Southeast and Southern agriculture and rural areas were very valuable for the Foundation."[22]

Will Erwin served as a "farmer member" on the Board of Trustees from 1981-1991. Hildreth recalled, "He represented the farmer's points of view on problems and opportunities for improving the well-being of farmers and rural people. He was active in farm and agricultural organizations and had contacts in government. Erwin was open to new and different ideas, but always gave them careful evaluation. He was close to Land Grant research and extension programs and made useful suggestions for Farm Foundation activities."[23]

Connie Greig of the Little Acorn Ranch in Estherville, Iowa, served on Farm Foundation's Board of Trustees from 1979-1984. Hildreth noted, "The Greigs operated the Little Acorn Ranch with her husband [John] as the crop manager and Connie the livestock manager. As a successful manager, she provided insight into farm and rural problems. Her suggestions and ideas for Foundation programming were often very innovative and useful."[24]

Roland Hendrickson, president of the Agricultural Division of Pfizer, Inc., served on the Board from 1982-1992. Hildreth noted, "He provided perspective and insight from the agricultural biochemical industry. His interests were nationwide as well as international. The biochemical industry was at the leading edge of new technology and methods for production agriculture. His interest and support of the Foundation program and his useful style of interaction with staff and Board made a large contribution."[25]

D. Gale Johnson was a member of Farm Foundation's Board of Trustees from 1979-1989. Hildreth recalled: "Johnson grew up on an Iowa farm, received his B.S. and Ph.D. from Iowa State University and joined the faculty at the University of Chicago. His research was in the area of agriculture and trade policies. He was Provost at the University during his term on the Foundation Board. Johnson combined farm, international trade, general economics and university perspectives in his suggestions and discussions of Foundation projects and programs."[26]

Orion Samuelson, agriculture and business broadcaster at WGN Radio, served on the Board from 1973-1999. Hildreth noted, "Samuelson was well known as an agricultural communicator in the Midwest as well as nationwide. He paid attention to the feedback from his audiences and thus provided useful predictions of emerging agricultural and rural problems and opportunities. Samuelson also had contact with advertisers and their points of view. His broad knowledge and his support of the Foundation's program was very helpful."[27]

Joseph P. Sullivan, executive vice president of Swift and Company and later CEO of the Vigoro Corporation, served on Farm Foundation's Board from 1975-1989. He was chairman of the Board twice during his service. Hildreth recalled, "Sullivan's knowledge of farm production problems and opportunities as well as the fertilizer industry and the Chicago business community was keen. This knowledge and his support for the goals of the Foundation made him a very valuable and useful member of the Board."[28]

Chapter 11

The Armbruster Era: Strategic Planning and Programming 1991-2007

"Farm Foundation's strategic plan has been designed... to address the difficult problems of rural America as it adjusts to the changes created by domestic and international forces."[1]

—Robert M. Book, Farm Foundation Trustee, 1993

The 1990s and the early years of the 21st century represented a new era at Farm Foundation. As the 1990s began, Farm Foundation found itself with new professional leadership for the first time in 22 years. At the same time, the staff and Board of Trustees were challenged to adapt the vision of the founders to a period of rapid change in agriculture. It could be argued that the economic and structural shocks experienced during this time were of a magnitude which had not occurred since the Great Depression. Farm Foundation adapted to the changing times in many ways, both large and small.

Walter J. Armbruster became managing director on December 1, 1991. Armbruster had been associate managing director of Farm Foundation since 1978, and had prior experience with USDA. While serving as associate managing director, Armbruster was active with the Finance Committee in revamping management of the Foundation's trust funds.

Up until then, the investment strategy had been highly conservative (see Chapter 12), and the endowment had consistently lost purchasing power for a generation. Working with the Finance Committee—which was then chaired by Joseph Sullivan—Armbruster helped initiate a new balanced, total-return investment strategy that led to unprecedented growth during the 1990s. The trust's value doubled from 1991 to 2007, net of annual program expenditures of approximately 5 percent of the trust value.

In 1992, the Board made another decision that initiated fundamental change within Farm Foundation—the adoption of a system of rotational, one-year terms

169

for chairs of the Board.[2] As a consequence, more individuals would chair the Board during Armbruster's tenure that during any previous managing director. Each new chair brought a new leadership style and priority issues, and the press for change was rapid.

Recent Trustees have served a maximum of two five-year terms.[3] Consequently, none of the Trustees serving in 2007 served with another managing director/president. This brought new ideas and faces to the boardroom, contributing to change in programs.

In June 1999, the titles of managing director and associate managing director were changed to president and vice president by action of Farm Foundation's Board of Trustees. The change was made to better communicate the duties and activities of these positions in more commonly used terminology. Armbruster became president and Steve Halbrook, who, in 1992, succeeded Armbruster as associate managing director, became vice-president.

Globalization and Agriculture. U.S. agriculture found itself in an increasingly globalized and competitive world throughout the 1990s. Trends continued which had begun in the Great Depression—declines in the number of farmers and farms, increases in average farm acreage, and development of various forms of supply chain management. In the 1990s, though, it became apparent that other forces were taking agriculture into a new era.

U.S. societal and demographic trends drove changes in the food system. New products were created, and traditional products were repackaged or prepared differently to appeal to an increasingly health-conscious, convenience-driven, ethnically-diverse population. The majority of U.S. households no longer fit the 1950s model. Fewer people had time to prepare elaborate meals as more spouses worked outside the home. Traditional products, like frozen whole broilers, lost market share while value-added products, such as whole rotisserie chicken and ready-to-cook chicken parts, gained market share.

Steve A. Halbrook
Farm Foundation Associate Managing Director/Vice President, 1992-present

Steve Halbrook received bachelor of arts and Ph.D. degrees in economics at the University of Arkansas and Iowa State University, respectively, and a J.D. at Drake University School of Law. Prior to joining Farm Foundation, Halbrook was in private legal practice and an economic consultant specializing in dairy marketing issues. He has served as an agricultural economist in the Agricultural Marketing Service, USDA; executive vice president of the National Dairy Promotion and Research Board; and as an economist for the Board of Governors of the Federal Reserve System. Halbrook, who joined Farm Foundation in July 1992, played a strong role in supporting Armbruster's leadership, and led Farm Foundation's efforts in the evolving area of bioenergy.

The changes in the 1990s impacted the entire food production and distribution system. At the corporate level, mergers and acquisitions reduced many traditional agricultural and food companies to subsidiaries of large, diverse corporations. Consolidation also occurred in seed, chemical and fertilizer companies. Companies began to look at integrating operations from production to distribution, consistent with the dictates of the globalized market and consumers with higher incomes. The supply chain business model evolved.

Producers began aligning their operations with processors/manufacturers/ wholesalers. Livestock operations, in particular, rapidly began to increase in size to take advantage of economies of scale and integrated systems. Cutting-edge advances, such as biotechnology and precision farming, became commonplace in agriculture.

Food safety and environmental concerns accelerated. Many long-used pesticides and chemical additives were banned. Products of biotechnology entered the market. Product recalls for pathogen contamination became more common. Recalls of ground beef, deli meat and chicken products totaled an astonishing 48 million pounds from July to October 2002.[4] In one instance, a major meat processor went out of business after selling products with pathogens, though no deaths resulted. Mad cow disease (bovine spongiform encephalopathy) and the virulent bacteria *E. coli* O157:H7 became household terms. In response, regulatory changes, proposals for tracing product from farm-to-table, and private initiatives to more effectively manage the supply chains were introduced. Regulation increased for confined animal feeding operations and non-point source pollution.

Internationally, trade agreements benefited some agricultural segments and created tensions in others. The North American Free Trade Agreement (NAFTA) took effect in 1994, liberalizing trade between the United States, Canada and Mexico. Completion of the Uruguay Round of the General Agreement on Tariffs and Trade (GATT) in 1994 set the rules for the world's trading partners and created the World Trade Organization (WTO) as a formal structure for settling international disputes.

The basic U.S. agricultural policy framework changed as well. In 1994, when the Republican Party took control of both houses of Congress for the first time in 50 years, one legislative focus was reforming agricultural policy. The "Freedom to Farm" legislation, in effect from 1996 to 2002, replaced the traditional target price mechanism with "transition payments." In retrospect, such a considerable revamping would not have been possible had it not been for record high commodity prices present during its passage. In the late 1990s, the Asian financial crisis substantially reduced export demand and commodity prices fell. Farmers once again looked to Washington for help. "Freedom to Farm" was abrogated through record levels of government payments to farmers.

Throughout all of this change, agriculture came to be viewed more like other business sectors. Farms began to develop business plans. Farm Foundation Board members were struggling to adapt to the rapidly changing environment in their own organizations. In the face of so much change, it was natural for Farm Foundation's programming approach to be re-examined.

Strategic Planning. Entering the 1990s, the Farm Foundation Board of Trustees saw the need for a more systematic approach to programming. The need for developing a strategic plan and areas for priority attention were discussed in the January 1992 Board meeting. Chairman of the Board Robert Thompson stated, "...the goal of the priority identification process was not to reinvent the wheel, but start from the conclusions of earlier discussions."[5] At the June 1992 Board meeting, a draft strategic plan was presented and adopted. It was implemented during 1992-1993. The strategic plan printed in the *1993 Annual Report*:

- Stated that the Foundation's mission "is to improve the economic and social prospects of agriculture and rural communities in America."
- Defined challenges resulting from economic and social changes in agriculture and rural communities. These included macroeconomics, trade, environmental issues, food safety and commodity programs.
- Reaffirmed the Foundation's catalytic leadership role to increase public knowledge of issues, promote communication about emerging agricultural issues, encourage better understanding of the issues and provide opportunities to explore new alternatives.
- Identified six program priority areas: Globalization, Environmental Issues, New Technologies, Consumer Issues, Role of Agricultural Institutions, and Changing Rural Communities.[6]

Program Implementation. Initial Board feedback on implementation of the strategic plan was positive. Chairman of the Board Arthur J. Fogerty stated in the *1994 Annual Report*, "This year, as we begin to test the elements of Farm Foundation's year-old Strategic Plan, we remember that Farm Foundation was established in another era marked by major structural changes in American agriculture. Now as then, technological advances and the resulting social changes have a profound impact on the science of agriculture as well as upon families living on and near America's farms. As we bring agricultural, government, academic and business leaders together to develop better public policy and stimulate creative thinking about these changes, our Strategic Plan renews our focus and gives us important feedback. Thus, we strive to achieve Farm Foundation's mission and continue to be an effective force in the field of agriculture."[7]

The adoption of the strategic plan in 1992 implied substantial change in programming, although the magnitude of change that would occur was not fully appreciated at the time. This redirection began a trend of Farm Foundation seeking new collaborators and working to a greater degree outside of its traditional

Land Grant partners. Additionally, Farm Foundation began to have a more international focus, due to the globalization priority area and the impact of the increasingly global economy on all priority areas. Farm Foundation also increased its association with USDA agencies through cooperative agreements, providing funding for collaborative projects of mutual interest.

It was recognized that catalytic leadership requires project involvement by both staff and the Board. Staff involvement in projects funded by the Foundation had always been a hallmark of its programming, which is different from many other foundations. The new strategic plan logically led staff to report to the Board on programs by priority area.

Semi-annual reports to the Board generated discussion that explored various elements of the priority area topics. These discussions provided staff ideas to communicate to contacts within the Land Grant universities and other organizations and institutions with whom Farm Foundation collaborated to implement projects. Farm Foundation's partners in research and education found the ideas informative in focusing on important economic policy issues affecting the future of agriculture and rural communities. While implementation of the strategic plan was left entirely to the discretion of Farm Foundation staff, Board input was integrated into implementation strategies.

When the strategic plan was being adopted in 1992, there was discussion of changing the name of Farm Foundation. The issue was first raised by John Block "so that the name of the Foundation is more description of its mission."[8] At the following Board meeting, divisions of views were evident, leading to a decision to study the issue in conjunction with implementing the strategic plan. The issue was dropped after research concluded that there were no alternative names that better described the major thrust of the Foundation that were not already being used by other entities.

1996 Strategic Plan Update. In 1996, the Board reviewed and updated the strategic plan. The new plan did not significantly change the priority areas, but provided greater detail on Farm Foundation's operating, management and financial procedures. It emphasized the Foundation's role as a catalyst for change:

> "Farm Foundation strives to provide a forum for open discussion, dialogue and debate on cutting-edge issues important to agriculture and rural people, emphasizing the long-term view. We seek participation by recognized leaders with divergent views to ensure that a wide range of interests are represented in all Foundation activities and we welcome disagreements. Farm Foundation acts as a catalyst to foster innovative solutions by empowering people through education and access to information, and creating an atmosphere that stimulates the development of thoughtful leadership."[9]

The 1996 vision statement contained in the strategic plan stated that Farm Foundation's mission was to be accomplished by "...stimulating economic and social sciences research on emerging topics, fostering education programs drawing on those research results and encouraging policy dialogue on the public- and private-sector issues involved."[10] This emphasis on dealing with economic and social issues confronting farmers and rural people, which is deeply rooted in the history of Farm Foundation, confirmed that the Foundation's major assets were "...its legacy, reputation for objectivity, and flexibility to respond to critical issues..."[11]

Following adoption of the revised 1996 strategic plan, the Board sought to track progress in implementation. The initial approach was to obtain "bench-mark studies" of each priority area by an independent authority. While Board Chairman Emmett Barker heralded this review in 1997 as "...the best summary of Farm Foundation programs produced during his association with the Foundation,"[12] the Board still wanted to be more involved in program evaluation and future program development.

Armbruster and staff developed Priority Area Advisory Committees comprised of Board members for each priority area. Each year, these committees review the objectives of the priority area, examine programs conducted during the previous year, and offer suggestions for future programming. At the Trustees' annual meeting, the chairs of each Advisory Committee make recommendations to the Board to adopt or update the strategic plan objectives and high priority topics. Interested members of the Farm Foundation Round Table participate in the Advisory Committee discussions. Program reports are also provided to the Round Table at their semi-annual meetings. The Advisory Committees:

- Directly involve the Board in setting and communicating priorities, with project management remaining a staff responsibility;
- Provide means to regularly review and update the strategic plan;
- Create opportunities to inform Round Table members of Foundation programs, and for Round Table members to voice opinions and ideas for future work.

Growing the Foundation. For several years in the late 1990s, the Board discussed the need for additional staff resources and the benefits of initiating a capital campaign. Underlying this discussion was the changing nature of the challenges facing agriculture:

- Ever-increasing government regulation of agriculture became an important concern. There was a fear that agriculture was losing the battle with environmental advocates and that the more urbanized, affluent population did

not understand agriculture's contributions as producer of food, fiber and
energy.

- The competitiveness of U.S. agriculture became a key concern as the
forces of globalization exposed farmers to ever-increasing economic pressures. Historically, U.S. farmers had depended on superior technology for
a competitive edge, but improved communication and other globalization
forces made technologies more rapidly available to farmers worldwide.
The need for a level international regulatory playing field also became a
concern.
- Farm policy continued to be a central concern as policy makers sought to
achieve a balance among competing demands for reduced government
spending, reduced trade-distorting effects of government payments to
farmers, increased support to make agriculture more environmentally
friendly, and reduced economic risk to farmers. While farm policy was once
the province of the U.S. Congressional Agriculture Committees, USDA and
the farm organizations, the new agenda also involved public interest groups
and other Congressional committees. Reapportionment of Congress every
decade meant that farmers increasingly had to play the politics of the minority, as urban replaced rural representation.
- Consumer demands for a safe and higher quality food supply became more
complex with increased trade and threats of bioterrorism. Satisfying these
demands led to greater interest in public- and private-sector strategies to
manage the food supply chain, increased opportunities for private firms to
satisfy particular consumer market niches, and a greater role for public
interest groups in farm and food policy issues.

If the Foundation were to deal more effectively with these challenges, more
financial resources would be required. In 2000, the Board directed the staff to
explore the feasibility of a capital campaign. An outside fund-raising consultant
was engaged to survey potential contributors, including current and past
members of the Board, recognizing that their commitment to and leadership
with substantial contributions would be a key factor in the success of the campaign. Based on the consultant's report and projected future project needs, the
Board voted in January 2001 to proceed, with the goal of generating $5 million
over three years. It also concluded that:

- A successful capital campaign to outside contributors called for a higher
level of Foundation visibility;
- A smaller number of problem-solving projects specifically targeted on key
issues would attract the interest of potential contributors; and
- Increased communication was required about the Foundation's work.

As a result, Mary Thompson joined the Foundation staff in 2002 as director of communications, and the emphasis in programming changed to focus available resources on fewer projects with a higher level of visibility.

The capital campaign was initiated during a time of significant financial pressure on individuals and businesses in agriculture and the food sector. The campaign failed to attract significant individual or business donors among Farm Foundation Board and Round Table members to jump start the effort. The campaign faltered in the early stages under ongoing examination of Farm Foundation's public visibility and operating approach. After two years, the Board terminated the formal phase of the campaign. The Board decided that further development efforts would have a three-pronged approach: the traditional annual campaign; increased project-specific funding tied to showcase or high-visibility projects; and endowment giving, targeting those most familiar with Farm Foundation's programs.

A New Business Plan. As Farm Foundation entered the new millennium, the staff and the Board believed that, while much had been accomplished, the Foundation's full potential as a catalyst for change had not been realized. There was general agreement that the long-standing mission of the Foundation was valid, but some Board members felt it should assume a more activist role in advocating specific remedies to issues facing agriculture, the food system and rural communities. Current and past Board members debated whether the Foundation should go beyond its traditional role of researching the facts and articulating options and consequences, to becoming an advocate of particular options. At a special Board meeting in April 2004, the staff presented three Foundation operating scenarios:[13]

- *Activist Catalyst Scenario,* essentially a status quo option, in which staff would initiate or solicit project proposals from professional networks and manage 80 to 100 projects averaging $10,000 to $15,000 in funding, and having potential long-term benefits for the priority areas identified by the Board.

Mary M. Thompson
Farm Foundation Communications Director and Project Manager, 2002-present

Mary Thompson received a bachelor of science degree in journalism from Iowa State University, and did graduate work at the University of Pennsylvania. Prior to joining Farm Foundation, she spent 11 years with *Farm Journal*, where she was business editor and features editor. Thompson was previously managing editor of *Agri Finance*, and farm editor and state editor of the *Waterloo (Iowa) Courier*. Thompson's focus has been on increasing awareness and understanding of Farm Foundation, maximizing communications and outreach activities of Foundation projects, and expanding its fund-raising efforts.

Alexander Legge

TIME

The Weekly Newsmagazine

Time magazine cover of Alexander Legge

International Harvester President Alexander Legge spearheaded the drive to create a private agency focused on agricultural and rural issues. His personal actions created and funded the trust that formally organized Farm Foundation in February 1933. Legge died in December 3, 1933, but his colleagues carried out his vision of the Foundation's work.

FIFTEEN CENTS

TIME

The Weekly News-Magazine

© International

VOL. II NO. 7.

FRANK O. LOWDEN
"Tact, moderation, scholarship"—
(See Page 3)

OCT. 15, 1923

Time magazine cover of Frank O. Lowden

Former Illinois Governor Frank Lowden worked closely with Legge in building the organization of Farm Foundation, and continued that work after Legge's death. Lowden and the other founding Trustees publicly announced the Foundation's creation on December 6, 1933, three days after Legge's death. A major benefactor of the Foundation, Lowden served as chairman of the Board, 1933 to 1943

Source: Time Life Pictures/Time & Life Pictures/Getty Images. Reproduced with permission.

Chris L. Christensen

Chris L. Christensen was
executive secretary of the
Federal Farm Board under
Alexander Legge and later
served as dean of the College of
Agriculture at the University of
Wisconsin. Christensen served
on the Farm Foundation Board
of Trustees from 1933 to 1964.

Source: Farm Foundation Archives

Henry C. Taylor

Henry C. Taylor founded the
Department of Agricultural
Economics at the University of
Wisconsin and the U.S.
Department of Agriculture's
Bureau of Agricultural
Economics, a precursor to the
Economic Research Service.
Taylor was Farm Foundation's
first managing director,
serving in that post from 1935
to 1945.

Source: Farm Foundation Archives

Frank W. Peck

Frank W. Peck was named president of the Federal Land Bank of St. Paul in 1938, and joined the Farm Foundation Board of Trustees in 1942. In 1945, he was named to succeed Taylor as managing director, serving in that position until 1954.

Source: Farm Foundation Archives

Joseph A. Ackerman

Joseph A. Ackerman was a land tenure specialist at Farm Foundation, 1939 to 1942; associate managing director, 1942 to 1954; and managing director, 1955 to 1969.

Source: Farm Foundation Archives

Farm Foundation's Board of Trustees

Farm Foundation marked its 30th anniversary in 1963. Participating in the May 28, 1963, Trustees meeting were standing from left: Oliver S. Willham, Robert B. Tootell, William R. Odell, Earl M. Hughes, Carroll P. Streeter, Earl L. Butz, R.S. Stevenson and Hobart Creighton. Seated from left: John M. Budd, C.W. Weldon, R.J. Hildreth, C.Y. Thomas, Edmund H. Fallon, C. Phillip Miller, Paul C. Johnson, Allan B. Kline, Joseph Ackerman and Jesse W. Tapp.

Source: Farm Foundation Archives

Charles Dana Bennett

Charles Dana Bennett and his wife, Edith, organized the Foundation for American Agriculture Program to bring together leaders to discuss agricultural issues. Farm Foundation took over management of the program in 1975, with Bennett continuing as a consultant until his retirement in 1983.

R.J. "Jim" Hildreth

R.J. "Jim" Hildreth was on the faculty at Texas A&M University before joining the staff of Farm Foundation as associate managing director in 1962. He was named managing director in 1970 and served in that post until his retirement in 1991.

Source: Farm Foundation Archives

Walter J. Armbruster

Walter J. Armbruster was an economist at USDA before being named associate managing director of Farm Foundation in 1978. He was named managing director/president in 1991. He plans to retire in 2008.

Source: Farm Foundation Archives

- *Cutting Edge Catalyst Scenario* in which staff would develop or solicit project proposals and manage 50 to 60 projects averaging $25,000 in funding, including several larger showcase projects designed to have more visible and immediate impacts.

- *Advocate Catalyst Scenario* in which a strategic agenda for agriculture, the food system and rural communities would be studied and articulated with recommendations by the Foundation for regulatory, administrative or legislative action.

Debate over these options was extensive and sometimes heated. At the June 12, 2004 meeting, the Board endorsed the "Cutting Edge Catalyst Scenario" as the operational model.

The 2004 strategic plan stated that the Foundation strives "...to stimulate creative thinking, objective analysis and innovative solutions to critical issues facing agriculture, the food system and rural communities in the short- and medium-term. Starting with staff expertise in agricultural economics and a network of professional associates, we develop multi-disciplinary activities to bring economic and social science analysis to these critical issues."[14]

The Foundation's strategic focus was further articulated in a three-year business plan which defined three types of projects:

- *Risk/Incubator* projects to build professional networks, incubate ideas and highlight new approaches;

C-FARE

The Council on Food, Agricultural and Resource Economics (C-FARE) is a non-profit organization dedicated to strengthening the national presence of the agricultural economics profession. Governed by a board that includes agricultural economists representing a wide range of public- and private-sector interests, C-FARE is widely recognized for helping agricultural economists contribute to private- and public-sector decision making on important agricultural, rural, environmental, food safety and other related societal issues. It communicates the value of economic contributions to agricultural research, funding institutions and national policy leaders. C-FARE is the voice of the agricultural economics profession in Washington, D.C. The organization is seen by leadership of the American Agricultural Economics Association (AAEA) as its primary outreach arm to policy makers. The planning committee that lead to the organization of C-FARE included Farm Foundation President Walt Armbruster; current Farm Foundation Trustee J.B. Penn; former and current USDA Economic Research Service Administrators Susan Offutt and Kitty Smith, respectively; and retired University of Illinois Professor Peter Barry. Armbruster , who continues as a member of the C-FARE Board, served as C-FARE's first chairman 1993-1996, and Barry served as the group's second chairman.

- *Keystone projects* to enrich project partnerships, extend the work of project partners to key stakeholder audiences and inform the policy debate;
- *Leadership/Showcase projects* — staff-directed projects addressing major issues facing agriculture, the food system and rural communities.

With approval of the three-year business plan, Armbruster and Halbrook began to develop the showcase project concept, drawing on ideas gathered from the annual Board reviews of the strategic plan and interactions with other leaders in the agricultural and food industries, the academic community and government agencies. The first significant showcase project, "Food Traceability & Assurance in the Global Food System," evolved from supply chain management and food safety concerns related to *E. coli* contamination, foot-and-mouth disease and mad cow disease. Funded by Farm Foundation at $80,000, this project was led by staff working with a task force of academics, industry specialists and policy leaders. There were no industry financial contributions to this project, although there was considerable in-kind support.

Another showcase project focused on renewable energy. Funded by USDA, "Agriculture as a Producer and Consumer of Energy" explored current and potential contributions of agriculture as a provider of energy, as well as its role as a user of energy. This was the first project in which the Foundation received compensation for project management. Since that 2004 conference, Farm Foundation has led three more conferences on bioenergy issues, with additional activities planned.

Farm Foundation, AAEA and IAAE

In 1920, 15 years before he became managing director of Farm Foundation, Henry C. Taylor served as president of the American Farm Economics Association, now the American Agricultural Economics Association (AAEA), a professional organization for U.S. agricultural economists. AAEA currently publishes two peer-reviewed research journals, as well as a policy outreach publication. Taylor was a founding member and organizer of the association in the early 1900s.[15] Taylor was also involved with the organization of the International Association of Agricultural Economists (IAAE) attending the first meeting in 1929.[16]

As one of the nation's foremost agricultural economists, Taylor continued to be involved with AAEA and IAAE throughout his career and initiated an association between Farm Foundation and the organizations which continues to this day. Taylor, Joseph Ackerman, Jim Hildreth and Walter Armbruster all served as president of AAEA and were elected fellows of the organization. Ackerman, Hildreth and Armbruster also have served as secretary/treasurer of IAAE, an office held by a member of Farm Foundation staff since 1958. Through these organizations, Farm Foundation has provided decades of leadership for agricultural social science research and education worldwide, helping to better inform public- and private-sector decision makers.

AAEA Food and Agricultural Marketing Policy Section (FAMPS)

In May 1992, Farm Foundation President Walt Armbruster provided leadership to organize a meeting of agricultural economists working in universities and government agencies who were concerned about food and agricultural marketing policy issues. A number of regional research committees existed that brought together academic researchers to address various segments of the food and agricultural marketing system. But there was no vehicle to bring that work together in a comprehensive fashion to address policy issues facing the industry and government agencies. The 1992 meeting led to formation of the Food and Agricultural Marketing Consortium to provide a forum for university, government and industry representatives to address the vitality and competiveness of the U.S. food and agricultural marketing system. The consortium has now become the Food and Agricultural Marketing Policy Section of the American Agricultural Economics Association and continues to organize annual conferences, serving an important role in assessing agricultural marketing programs and policy.

These initial showcase projects were highly successful and drew substantial public attention. The next showcase project, "The Future of Animal Agriculture in North America," addressed critical policy issues, attracted significant financial support from multiple sources, and introduced the Foundation to broader audiences.

"The Future of Animal Agriculture in North America" examined the major issues affecting the competitive position of the North American livestock industry. Like previous showcase projects, it relied heavily on the staff's expertise and leadership in directing the project. The project's $350,000 budget was designed to cover a portion of staff costs in development and implementation. It differed from other showcase projects both in its scope and the wide diversity of funding sources.

The project was also notable for examining industry challenges and opportunities across North America—Canada, Mexico and the United States—with participation and funding support from organizations and agencies in all three nations. Project findings were introduced during one week in April 2005, with press and industry events in Washington, D.C., Mexico City and Ottawa.

The project report was widely shared with project partners, and disseminated broadly within their national networks. Findings of the study have been used in strategic planning efforts by several industry sectors. In the year following the project's completion, project representatives, including Farm Foundation staff, presented reports to various industry audiences. The full project report was widely disseminated in electronic and print formats in English, Spanish and French.

The Armbruster Legacy. In late 2005, Walt Armbruster informed the Board he would retire in early 2008. A Transition Committee was appointed to identify a successor. Even more change had come to Farm Foundation.

Looking back, Armbruster was one of the few constants during the prior 15 years. His calm and pragmatic style—focusing on cooperation and consensus-building—enabled the Foundation to partner with a wide range of other organizations and individuals. His social consciousness, vast network of professional contacts, and leadership skills gave Farm Foundation the ability to tackle virtually any policy issue. Armbruster and the Board of Trustees provided astute financial management, continuous strategic planning and adaptation of programs to rapidly changing times.

Under Armbruster's leadership, the Foundation maintained its reputation for objectivity while substantially expanding the scope and reach of its programs. While the Foundation supported some of the same types of programs it did a decade before, the focus on impacts and the presentation to broader audiences increased dramatically. It would have been hard to envision a project the scope of the "Future of Animal Agriculture in North America" in 1991.

Armbruster and the Board also recognized that the new economic and policy issues facing agriculture and rural communities fit the Foundation's strategic advantage. The 1993 strategic plan, and the periodic revisions throughout the 1990s, gave Farm Foundation a Board-endorsed programming agenda, which was used to generate new program ideas and push traditional program partners to address the issues identified. Farm Foundation became a much more active participant in program planning and development, and its programs became more visible, focused and outreach oriented.

Farm Foundation was also largely remade as an organization under Armbruster's leadership. The key to success in organizational change was integration. The development of Priority Area Advisory Committees was an institutional innovation designed to integrate Trustees and Round Table members more fully into Farm Foundation programs. This made Farm Foundation a more proactive, effective and visible organization.

Chapter 12

Farm Foundation's Financial History

"While income is important, neither the Corporate Trustee nor the [Finance] Committee has in its judgment sacrificed security of principal for income."[1]
—Farm Foundation Board Minutes, 1953

Farm Foundation's 75-year history of service to agriculture has been dependent on prudent financial management of its trust and the ability to attract additional capital.

The heart of Farm Foundation's present endowment can be traced to four major sources in the 1930s and 1940s: a bequest of cash and securities from Alexander Legge; donations by other founding Board members and sponsors; the sale of the Fairway Farms Corporation, donated by John D. Rockefeller, Jr.; and the sale of real estate holdings willed by Frank Lowden (Table 12.1). In addition to outright capital contributions, many individuals, particularly Trustees, contributed their time and expenses to grow the Foundation.

Several founders made contributions for the operation of the organization committee in the early 1930s, before the execution of the Farm Foundation Trust Agreement. No formal record of these contributions exists. Dan A. Wallace wrote Frank E. Mullen about these contributions in 1943:

> "Of course, there were many meetings with such people as Mr. Legge, Governor Lowden, Magnus Alexander, Cliff Gregory and other editors, and Mrs. Rumsey and Mr. McDonald. I made several trips to Chicago and at least three trips East at my own expense, other than certain reimbursements for wires, telephone calls and rail fare. As I recall, Mrs. Rumsey paid $500 to cover a portion of this and other expenses. As I recall, one of your trips was paid out of this fund, which was set up at the suggestion of Governor Lowden. I am not positive about the total amount of the contributions of this sort, but there seems to be no record

in the files of the Foundation or the Trust Company. This is quite natural because it was a generous personal contribution turned over for the use of the organized group which operated for a year or more before the Foundation was set up. All of us made some personal contributions of the same sort which is one explanation of the fact that a few of us like you, Cliff Gregory and I were not asked to turn over money as founders because of our previous contributions in time, effort and expense involved in working out an idea which we all sincerely believed."[2]

Alexander Legge. As noted in Chapter 2, on October 12, 1931, Alexander Legge created a trust containing securities and cash subscribed by him and naming as trustees himself, Addis E. McKinstry, George A. Ranney, William M. Gale and William S. Elliott.[3] The trust agreement provided for the transfer of the funds to a foundation to be created for the general welfare of the rural population of the United States.

When Farm Foundation's trust was executed February 10, 1933, Legge transferred from his 1931 trust $21,673.74 in cash, and International Harvester and U.S. Steel Company securities with a face value of $390,150. Legge's will, dated February 18, 1932, included this clause:

"*Sixth,*—One-half of the residue of my estate, real, personal and mixed, but not to exceed five hundred thousand dollars ($500,000) in value, I give, devise and bequeath in trust for charitable purposes as follows: I am now interested with others in the formation of a foundation to be devoted to the general welfare of the farming population of the United states and improvement of the conditions of rural life. If, prior to my death, such a foundation shall have been formed and I shall have taken part in its formation or contributed to its endowment, this residuary devise and bequest shall go to said foundation to be used and applied for charitable purposes in accordance with the provisions of the charter or trust agreement creating the same..."[4]

Table 12.1
Major Sources of Farm Foundation's Endowment (1933-1943)

Donor(s)	Donation	Year	Value
Alexander Legge	stocks and cash	1933	$979,440 (1935 value)
Other Contributions	stocks and cash	1933	$14,450 (1933 value)
John D. Rockefeller, Jr.			
Fairway Farms Corporation	Promissory Notes ($150,000)	1937	$62,670 (1946 value)
Frank O. Lowden	South Bend Plantation	1943	$320,000 (1947 value)

According to the records of the trust company, The First National Bank of Chicago, Legge bequeathed Farm Foundation a further $500,000 in cash and Illinois Steel Company bonds and U.S. Steel Company securities with a face value of $50,000. The 1938 value of Alex Legge's total contribution was $961,823.74, or 98.5 percent of the Farm Foundation trust value at that time.

Also contributing to the Farm Foundation trust, (Table 12.2) in cash or securities were: Ralph Budd, William L. Clayton, Chris L. Christensen, Sam R. McKelvie, Paul A. Draper, Harold F. McCormick, Robert E. Wood, William S. Elliott, Arthur M. Hyde, Frank O. Lowden, Cyrus H. McCormick and Bernard M. Baruch. The sum of these contributions had a market value of $114,450 in 1938. The failure to secure additional funds was disappointing to the founders, but reflected prevailing Depression conditions.

Illinois Supreme Court Decision. Farm Foundation's trust faced a significant challenge in 1935. On November 4, 1935, the DuPage County Court at Wheaton, the jurisdiction in which Alexander Legge formally resided, ruled that Legge's $500,000 bequest to Farm Foundation was subject to Illinois inheritance taxes. The decision dealt with the interpretation of a statute of Illinois law: "Gifts to foreign corporations or to non-residents, to be expended outside the State, are not exempt from taxation under section 28 of the *Inheritance Tax Act*."[5] This decision resulted in a state inheritance tax assessment of $122,750, a value roughly equal to the total contributions of all of Farm Foundation's other donors at that time.

The original hearing included testimony by Frank Lowden and Paul Mathias, secretary and assistant to the general counsel of the Illinois Agricultural Association, that: "fundamental farm problems are not local; that it was impossible to help Illinois farmers by study and education without helping farmers in every other State where similar problems occur, and that a program for the solution of farm problems confined to Illinois could not possibly be effective; that the Farm Foundation will be of substantial benefit to the farmers of Illinois, and that Chicago, the agricultural capital of the nation, will also benefit by improved conditions of the farmers in this and other States..."[6]

The decision was appealed to the Illinois Supreme Court, which reversed the judgment in an October 14, 1936, decision. The court ruled: "...Farm Foundation is a charitable and benevolent trust organized and operating within the jurisdiction of the State of Illinois to benefit the rural population of the State and that such legacy given to that trust under the will of Alexander Legge is exempt..."[7]

Fairway Farms. John D. Rockefeller, Jr. gifted Farm Foundation 12 promissory notes of the Fairway Farms Corporation of Montana in 1937. The notes were valued at $150,000 (principal and interest). The notes were transferred not merely as a gift, but also to enable Farm Foundation Board of Trustees to control and direct the orderly liquidation of the Fairway Farms Corporation and provide for the analysis and preservation of the results of its experiments.

Table 12.2
Subscriptions and Donations Made to the Farm Foundation Trust, April 30, 1938[26]

Donor	Cash	Description	Number of Shares or Principal Amount	Book Value
Alexander Legge	$500,000.00	Unites States Steel Corporation 7% cumulative preferred stock	400 shares	$40,000.00
		Illinois Steel Company debenture gold bonds 4-1/2%	$10,000.00	$10,000.00
Alexander Legge, Addis E. McKinstry, George A. Ranney, William M. Gale, and William S. Elliott, as Trustees	$21,673.74	International Harvester Company 7% cumulative preferred stock.	3,300 shares	$330,000.00
		International Harvester Company common stock.	150 shares	$150.00
		United States Steel Corporation 7% cumulative preferred stock.	600 shares	$60,000.00
Harold F. McCormick		International Harvester Company common stock.	1000 shares	$1,000.00
Cyrus H. McCormick		International Harvester Company common stock	1000 shares	$1,000.00
Frank O. Lowden		Swift and Company capital stock	250 shares	$6,250.00
Bernard M. Baruch		Great Northern Railway Company preferred	1,400 shares	$1,400.00
Robert E. Wood	$100.00			
Ralph Budd	$1,000.00			
William L. Clayton	$1,000.00			
Paul A. Draper	$1,000.00			
William S. Elliott	$1,000.00			
Arthur M. Hyde	$500.00			
Chris L. Christensen	$100.00			
Sam R. McKelvie	$100.00			
Total	$526,473.74			$449,810.00

John D. Rockefeller, Jr.
Farm Foundation donor

John D. Rockefeller, Jr. was the only son of billionaire Standard Oil Company founder John D. Rockefeller. Making money held little appeal, so he dedicated his life to philanthropy. During his 86 years, he donated an estimated $537 million. His largess included sponsoring Rockefeller Center in New York, funding the restoration of Colonial Williamsburg, and donating the land for the United Nations complex. He gave millions to public health campaigns and universities. Rockefeller was very interested in conservation, providing funds or donating lands which are now included in Great Smoky Mountains, Acadia, Shenandoah and Grand Teton National Parks. His generosity also financed museums in Mesa Verde, Grand Canyon and Yellowstone National Parks.

Founded in 1924 in cooperation with Montana State College of Agriculture, Fairway Farms was a non-profit experimental study of the problems of land tenure and land utilization in the Northern Great Plains. Montana was one of the last areas of the United States to be homesteaded, with a boom occurring there from 1907 to the early 1920s. Homesteaders adopted a farming style prevalent in the Eastern United States and, until 1917, were generally successful due to unusually favorable climatic conditions, the fertility of the virgin sod, and a lack of pests and disease. Then a succession of droughts, pests and lower prices doomed many farmers.

In 1923, 12 years before he was employed by Farm Foundation, Henry Taylor was dispatched by Secretary of Agriculture Henry C. Wallace to investigate Montana's agriculture situation. Taylor and Milburn L. Wilson of Montana State College, devised an experiment in which the best machinery and farm management practices would be tested in the semi-arid lands of Montana to determine if farming could be made profitable.

In 1924, Wilson organized a corporation with the purpose of "...acquiring agricultural lands in the State of Montana, and elsewhere, and of settling the same, encouraging the development thereof according to the best practices of agriculture, horticulture, and animal husbandry, and providing means for acquisition of title by tenants, and generally of encouraging and promoting efficient agricultural and horticultural methods and practices, and disseminating information thereon."[8] Taylor was one of the corporation's nine directors.

By 1926, with the financial assistance of John D. Rockefeller, Jr., nine farms totaling 3,500 acres were purchased in diverse areas across the state. The corporation worked with tenants to improve profitability by utilizing "...the best known methods of agricultural production under semi-arid conditions and to develop improved farm organization and management."[9]

The experiment immediately suffered from low commodity prices, drought and a poor selection of tenants. As Ronald Kenney noted in his 1969 master's

The Great Depression

The Great Depression is generally defined as starting after the October 29, 1929, stock market crash and ending sometime during World War II. Frequently overlooked is the fact that there was a succession of stock market crashes during the Great Depression.[25] That fact makes Farm Foundation's maintenance of its endowment through the period all the more remarkable.

The first downturn, which was punctuated by the famous "Black Tuesday" crash, began September 3, 1929, and lasted 71 days through November 13, 1929. The Dow Jones Industrial Average lost 47.9 percent of its value during this period. After some recovery, the market suffered its most severe crash in history on April 17, 1930. From that day to July 8, 1932, the market lost 86 percent of its value.

The next crash occurred during the 173 days from September 7, 1932, to February 27, 1933. The Dow Jones Industrial Average lost 37.2 percent of its value during this period, which corresponded with the uncertainty associated with the election of Franklin Roosevelt and the start of the New Deal. After some recovery, the stock market fell again beginning March 10, 1937, and ending 386 days later on March 31, 1938. During this period, the market lost 49.1 percent of its value. In percentage terms, this was the second worst crash in the history of the New York Stock Exchange.

After a brief recovery, from September 12, 1939, through April 28, 1942, the market crashed again, losing 40.4 percent of its value. This collapse corresponded with the start of World War II in Europe through the Pearl Harbor attack and the United States' entry into the conflict.

Only the crashes in 1932 and later had implications for Farm Foundation as the initial trust fund was first made available in October 1931. However, the earlier turmoil undoubtedly affected the contributions of various donors.

thesis on the Fairway Farms Experiment: "Wilson sought ordinary men with average capabilities for farm tenants. He attempted to choose former tenants of proven managerial capacity, thrift, and knowledge of practical farming. He believed that, if the Fairway concept were to prove useful, it had to demonstrate that average men could succeed at farming once they had proper land units and adequate equipment." However, Kenney continued, "Many of them had been unsuccessful farmers before signing with the Fairway Farms and continued to be just as unsuccessful as tenants."[10] Considering the prevailing conditions, the experiment would have required extraordinary tenants to have been fully successful.

In February 1933, eight years after its founding, "...the drought and changed economic conditions had disastrously affected the experiment....it is evident that the existing tenant-purchasers will not be able to become owner operators as was originally contemplated."[11] After giving notice to Rockefeller, the Fairway Farms Corporation began selling the least-performing farms and reorganizing its financial structure. Taylor later worked out an agreement with Rockefeller for the delinquent notes to be transferred to Farm Foundation. In 1942, the Fairway Farms Corporation board voted to liquidate all remaining farms in the experiment. Over the next few years, the farms were sold and a total of $62,670.01 was paid to Farm Foundation. On May 27, 1946, Fairway Farms Corporation was formally dissolved.

Lowden Plantation. Frank Lowden willed his South Bend plantation near Gould, Arkansas, to Farm Foundation at his death in 1943. The will stated:

> "<u>TWENTIETH:</u> I give, devise and bequeath to the FARM FOUN-
> DATION all real estate owned by me in Lincoln and Desha Counties,
> in the State of Arkansas, consisting of about 21,000 acres of alluvial land,
> 13,000 acres of which are protected by a levee and are suited for small
> farms, the other 8,000 acres of which are in timber which I desire
> handled in accordance with the best forestry practices; together with all
> buildings, improvements, farm equipment and other personal property
> located thereon and owned by me; subject to all leases or other con-
> tracts affecting said lands existing at the time of my decease."[12]

Farm Foundation accepted the bequest under the terms of Lowden's will and assumed ownership and operation of the plantation property, including all farm and timber operations. A Lowden Plantation Advisory Committee, appointed by the Farm Foundation Board each year, and Joseph Ackerman were responsible for operating decisions. Net operating income varied year-to-year: a loss of $3,000 in 1946-1947 and a gain of $24,276 in 1947-1948. In 1946, the Board approved the sale of just over 1,000 acres to the Mississippi River Commission for about $20,000 for a levee enlargement project on the south bank of the Arkansas River.

It was Lowden's wish that the Board consider operating the property in the interest of the tenants and sharecroppers so they might own and farm family-sized units of land, and improve their economic and social status. Lowden recognized that two important factors would influence the experiment he had in mind. One was the relatively large amount of capital required to maintain optimal production on the farm, equip it with mechanical power, and provide family-unit housing for the operators. The second factor was the time needed to develop the tenants to be able to manage and pay for their own farms.

Estimates of the capital needed exceeded the resources of Farm Foundation, and the time required to develop the experiment out of plantation's income appeared impracticable. The Trustees determined that greater progress would be made toward improving living conditions of tenant farmers and sharecrop-pers by cooperating with existing research and educational agencies and through other Farm Foundation programs. In 1947, the Trustees accepted an offer of $300,000 for the remaining land.

The Farm Foundation Trust. The economic conditions preceding Farm Foundation's formal organization on February 10, 1933, influenced the founders' levels of contribution. The wealth of Farm Foundation's principal founder, Alexander Legge, was primarily in International Harvester stock. Harvester weathered the Depression comparatively well. If Legge's holdings had been more diversified, it is possible there never would have been a Farm Foundation. Credit should also be given to Farm Foundation's trust managers. The trust's value decreased only 8 percent from 1933 to 1942. Considering the economic conditions, and that projects were sponsored and salaries paid during that period, they did an exemplary job.

The founders choose as Farm Foundation's corporate trustee the First Union Trust and Savings Bank (later First National Bank) of Chicago, Illinois. After establishing Farm Foundation, one of the Board's first activities was ensuring exempt status for federal income taxation under the Revenue Act of 1932. That status was granted by the Treasury Department on June 1, 1933, so long as Farm Foundation's "...purposes and actual activities remain unchanged."[13] As specified in the bylaws, the Finance Committee was also established.

Since International Harvester preferred stock represented a large percentage of Farm Foundation's investments, one of the corporate trustee's first recommendations was to diversify the Foundation's holdings. With the additional funds received from the Legge estate, this matter became more pressing. The Finance Committee concurred, but the full Board of Trustees could not reach a consensus as to which securities were worthy of investment. Consequently, the first several years of Board minutes note the lack of consensus and state, "...all matters of investment policy and specific investments were left to the Corporate Trustee and the Finance Committee to be determined according to their best judgment."[14] With the uncertainty of prevailing economic conditions and the lack of consensus of the Trustees, few if any changes were made to Farm Foundation's portfolio for the first several years.

In 1938, the Finance Committee used accumulated income to purchase U.S. Savings Bonds with a maturity value of $10,000. The Board also authorized the committee to sell 1,000 shares of International Harvester Preferred shares and reinvest the proceeds in short-term high grade bonds. Diversification activities continued after that date.

During the 1940s, Farm Foundation continued to diversify its holdings. At the 1949 Board meeting, R.G. Collins of the First National Bank of Chicago reported on Farm Foundation's endowment performance:

"The current value of the Fund is $1,840,000. At no time during the history of the Fund has its market value been less than its original value plus the assets added as of any given date. At the time the Endowment Fund was established it was producing an annual income of $27,000. The present income of $80,000 is the highest the Fund has produced during its history and is close to three times the 1933 income. Initially

Early Financial Management

At the June 1942 meeting of the Farm Foundation Board of Trustees, R.G. Collins, a representative of the First National Bank of Chicago, presented a detailed summary of the management of the trust fund up to that date:

"The original security holdings of the Farm Foundation as of the date of acquisition in February, 1933 had a market value of $420,650. Subsequent donations in cash of $519,973.74, received at various times, give a valuation of $940,623.74 at the time the assets were received by the Trustees. If the original assets had been held intact their value as of April 30, 1942 would have been $1,252,985. The account as of April 30, 1942 had a value of $1,153,178, or about $100,000 less than its value would have been if none of the original securities had been sold and the cash had remained uninvested.

In 1933 the securities produced an income of $28,271. Approximately 80% of their value was in International Harvester preferred and common stocks, and about 2% was represented by bonds.

During the early years of the account, only a part of its income was being used, the original securities were held intact, and as cash was received it was largely invested in high-grade short-term securities. In June, 1939 and through May, 1940, with an isolated sale in October of that year, in order to bring about some obviously needed diversification the following sales of original security holdings were made:

	Original Share Holdings	Shares Sold
International Harvester, preferred	3,300	1,500
International Harvester, common	2,150	1,650
United States Steel, preferred	1,000	750

These shares sold had an original market value of $210,768; the proceeds from their sales were $408,839, which was $51,189 in excess of their market value as of April 30, 1942.

During the first ten months of 1940 (with one small purchase in October, 1941) when the need for income grew and common stocks were selling generally at around their long term average levels, $426,412 was invested in a diversified list of high grade common and preferred stocks, although only about 10% of this amount was invested in preferred stocks. On April 30, 1942, with stock averages at around their lowest prices since 1935, these stocks had a market value of only $287,995, a decline of a third of their cost. Since the latter date they have recovered 25% of that decline and show a current value of $322,629. With this recovery, industrial stocks are still at only about 73% of their long term average level, and are, we think, currently being appraised at less than their intrinsic worth.

The balance of the investments have been in high grade bonds. Those now held as of April 30, 1942 were quoted as slightly in excess of their cost.

It will be noted that as of that date 44.6% of the portfolio was invested in bonds, 29.4% in preferred, and 26% in common stocks; that none of the last named holdings exceeded 3% of the value of the Fund; that the only out-of-proportion holding was 1,800 shares of International Harvester preferred which still represents 25% of the value of the portfolio; and that the estimated gross income is 5% of the April 30, 1942 market value. The proportions of fixed income and equity securities in the account are in line with accepted conservative investment standards, and we would not wish to see them changed in any substantial way. The general quality of the securities in the portfolio is, we think, definitely above average."[24]

the income represented a return of 4.7 percent on the market value; in the interim, on the basis of market value, the income has varied from 2.8 percent to 5 percent; and it is currently 4.5 percent. On the basis of original market value plus the capital added to a specified date, the income return was initially 4.7 percent; in 1936 it had reached its low of 3.6 percent; and it is now [1949] 5.8 percent."[15]

New Funds Committee. Farm Foundation's New Funds Committee had existed, at least informally, since the late 1930s. The 1941 Board minutes note that no report from the committee was forthcoming, but that Robert E. Wood was succeeding George MacDonald as chairman. Under Wood, Farm Foundation received 600 shares of Goodyear Tire and Rubber Company common stock from Sears, Roebuck and Company in 1943.

On May 1, 1944, under the leadership of New Funds Committee Chairman Arnold B. Keller, Farm Foundation began its first capital campaign—a five-year effort to raise $300,000. The funds were to be used to support and expand the current work of the Foundation, allowing the endowment income to accumulate. A 16-page informational publication, *Looking Ahead with The Farm Foundation*, was produced in 1946 to support the effort.

More than $267,000 was raised (Table 12.3), short of the initial goal of $300,000. In 1949 it was decided to extend the campaign another five years. Two additional publications, *Improving Farm Life* and *Reaching the Grass Roots: An Investment in Enduring Values*, were produced in 1950 and 1951 respectively for the fund raising campaign. By 1954, more than $527,000 had been raised.

After the 10-year capital campaign, Farm Foundation continued to solicit and receive donations. Between 1955 and 1970, the New Funds Committee raised annual amounts ranging from a low of $19,000 to a high of $60,000.

Management of the Trust in the 1950s and 1960s. Farm Foundation's corporate trustee, First National Bank of Chicago, continued to manage Farm Foundation's endowment under the direction of the Board's Finance Committee. The 1950 Board minutes state: "In the opinion of the Finance Committee, the portfolios as presently constituted are well diversified and the securities held are all of investment merit, and the maturity calendar in each Fund adapted to the short and long term budget requirements of the Foundation."[16]

In 1951, Farm Foundation's trust had a market value of more than $2.6 million, which provided about $96,000 in gross income for the year. At that time, Farm Foundation's yearly budget was approximately $145,000, with the remainder of the budget covered through corporate contributions. This funding arrangement worked fairly well through the 1950s and 1960s. The 1957 minutes offer insight into Farm Foundation's management style at that time: "While the proposed budget for 1957-58 now totals $199,985, the experience in the past has been that the full amount [of the] budget has never been spent. No more will be spent this year than can be used productively."[17] It was not uncommon for five to 10 percent of the budget to be returned.

The Perils of Inflation.[18] From the late 1960s to the mid-1980s Farm Foundation faced a great challenge to the security of its endowment. A period of high inflation, low returns on trust income, and decreased contributions

Table 12.3
Gifts Designated for First and Second Current Use Campaigns, 1944-1954[27]

Company	1944-1948	1949-1954
International Harvester Company	$50,000	$60,000
Wilson and Company, Inc.	$15,000	—-
Quaker Oats Company	$10,000	$10,000
Oliver Farm Equipment Company	$5,000	—-
Swift and Company	$15,000	$7,500
Armour and Company	$15,000	—-
International Minerals and Chemical Corporation	$500	$1,000
Allis-Chalmers Mfg. Company	$15,000	$15,000
Sears, Roebuck and Company	$25,000	$25,000
Standard Oil Company of Indiana	$15,000	$15,000
Deere & Company	$10,000	$10,000
Goodyear Tire and Rubber Company	$7,500	$15,000
Firestone Tire and Rubber Company	$7,500	$15,000
B.F. Goodrich Company	$7,500	$15,000
United States Rubber Company	$7,500	$7,500
J.I. Case Company	$7,500	$7,500
First National Bank of Chicago	$5,000	$10,000
Harris Trust and Savings Bank	$1,500	$1,500
Northern Trust Company	$1,500	$1,500
City National Bank and Trust Company	$1,000	$1,000
Aldens Foundation	$2,000	$1,000
Continental Illinois National Bank and Trust Co.	$5,000	$6,000
Beech Nut Packing Company	$1,000	—-
Proctor and Gamble Company	$5,000	$5,000
Western Association of Railway Executives	$16,672	$12,553
General Motors Corporation	$15,000	$15,000
General Mills	$1,000	$2,500
Kraft Foods, Inc.	$3,000	—-
Total	**$267,672**	**$259,553**

resulted in the Farm Foundation trust being valued at less than its original value in real (adjusted for inflation) terms. Although the trust continued to increase in nominal value, the increases were offset by inflation to the degree that the trust was worth less in current dollars than it had been during the 1930s (Figure 12.1).

Prior to this period in U.S. history, inflation, or a sustained rise in average prices, had been seen during war periods, but was followed by a post-war deflation. After World War II, prices slowly but steadily increased. By the mid-1960s, it was apparent that inflation was becoming a problem. Various remedies were attempted. President Nixon's 1971 price-wage freeze and President Ford's Whip Inflation Now (WIN) campaign were largely ineffective at curtailing basic economic pressures. Average inflation was about 1.4 percent from 1961 to 1965, jumping to 6.7 percent during 1971-1975 and 8.9 percent from 1976-1980. Interest rates increased correspondingly. At times, during 1980-1981, the weekly Federal Reserve federal funds rate exceeded 20 percent.[19]

By the late 1970s, Trustees began to express concern about the performance of Farm Foundation's trust. In 1981, the Finance Committee, in conjunction with the Corporate Trustee, the First National Bank of Chicago, reviewed Farm Foundation's stock and bond portfolio. The Board minutes record that the bond portfolio was "substantially strengthened" and actions were undertaken to "improve the prospects for financial performance of the common stock portfolio over the next three to five years."[20]

Farm Foundation's annual fundraising suffered. In 1980, only $22,900 was raised for programming, with $23,950 raised in 1981. But in 1982, contributions rebounded, totaling $50,239. The Board minutes state: "Discussion indicated that the Board was pleasantly surprised by the gifts and contributions, especially in today's economic environment."[21] Bolstered by that success, a three-year fundraising campaign was initiated in conjunction with Farm Foundation's 50th anniversary in 1983.

Foundation Excise Tax and Fundraising. In the late 1960s, Congress imposed on private foundations an excise tax of two percent of a foundation's net investment income (26 U.S.C. §4940). Foundations can avoid this tax if they meet the definition of a "publicly supported organization" by, among other requirements, receiving at least 10 percent of total income from "public" sources averaged over a 5-year period (see 26 U.S.C. §509(a) and 26 U.S.C. §170(b)(1)(A)(vi)). During the early 1970s, Farm Foundation struggled to obtain sufficient income from public sources to avoid the excise tax, and paid this tax from 1970 to 1974. The payments were about $11,000 per year.

The merger with the Foundation for American Agriculture (see Chapter 9) in 1975 provided Farm Foundation with a larger group of potential individual and corporate donors. During this same period, Farm Foundation started organizing cooperative projects with government agencies, for which the agencies

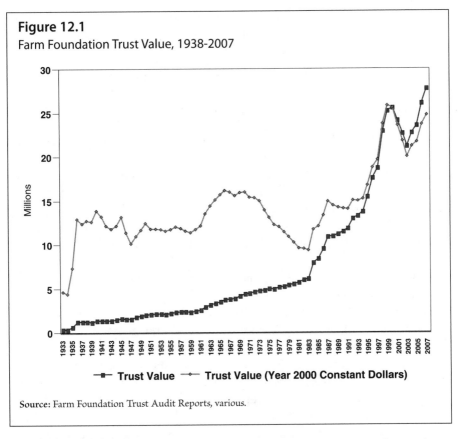

Figure 12.1
Farm Foundation Trust Value, 1938-2007

Trust Value — Trust Value (Year 2000 Constant Dollars)

Source: Farm Foundation Trust Audit Reports, various.

reimbursed the Foundation for some or all of its project expenses. The combination of individual and corporate donations and the "cooperative agreement" payments from government agencies helped Farm Foundation qualify as a publicly supported charity. In 1983, the five-year average of gifts and contributions was 10.4 percent of total income. Contributions have varied from year to year, but Farm Foundation has met the IRS definition of a publicly supported charity every year since 1975.

A New Investment Strategy. Beginning in 1984, the Finance Committee began to play a more active role in managing Farm Foundation's assets. On the recommendation of the Finance Committee, the Board voted by mail ballot to modify Farm Foundation's bylaws to change the way the trust fund was managed.

Until this time, management of the trust had remained with First National Bank of Chicago, Farm Foundation's original corporate trustee. After a period of the Committee itself making investment decisions, the responsibility for operating decisions was transferred from the Finance Committee to professional management who reported to and were closely monitored by the Finance

Committee. The January 1984 Trustee minutes state: "The goal is to put management of the Trust Fund on a total return basis and provide responsibility for managing it for greater long-term value."[22]

In 1985, though, disappointment with the results of the First National Bank of Chicago's professional fund managers resulted in a decision to limit its role to providing custodial services, thus severing the 52-year relationship as trust manager. From 1985 to 1991 the endowment was conservatively managed by the Finance Committee, generally through laddering treasury notes which returned fairly high returns due to market conditions.

In 1991, the Finance Committee solicited bids for managing the funds. The Committee selected the Pacific Investment Management Institutional Trust (PIMIT/PIMCO) to manage half the funds in bonds. A private equity manager, Bjurman and Associates, of Los Angeles, California, was selected to invest the other half in equities. The fund had a total value of $12.2 million at the time.[23]

First National Bank of Chicago continued to provide custodial services until 1994 when those services were put out for bid and Norwest (now Wells Fargo) of Minneapolis, Minnesota, was selected. Norwest's fees were one-third those of First National Bank of Chicago, and the service was much better.

In the 1997, following several years of under-market performance by Bjurman and Associates, the Trustees approved a Finance Committee recommendation to move the equities to the Vanguard Index 500 Fund. Equities were kept in the range of 50 percent to 60 percent of the total portfolio. During the period of relatively rapid increases in stock market values preceding the 2001 crash, there was often discussion in the Trustees' meetings of the desirability of increasing the percent of equities in the portfolio.

By April 2000, the value of the trust had reached $26 million. The bursting of the dot.com bubble and the terrorism events of September 2001 caused a significant downturn in the market. The value of Farm Foundation's portfolio dropped to $23 million at the end of the 2002 fiscal year and $21 million at the 2003 fiscal year-end. During the market downturn, the Finance Committee continued to rebalance the portfolio to the 60 percent equities, 40 percent bonds guidelines. This strategy proved successful and by April 2007, the portfolio had a market value of $27 million. During the market downturn and rebound, the portfolio continued to provide about $1.2 million per year to Farm Foundation operations. When funding of Foundation operations is taken into consideration, the portfolio weathered the turbulent market with less than a five percent loss of value.

Five Percent Spending Rule. The Farm Foundation Trust Agreement contains a typical, if vague, provision against raiding the corpus of the Trust.

"At any time after five years from the date of this agreement, the Board of Trustees may, in its discretion, use a portion of the principal funds of the Foundation for the financing and extension of the current work and activities conducted by or for the Foundation or for the endowment of other agencies which, in the judgement of the Board of Trustees, are fitted to carry on and continue work in any beneficial field within the Foundation purposes, provided that no principal shall be so used for current expenses and activities without the approval in writing of all members of the Board of Trustees, or for the endowment of other agencies, without the approval in writing of three-quarters of all of the Trustees. The portion of the principal fund which may be expended or transferred under this provision in any calendar year, shall not exceed five per cent (5%) of the sum arrived at by valuing the principal assets on hand at their average market value during the preceding calendar year and adding thereto any amounts of principal previously distributed under this provision. The Corporate Trustee's determination of the amount of principal available for use hereunder in any year shall be final. The Corporate Trustee shall payout or transfer portions of the principal funds permitted to be expended or transferred hereunder as and when directed by the Board of Trustees."

—Farm Foundation Trust Agreement, Feb. 10, 1933
as amended April 2000, Article IV, Section 7

While this provision has only indirect application to annual spending, the Board of Trustees has used it as a guide for budgeting. Over the years, annual budgets have averaged about five percent of the value of the portfolio.

In 2002, the Trustees adopted a more formal spending rule. Future operating budgets would be limited to five percent of the value of the portfolio, based on a rolling average of the most recent three years, plus anticipated annual gifts. The Trustees made exceptions to this rule for expenditures directly related to fundraising activities. This spending rule complements the "total return" investment policy adopted in the early 1990s. Budgets are based on the value of the portfolio plus anticipated gifts, rather than cash income from the portfolio. The policy was adopted at a low point in equity markets which acted to constrain budget growth. The operating budget has grown from about $1.5 million in 2002 to about $1.8 million in 2007. During this period, income from gifts and contributions increased from $167,000 to $577,000 in 2006 before declining slightly in 2007.

In 2002, the Trustees initiated a second capital campaign. As noted in Chapter 11, this campaign met with limited success. Pledges of $376,000 were received and by 2007, 80 percent of those pledges had been paid. The business plan adopted in 2004 and extended in 2007 places more emphasis on securing annual gifts and gifts to fund specific projects. Project-specific funding has grown significantly in recent years with the development of higher profile leadership/showcase projects. "The Future of Animal Agriculture in North America" project attracted more than

$300,000 in support from industry, government agencies and other foundations. A series of bioenergy projects initiated in 2004 generated more than $250,000 in support with an equal amount pledged for activities in 2008 and beyond. Attracting partner support for projects will be a significant element of Farm Foundation's development strategy for the foreseeable future.

Legacy and the Future. From its origins in the Depression of the 1930s, Farm Foundation has grown its asset base from Legge's original gift of roughly $1 million to more than $26 million. The spending power of the original trust has been maintained through the Depression, a world war, a technological revolution in agriculture, a period of rapid inflation and 12 administrations in Washington, D.C. Over 75 years, the Trust has generated about $100 million (today's dollars) in income for projects and activities designed to improve the economic and social well-being of agriculture, the food system and rural America.

The financial success of Farm Foundation has been the result of prudent management by the staff and Trustees. Investments have been managed conservatively, but in ways that have allowed the portfolio to grow with the market. Spending of trust income has been limited to cash income or five percent of value. There has been a continuous effort to raise additional funds, with varying degrees of success. While fundraising has not increased the real value of the trust portfolio, it has allowed for additional programs and prevented the loss of portfolio value when markets drop.

Farm Foundation's financial history is the story of a few benefactors with a vision, and generations of Trustees willing to spend the time, raise the funds and make the decisions to continue that vision. In all likelihood, the financial success of the next 75 years will also depend on a few benefactors who share the vision and generations of Trustees willing to nurture that vision.

Chapter 13

The Future

"What will the future hold for agribusiness and rural America? I don't know. But you can be assured that Farm Foundation will be addressing these issues before most of us know what they are."[1]

—Dan Smalley, Alabama agribusiness leader, 2007

Seventy-five years ago, leaders in agriculture, business, the media and society at large shared ideas, debated perspectives and laid the groundwork for what is today Farm Foundation. Those leaders were not in full agreement on the original vision of this new organization. Yet through respectful discussions of the diverse opinions, they found a common ground on which they could move forward.

This book summarizes the 75-year history of Farm Foundation, chronicling the activities of the people who founded Farm Foundation and who carried out the work of the organization. It is appropriate here to address the extent to which Farm Foundation's programs have been true to the vision of its founders, the impact of the organization, and its future role.

The Vision. Perhaps one of the greatest insights of Farm Foundation's founders was to arm the organization with a mission that was responsive to change, specifically the ever-evolving challenges and opportunities for agriculture, the food system and rural communities. As previous chapters have described, the mission of an independent, objective Foundation serving agriculture, the food system and rural communities has never waivered. Farm Foundation has remained focused on relevance and effectiveness, continually adapting programs to respond to needs generated by changing economic, technological and social forces.

Alexander Legge was Farm Foundation's principal founder and primarily responsible for its organization in February 1933. His legacy provided the majority of the Foundation's endowment.

Legge, who died before the Foundation was fully organized, had definite opinions about what Farm Foundation was to become, but was fairly ambiguous about specific details. He desired that Farm Foundation be a permanent institution. He also wanted it to have a larger endowment than he could provide so that it would have the resources to conduct substantive work. Legge described the types of activities he believed the Foundation should pursue:

"1. To conduct research and experimental work for the study of any social, mechanical, physical or economic problem of importance to any substantial portion of the agricultural population of the country, including problems of production, marketing and purchasing, the sound coordination of the agricultural with the industrial and mercantile life of the country, living conditions and human, animal and plant diseases.

2. To finance any such research or experimental work conducted by the staff of any university or college, or other institution, corporation or person calculated, in the judgment of the Board of Trustees, to lead to useful results.

3. To disseminate education and useful information developed as a result of any such study, research and experimentation, or otherwise, in such manners to be of practical value to the farming population."[2]

Farm Foundation has fulfilled Legge's vision. It is a permanent institution and the types of activities which have been sponsored correspond exceedingly well to his wishes.

One of the most significant departures from Legge's vision was the decision not to undertake basic research, but rather to act as a catalyst. At the 1954 Board meeting, F.D. Farrell, one of the founding Trustees, explained: "Shortly after Dr. Taylor became Managing Director in 1935, the Trustees decided, upon Dr. Taylor's recommendation, to conduct directly little or no research and educational work, but to stimulate and aid established research and educational institutions–chiefly the Land Grant colleges–to 'find the truth and to tell it' in areas within the terms of our charter. This has proved to be one of the most important and wisest decisions ever made by the Trustees."[3]

This decision was based principally on what was probably the Farm Foundation Board's greatest shortfall—the inability to increase its endowment in its early years. Legge envisioned an endowment of $10 million or more in 1933. Farm Foundation's endowment would not surpass $10 million until 1987.

The founders did the best with what they had. William Waymack, a Board member from 1939-1949, provided an interesting perspective: "... I find myself concluding that relatively modest resources have actually, in this rare case, been an advantage…A unique kind of program has been devised, 'cut according to the cloth available,' based on doing things with people primarily rather than with dollars primarily. Stimulating and catalyzing, when it is really made to work, can produce exceptional values. I doubt whether there is another organization in the country that has made it work better."[4]

Several founding Trustees provided perspectives on Farm Foundation over the years. Joseph Ackerman summarized remarks made at a 1953 Trustees' meeting by Chris L. Christensen: "Mr. Christensen said that through the twenty years of his service as a Trustee of the Farm Foundation, the intent, the concept, and the fundamentals with respect to this country and, in particular, to our rural people as they were envisioned by Mr. Legge and Governor Lowden, have served as a guide in the planning and in the development of the work of the Farm Foundation."[5]

The minutes of the same meeting include this report of comments by Roy Johnson: "The founders believed that a private agency was needed to supplement the work of the federal and state governments and to help coordinate the work of other agencies. Mr. Johnson felt that the Farm Foundation has done a remarkable job in coordinating research and extension activities."[6]

After receiving a copy of *The Farm Foundation: 1933-1943*, Owen Young wrote Henry Taylor: "I well recall my talks with Alex Legge in which he outlined with enthusiasm the field in which he hoped a trust fund might be productive. I am sure that he would be pleased with the advances which you have made."[7]

At least one founding Board member disagreed. In 1943, Dan Wallace wrote Frank Mullen: "Frankly speaking, I feel that the Foundation and its operations to date has fallen far short of the splendid idea that inspired it. Perhaps back at the time when such folks as yourself, Mary Rumsey, Cliff Gregory and some of the forward thinking Master Farmers, were dreaming about an all around service to agriculture, was not the time to carry such dreams into positive action."[8]

Wallace harkened back to the nebulous "New York Group" and their efforts to address the social, rather than economic problems confronting agriculture in the early 1930s. While the efforts of the "New York Group" were noble, they were idealistic and judged by the other founders as too broad to undertake. Farm Foundation simply did not have the resources to address the issues the "New York Group" championed.

While Legge or Frank Lowden may not have liked every specific program, they would likely be pleased that their legacies have extended into the 21st century, that Farm Foundation has had a significant role through a remarkable period of change in agriculture, and that the organization continues to carry out programs supportive of their goals as interpreted by the founding Board.

The Foundation's Impacts. In the early days of Farm Foundation, Managing Director Henry Taylor and Associate Managing Director Joe Ackerman were at a meeting. "A colleague of Joe's came up and said, 'It seems to me that I see you at every meeting I go to. What is your racket?' Taylor heard the question and answered before Ackerman could. He said, 'Oh, he has the same function that yeast has in the making of bread.'"[9]

Farm Foundation has made a difference to agriculture and rural America. But if Farm Foundation is the "yeast," accurately measuring the yeast's effect requires envisioning a world without Farm Foundation.

In that scenario, there would have been no central coordinating agency in the agricultural social sciences. There would be no national organization addressing issues in agriculture, the food system and rural communities. Hundreds of fellowship recipients would have had to look elsewhere for additional funding for graduate training that enabled them to help agriculture and rural people. There would not have been funding and seed money for thousands of projects. Farm Foundation has directly impacted innumerable lives through its programs.

Barry Flinchbaugh of Kansas State University, identified four areas where Farm Foundation has had lasting impact: "1. Seed money for projects, benefitting farmers and rural people. 2. An objective, respected voice on agricultural and rural issues. 3. Bringing together the 'movers and shakers' to discuss issues and enhance input. 4. I can't think of a major issue facing rural America in the last 30 years in which Farm Foundation events, publications and sponsored-dialogue didn't make a difference."[10]

"A subtle but important product of Farm Foundation activity has been its contribution to the development of professional staff in the Land Grant system and in the social science parts of USDA," according to Howard W. Ottoson, a retired professor at the University of Nebraska. "Young staff members have been exposed to more experienced peers in other institutions through the regional committees in ways different than contacts through professional societies. They have learned new methodologies. They have become acquainted with senior members of the profession. State and federal staff people have been more effective and productive research and extension people because of experiences in Farm Foundation sponsored committees and activities."[11]

"Without doubt, the Farm Foundation made a difference," according to Neil Harl, emeritus professor of economics at Iowa State University. "The publications represented tangible contributions to the literature and were widely used and cited. The publications were uniformly relevant, state-of-the-art and appropriately balanced in tone and tenor. The Foundation also made a contribution to the human family by providing a forum for the ongoing debates on important issues."[12]

Ann Veneman was a Farm Foundation Trustee when she was named U.S. Secretary of Agriculture in 2001, a post in which she served until 2005. "When a Farm Foundation publication or report crossed my desk, I knew it contained comprehensive, objective information. The value of that is immense, especially for a public official who is constantly bombarded with special interest materials."[13]

Alabama agribusiness leader Dan Smalley values Farm Foundation's ability to look around the corner. "Farm Foundation has a long history of identifying opportunities and challenges which America's agriculture and rural people will be facing *before* the issues are being discussed in mainstream agricultural, governmental, academic or rural organizations," says the former Trustee. "Globalization, consolidation, bio-technology, nutraceuticals and renewable energy are just a few of the topics that have been identified and brought to the table for discussion over the 18 years that I have been involved with Farm Foundation. What will the future hold for agribusiness and rural America? I don't know. But you can be assured that Farm Foundation will be addressing these issues before most of us know what they are."[14]

The challenge of measuring quantifiable impacts highlights the unique role Farm Foundation has played in U.S. agriculture. The Foundation has not funded tangible projects like building hospitals or feeding the hungry, but rather has worked with intangible projects that build human capital, identify emerging issues in agriculture, and advance the public policy debate. Universities, non-profit organizations and other foundations have also long struggled with how to appropriately measure the impacts of similar programs.

"Farm Foundation made a difference because it developed and conducted activities that educated the educators," says Lee Kolmer, retired dean of agriculture at Iowa State University, and a former Farm Foundation Trustee. "It helped us to look out of our small cell and observe and interact with the forces that were changing the agricultural economy, the community and the family...We were better attuned to the forces that were changing agriculture and the rural community. This, in my mind, was how the Farm Foundation 'made a difference.'"[15]

"There can be no questioning of the fact that the Farm Foundation has made a difference over the last 75 years," says former Texas Congressman Charles Stenholm. "From the complexity of the global marketplace to the frustration of the political marketplace the Farm Foundation has repeatedly stepped in to provide constructive and, many times, alternative approaches for consideration of farmers, ranchers, consumers and policy makers. Contributions from and to the academic world, as well as the domestic and international political worlds, have often gone unnoticed but can be found in many of the successful policies that have been implemented.

"In a world that is gaining three people per second and losing one hectare of arable land every 7.6 seconds, finding new and better ways to make two blades of grass grow where only one grew before will be even more critical," Stenholm continues. "There is no doubt that the research and education communities will provide the recipes for success. Farm Foundation will be there to interpret and translate into usable and understandable language with its usual pinch of common sense."[16]

At a time of expanding world populations that increase demand for food, an evolving biofuels market, global food markets, food safety issues, including the potential for bioterrorism in the food system, "the role of education and understanding cannot be understated," says William Boehm, president of Kroger Manufacturing and a Trustee of Farm Foundation. "If there ever was a need for a facilitating body in this broad industry, this is it. In this environment, the successful facilitating body will need to welcome people with different views and different data. To make a difference, an impact, it will have to be seen as credible and inviting to all points of view. Farm Foundation can perform this role in its next 75 years."[17]

The Future. One of Farm Foundation's greatest strengths has been its ability to stay true to its original mission while evolving with changing times. In the Henry Taylor years, Farm Foundation hired specialists to address under-served topics, such as land tenure, rural health and rural education. Later, it coordinated research between USDA and university scientists. In the 1960s through the 1980s, an additional focus was developing methodologies and promoting public policy education as tools for applying research results to important issues facing agriculture, the food system and rural people. From the 1990s through today, the Foundation has focused on projects within designated program priority areas to address timely, evolving societal issues, collaborating with academia, government and industry to maximize human and financial resources devoted to these issues.

Despite being a small foundation with limited resources, Farm Foundation's agility and ability to identify new opportunities has kept it relevant and effective across a period of continuous and at times breathtaking change, while staying true to its founding vision.

Farm Foundation's future is tied to the future of U.S. agriculture, the food system and rural communities in a global economy. Change remains the constant. New technologies continue to revolutionize not only agricultural production but the entire food system. The roles of traditional institutions—the U.S. Department of Agriculture, state departments of agriculture, Land Grant colleges and universities, and farm and commodity groups—are evolving to meet broader societal needs. Special interest groups, including environmentalists and consumers, are taking a much more active role in issues related to agriculture, the food system and rural communities.

The changes in the Land Grant community, Farm Foundation's long-standing partners, are pronounced. With an increasing focus on budgets and performance measures, extension positions are vulnerable and being eliminated in many institutions. Competition for research grants has replaced cooperation between institutions and professionals in some instances, yet in other cases forced more multi-state collaboration.

Farm Foundation's long history with university and USDA agricultural social scientists will undoubtedly continue. Farm Foundation must also continue to further leverage its resources by seeking new partners and relationships.

Another challenge of the Foundation is sustaining its financial health through continued prudent management and growth of its trust, and leveraging that endowment with funding support from other public and private sources.

The latter has been increasingly successful, especially as the Foundation raises its visibility and the impact and influence of its work. This provides a sound basis for continued collaborative project funding and enhances the potential for additional endowment growth.

In 1929, Alexander Legge wrote Frank Lowden "about a dream that [he] had been indulging in for some time past, and that is the forming of some kind of business organization that might be helpful in the big problem of agriculture."[18]

Today, Farm Foundation is the nation's only foundation devoted exclusively to agricultural and rural interests. Seventy-five years after its founding, Legge's dream is still alive, pertinent and valued. A statement written for Farm Foundation's 50th anniversary in 1983 remains relevant today: "In sum, there is every reason to believe that the next fifty years will offer as many or more opportunities and challenges for agriculture and agribusiness as have the past fifty years. Likewise, there is every reason to expect that an independent organization such as Farm Foundation will find ample opportunities to help foster innovative thinking and insights into solutions to problems and issues facing agriculture and rural people in the coming decades."[19]

Acknowledgments

The authors gratefully acknowledge the assistance of the following individuals whose support and encouragement made this book possible:

Farm Foundation's Institutional Memory
Walter Armbruster, Howard Diesslin, Steve Halbrook, Rita Dohrmann MacMeekin, Maudie Noma, Esther Olsen, Toni Purves Russin, Neill Schaller, Mae Ramclow Tappendorf, Mary Thompson and Sandy Young.

Farm Foundation and its Partners
Duane Acker, Daniel Badger, Emery N. Castle, Joe Coffey, Larry J. Connor, Bob Cropp, Vernon Eidman, Dennis U. Fisher, Barry Flinchbaugh, Bernal L. Green, Harold Guither, Neil E. Harl, Hal Harris, J.C. Headley, Lowell Hill, Jimmye S. Hillman, Verne W. House, Verner G. Hurt, Ed Jesse, Lee Kolmer, John Lee, Larry Libby, Ardelle A. Lundeen, Warren McCord, Howard J. Meenen, Susan Offutt, Howard Ottoson, Daniel B. Smith, Robert G.F. Spitze, Luther Tweeten, Hank Wadsworth and Fred Woods.

Bennett Agricultural Round Table History
Emmett Barker, Gary H. Baise, Orville Bentley, William Erwin, Don Fites, Connie Greig, Lorenzo N. Hoopes, Donald Lerch, Robin Smith, Jocelyn K. Wilk and Clayton Yeutter.

Research Support
Lee Gady (Alexander Legge, International Harvester, Henry C. Taylor); Glenn Johnson (Farm Foundation's role in farm management and production economics); David Ruesink (Farm Foundation rural church projects); Jay Satterfield (Frank Lowden, early Farm Foundation history); and Gene Wunderlich (Farm Foundation and the American Country Life Association).

Manuscript Support and Preparation/Research Support
Kelli Shea Armstrong, Annie Hernandez, Chandra Orr, Madeline Palla, Kendra Redmon and Brandi Taylor.

Without the assistance of Farm Foundation, this book would not have been possible. Walt Armbruster and Steve Halbrook proposed the project and offered valuable guidance and suggestions. Mary Thompson served as editor and nurtured the manuscript through the publishing process. It was a thankless job and this book is much improved because of her. Julia Walski contributed copy editing expertise. The assistance of Tony Purvis Russin and Sandy Young with research queries is also gratefully acknowledged.

While Farm Foundation's archives contain few documents predating the 1950s, we were pleased to discover that the Joseph Regenstein Library at the University of Chicago had a significant collection of early Farm Foundation documents in its Frank Lowden collection. Likewise, the Archives of the State Historical Society of Wisconsin had a small collection of early Farm Foundation documents. The support of these two archives was invaluable and essential.

Of the many people who told us their stories for this book, there are a few that deserve special recognition. Mae Ramclow Tappendorf and Rita Dohrmann MacMeekin went to work for Farm Foundation a few years after graduating from Northwestern in 1941. They remain friends to this day. Later, Maudie Noma and Esther Olsen joined the staff. They graciously lent their memories and brought to life the years of Henry C. Taylor, Frank Peck and Joseph Ackerman. We know there are some members of the Farm Foundation family who, for whatever reason, were never contacted. We sincerely regret that this manuscript could not benefit from their recollections.

We hope that you will find, as we have, that Farm Foundation has a proud and interesting history. We are pleased that we were able to bring the remarkable personalities and accomplishments of this unique organization to a wider audience.

—David Ernstes and Ronald Knutson

Endnotes

Chapter 1

1. "The Will of Alexander Legge." Quoted in *The People of the State of Illinois vs. The First National Bank of Chicago et al.* 364 Ill. (1936), p. 264.

2. The main narrative of this section is extensively based on *Alexander Legge: 1866-1933* by Forrest Crissey, Chicago, IL: Lakeside Press, 1936. This book was written for the Alexander Legge Memorial Committee shortly after Legge's death. Crissey interviewed scores of Alex Legge's friends and associates. The description of Legge's activities as president of International Harvester greatly benefited from Barbara Marsh's *A Corporate Tragedy: The Agony of International Harvester* (New York, NY: Doubleday & Company, 1985).

3. William T. Hutchinson, *Lowden of Illinois* Chicago, IL: The University of Chicago Press, 1957.

4. Sam R. McKelvie, "My Memories of Alex Legge," *The Nebraska Farmer*, February 17, 1934.

5. Several predecessor organizations had existed in anticipation of the United States entering the conflict.

6. Crissey, p. 127-128.

7. Robert D. Cuff, *The War Industries Board; Business-Government Relations During World War I.* Baltimore, MA: Johns Hopkins University Press, 1973, p. 271.

8. Crissey, p. 138.

9. After his Army service, Johnson was an executive with the Moline Plow Company and along with George N. Peek proposed and advocated a two-price agricultural policy which when introduced in Congress would be called the McNary-Haugen bills.

10. Crissey, p. 135.

11. Crissey, p. 141.

12. Cuff, p. 271.

13. Cuff, p. 271.

14. Benedict Crowell and Robert Forrest Wilson. *The Giant Hand: Our Mobilization and Control of Industry and Natural Resources, 1917-1918.* New York NY: J.S. Ozer, 1974. Reprint of the original, New Haven CN: Yale University Press, 1921, pp. 162-163.

15. Crissey, pp. 153-154.

16. Crissey, p. 157.

17. Barbara Marsh. *A Corporate Tragedy: The Agony of International Harvester Company.* Garden City, NY: Doubleday & Company, 1985, p. 52-53.

18. Marsh, p. 53.

19. Crissey, p. 166.

20. Searching for a suitable way to honor his wife, Legge established the Katherine Legge Memorial in Hinsdale, Illinois. The memorial consists of a lodge and 52 acre park which was created to offer a site for rest and relaxation for the women employed at Harvester. In 1973, it was donated to the Village of Hinsdale.

21. Marsh, p. 55.

22. Marsh, p. 57.

23. Marsh, p. 49-50.

24. Crissey, p. 184.

25. Crissey, p. 200.

26. Crissey, p. 196.

27. Crissey, p. 207.

28. Crissey, p. 212.

29. Crissey, p. 216.

30. Crissey, p. 216.

31. *Time*. Volume XVI, Number 5, August 4, 1930. In January 1930, Legge was considered for *Time's* 1929 "man of the year," losing to Owen D. Young.

32. Crissey, p. 213-214.

33. Crissey, p. 147.

34. Crissey, p. 83.

35. Crissey, p. 150.

36. Crissey, p. 138.

37. "Ex-Gov. F.O. Lowden of Illinois is Dead," *The New York Times*, March 21, 1943, page 26.

38. Union College was jointly administered by Northwestern University and the first University of Chicago.

39. Hutchinson, p. 78.

40. Hutchinson, p. 191.

41. Prior to the 17th Amendment to the United States Constitution, ratified in 1913, Senators were elected by the state legislatures.

42. Hutchinson, p. 217.

43. Hutchinson, p. 215.

44. Portions of Sinnissippi are now Lowden Miller State Forest in Illinois. It was purchased in the early 1990s from Warren and Nancy Miller and Philip Miller, descendants of Lowden. Lowden's "farm house" is privately owned.

45. Hutchinson, p. 234.

46. Hutchinson, p. 291.

47. Hutchinson, p. 319.

48. Steve Neal. "Illinois Governor Winners and Sinners." *Chicago Sun-Times*. Wednesday, January 15, 2003, p. 47.

49. Hutchinson, p. 510.

50. "Ex-Gov. F.O. Lowden of Illinois is Dead."

51. Diary of Florence Pullman Lowden, May 2, 1924, quoted in Hutchinson, p. 536.

52. Hutchinson, p. 650.

53. "Iowa and America Lose a Great Man," *The Des Moines Register*, March 22, 1943.

54. Hutchinson, p. 691.

55. Hutchinson, p. 740.

56. Sam R. McKelvie. "My Memories of Alex Legge III." *The Nebraska Farmer*, March 17, 1934.

Chapter 2

1. *Letter from Mangus W. Alexander, National Industrial Conference Board to Dan A. Wallace, Web Publishing Company, December 14, 1931.* (Archives of Farm Foundation, 1301 West 22nd Street, Suite 615, Oak Brook, IL.

2. F. Emerson Andrews. *Philanthropic Foundations.* New York, NY: Russell Sage Foundation, 1956, p. 14.

3. Murray R. Benedict, *Farm Policies of the United States 1790-195.* New York: The Twentieth Century Fund, 1953.

4. Benedict, p. 159.

5.. Economic Research Service/U.S. Department of Agriculture. *U.S. and State Farm Income Data.* http://www.ers.usda.gov/Data/FarmIncome/FinFidMu.htm

6. U.S. Department of Agriculture. "Annual Report of the Secretary." *U.S. Department of Agriculture, Yearbook, 1920.* Washington, D.C.: U.S. Department of Agriculture, 1921. pp. 9-10.

7. Business Men's Commission on Agriculture. *The Conditions of Agriculture in the United States and Measures for its Improvement.* New York, New York: Published jointly by the National Industrial Conference Board, Inc. and the Chamber of Commerce of the United States of America, 1927.

8.. Business Men's Commission on Agriculture, p. 36.

9. *Letter from Mangus W. Alexander.*

10. *Letter from Dan A. Wallace, United States Department of Agriculture/Food Distribution Administration to Frank E. Mullen, National Broadcasting Company, April 27, 1943.* (Archives of Farm Foundation, 1301 West 22nd Street, Suite 615, Oak Brook, IL).

11. *Constitution of the Agricultural Service Foundation.* Typewritten 7-page document with handwritten notation, "Copy for Mr. Lowden," developed by Alexander Legge, International Harvester Company. (Frank O. Lowden Papers, Department of Special Collections, Joseph Regenstein Library, 1100 East 57th Street, The University of Chicago, Chicago, IL).

12. Peek was a recognized authority on agricultural policy. He along with General Hugh Johnson originated and were strong advocates for a two-price agricultural policy which became the McNary-Haugen bills. Peek tried throughout the 1920s to introduce the parity price concept and would later be the first administrator of the Agricultural Adjustment Administration.

13. *Letter from George N. Peek to Alexander Legge, May 2, 1929.* (Frank O. Lowden Papers, Department of Special Collections, Joseph Regenstein Library, 1100 East 57th Street, The University of Chicago, Chicago, IL).

14. *Letter from Alex Legge to Frank O. Lowden, July 11, 1929.* (Frank O. Lowden Papers, Department of Special Collections, Joseph Regenstein Library, 1100 East 57th Street, The University of Chicago, Chicago, IL).

15. *Carbon copy of letter from Frank Lowden to Alexander Legge, July 12, 1929.* (Frank O. Lowden Papers, Department of Special Collections, Joseph Regenstein Library, 1100 East 57th Street, The University of Chicago, Chicago, IL).

16. *Constitution of the Agricultural Service Foundation.* Printed 12-page 8" x 5" document developed by Alexander Legge. (Frank O. Lowden Papers, Department of Special Collections, Joseph Regenstein Library, 1100 East 57th Street, The University of Chicago, Chicago, IL).

17. *Carbon copy of letter from Frank Lowden to Alexander Legge, Federal Farm Board, June 13, 1930.* (Frank O. Lowden Papers, Department of Special Collections, Joseph Regenstein Library, 1100 East 57th Street, The University of Chicago, Chicago, IL).

18. *Letter from Alex Legge, Federal Farm Board to Frank Lowden, June 23, 1930.* (Frank O. Lowden Papers, Department of Special Collections, Joseph Regenstein Library, 1100 East 57th Street, The University of Chicago, Chicago, IL).

19. *Carbon copy of letter from Frank Lowden to Alexander Legge, Federal Farm Board, June 25, 1930.* (Frank O. Lowden Papers, Department of Special Collections, Joseph Regenstein Library, 1100 East 57th Street, The University of Chicago, Chicago, IL).

20. *Letter from Cyrus H. McCormick, Jr. to Anita Blaine, January 17, 1930.* (Cyrus H. McCormick, Jr. Papers, Archives of the State Historical Society of Wisconsin, 816 State St, Madison, WI).

21. *Letter from Cyrus H. McCormick, Jr.*

22. *Letter from Cyrus H. McCormick, Jr.*

23. William T. Hutchinson. *Lowden of Illinois: The Life of Frank O. Lowden.* Chicago: University of Chicago Press, 1957. Vol. 2, p. 695.

24. Hutchinson, p. 625.

25. M.J. Bonn quoted in Robert B. Davis. *George William Russell ("AE").* Boston, MA: Twayne Publishers, 1977, p. 36. Æ was Russell's spiritual identity and was used more frequently than his given name by his acquaintances. It is derived from the Gnostic concept "Æon" or an emanation sent forth by god. For a complete account of how Russell chose the name Æ, see Henry Summerfield, *That Myriad Minded Man.* Totowa, NJ: Rowman and Littlefield, p. 30-31.

26. George Russell. "Building A Rural Civilization." *Standards of Living: Proceedings of the Thirteenth American Country Life Conference.* Chicago, IL: The University of Chicago Press, April, 1931, p 41.

27. Mary Harriman Rumsey. "Notes of Meeting, December 9, 1930." Attachment to *Letter from Mary Harriman Rumsey to Frank O. Lowden,* January 19, 1931. (Frank O. Lowden Papers, Department of Special Collections, Joseph Regenstein Library, 1100 East 57th Street, The University of Chicago, Chicago, IL), p. 1.

28. *Prospectus for A National Broadcasting Service for the Rural Audience and A National Agricultural Foundation.* Original undated 12-page document with handwritten note by Henry C. Taylor, "This paper was given to HCT by Dan Wallace. It purports to be a forerunner of the Farm Foundation." (Archives of Farm Foundation, 1301 West 22nd Street, Suite 615, Oak Brook, IL).

29. *The Need for an American Farm Foundation with Suggestions Concerning: The Field to be Covered, Possible Accomplishments & Possible Procedure.* Original undated document. (Archives of Farm Foundation, 1301 West 22nd Street, Suite 615, Oak Brook, IL), p. 1.

30. Mary Harriman Rumsey. "Notes of Meeting, January 15, 1931." Attachment to *Letter from Mary Harriman Rumsey to Frank O. Lowden,* February 6, 1931. (Frank O. Lowden Papers, Department of Special Collections, Joseph Regenstein Library, 1100 East 57th Street, The University of Chicago, Chicago, IL), p. 1-2.

Farm Foundation

31. Mary Harriman Rumsey. "Notes of Meeting, January 15, 1931," p. 13.

32. *Letter from George N. Peek to Alexander Legge, May 2, 1929.* (Frank O. Lowden Papers, Department of Special Collections, Joseph Regenstein Library, 1100 East 57th Street, The University of Chicago, Chicago, IL).

33. *Prospectus for A National Broadcasting Service for the Rural Audience and A National Agricultural Foundation,* p. 2.

34. *Letter from Edward M. Tuttle, The Book of Rural Life, to Dan A. Wallace, The Farmer-Webb Publishing Co., December 31, 1930.* (Archives of Farm Foundation, 1301 West 22nd Street, Suite 615, Oak Brook, IL).

35. *The Need for an American Farm Foundation with Suggestions Concerning: The Field to be Covered, Possible Accomplishments & Possible Procedure.* Original undated document. (Archives of Farm Foundation, 1301 West 22nd Street, Suite 615, Oak Brook, IL), p. 5.

36. *The Need for an American Farm Foundation,* p. 3

37. *Carbon copy of letter from Charles Nagel to Dan A. Wallace, January 19, 1931.* (Frank O. Lowden Papers, Department of Special Collections, Joseph Regenstein Library, 1100 East 57th Street, The University of Chicago, Chicago, IL).

38. *Minutes of the Agricultural and Community Foundation, Chicago Meeting, February 15, 1931.* (Frank O. Lowden Papers, Department of Special Collections, Joseph Regenstein Library, 1100 East 57th Street, The University of Chicago, Chicago, IL), p. 2.

39. *Minutes of the Agricultural and Community Foundation,* pp. 13-14.

40. *Minutes of the Agricultural and Community Foundation,* p. 14.

41. Letter from Dan A. Wallace, The Farmer, to Frank O. Lowden, February 7, 1931. (Frank O. Lowden Papers, Department of Special Collections, Joseph Regenstein Library, 1100 East 57th Street, The University of Chicago, Chicago, IL).

42. *A Proposal for an American Farm Foundation.* Typewritten 6-page document. Part of a packet given to Cyrus H. McCormick, Jr. by William S. Elliott, January 27, 1933. (Cyrus H. McCormick, Jr. Papers, Archives of the State Historical Society of Wisconsin, 816 State St, Madison, WI).

43. *Minutes of the Agricultural and Community Foundation, Chicago Meeting, February 15, 1931.* (Frank O. Lowden Papers, Department of Special Collections, Joseph Regenstein Library, 1100 East 57th Street, The University of Chicago, Chicago, IL), pp. 45-46.

44. *Letter from Dan A. Wallace, The Farmer's Wife, to Frank O. Lowden, February 19, 1931.* (Frank O. Lowden Papers, Department of Special Collections, Joseph Regenstein Library, 1100 East 57th Street, The University of Chicago, Chicago, IL).

45. *Letter from Dan A. Wallace, The Farmer's Wife, to Frank O. Lowden, February 19, 1931.*

46. *Letter from Dan A. Wallace, The Farmer's Wife, to Frank O. Lowden, February 19, 1931.*

47. *Constituent Agreement Creating the American Farm Foundation.* Typewritten 12-page document. Part of a packet given to Cyrus H. McCormick, Jr. by William S. Elliott, January 27, 1933. (Cyrus H. McCormick, Jr. Papers, Archives of the State Historical Society of Wisconsin, 816 State St, Madison, WI).

48. *Excerpt from Minutes of the Executive and Legal Committee Meeting, April 25, 1931.* (Frank O. Lowden Papers, Department of Special Collections, Joseph Regenstein Library, 1100 East 57th Street, The University of Chicago, Chicago, IL).

49. *Letter from Mary Harriman Rumsey to Frank O. Lowden, May 4, 1931.* (Frank O. Lowden Papers, Department of Special Collections, Joseph Regenstein Library, 1100 East 57th Street, The University of Chicago, Chicago, IL).

50. *Letter from Alexander Legge to Frank O. Lowden, July 24, 1931.* (Frank O. Lowden Papers, Department of Special Collections, Joseph Regenstein Library, 1100 East 57th Street, The University of Chicago, Chicago, IL).

51. *Carbon copy of letter from Frank O. Lowden to Alexander Legge, July 27, 1931.* (Frank O. Lowden Papers, Department of Special Collections, Joseph Regenstein Library, 1100 East 57th Street, The University of Chicago, Chicago, IL).

52. *Letter from Mangus W. Alexander.*

53. "Averell Harriman Remembers Mary." Unidentified copy of *Junior League Review,* p. 11. Provided to the authors by the Junior League of the City of New York, Inc.

Chapter 3

1. *Copy of letter from C.E. Woodward, Northwest Farm Equipment Journal, to Mrs. Mary Harriman Rumsey, January 16, 1934.* The copy was forwarded to Frank O. Lowden. (Archives of Farm Foundation, 1301 West 22nd Street, Suite 615, Oak Brook, IL).

2. *Letter from Alex Legge to Frank O. Lowden, December 22, 1932.* (Frank O. Lowden Papers, Department of Special Collections, Joseph Regenstein Library, 1100 East 57th Street, The University of Chicago, Chicago, IL)

3. *Carbon Copy of Letter from Dan A. Wallace, The Farmer, to George MacDonald, February 3, 1933.* (Archives of Farm Foundation, 1301 West 22nd Street, Suite 615, Oak Brook, IL)

4. *Carbon Copy of Letter from Dan A. Wallace, The Farmer, to C.C. Webber, February 2, 1933.* (Archives of Farm Foundation, 1301 West 22nd Street, Suite 615, Oak Brook, IL)

5. *Carbon Copy of Letter from Dan A. Wallace, The Farmer, to George MacDonald, February 3, 1933.* (Archives of Farm Foundation, 1301 West 22nd Street, Suite 615, Oak Brook, IL)

6. *Carbon Copy of Letter from Dan A. Wallace, The Farmer, to Frank Mullen, National Broadcasting Company, February 7, 1933.* (Archives of Farm Foundation, 1301 West 22nd Street, Suite 615, Oak Brook, IL)

7. *Letter from William S. Elliott, International Harvester to Dan A. Wallace, Web Publishing Company, January 31, 1933.* (Archives of Farm Foundation, 1301 West 22nd Street, Suite 615, Oak Brook, IL)

8. *Attachment to Memorandum from Cyrus H. McCormick, Jr. to F.A. Steuert, February 16, 1933, listing attendance list for the Farm Foundation organization meeting.* (Cyrus H. McCormick, Jr. Papers, Archives of the State Historical Society of Wisconsin, 816 State St, Madison, WI)

9. The designation of Board members by area has continued up to the present in roughly the same proportions as designated in the trust agreement.

10. Farm Foundation. *Trust Agreement Creating the Farm Foundation.* Chicago, IL: The Gunthorp-Warren Printing Company, February 10, 1933, p. 1-2. (Archives of Farm Foundation, 1301 West 22nd Street, Suite 615, Oak Brook, IL)

11. Farm Foundation. p. 2-3.

12. *Copy of letter from Chris Christensen, University of Wisconsin, to H.C. Taylor, Rome Italy, March 28, 1935.* (Frank O. Lowden Papers, Department of Special Collections, Joseph Regenstein Library, 1100 East 57th Street, The University of Chicago, Chicago, IL)

13. *Letter from Mary H. Rumsey to Daniel Wallace, February 14, 1933.* (Archives of Farm Foundation, 1301 West 22nd Street, Suite 615, Oak Brook, IL)

14. *Carbon Copy of Letter from Dan A. Wallace, The Farmer to Mary Harriman Rumsey, February 21, 1933.* (Archives of Farm Foundation, 1301 West 22nd Street, Suite 615, Oak Brook, IL)

15. *Letter from Alexander Legge, International Harvester Company to Dan Wallace, The Farmer, March 2, 1933.* (Archives of Farm Foundation, 1301 West 22nd Street, Suite 615, Oak Brook, IL)

16. "The First 100 Days." *Gilder Lehman History Online.* http://www.gliah.uh.edu/database/article_display.cfm?HHID=468

17. Forrest Crissey. *Alex Legge: 1866-1933.* Chicago, IL: The Lakeside Press, 1936, p. 225.

18. Crissey, p. 226.

19. *Copy of letter from Chris Christensen, University of Wisconsin, to H.C. Taylor, Rome Italy, March 28, 1935.* (Frank O. Lowden Papers, Department of Special Collections, Joseph Regenstein Library, 1100 East 57th Street, The University of Chicago, Chicago, IL)

20. *Carbon Copy of Letter from Frank Lowden, to Mary Harriman Rumsey, December 26, 1933.* (Frank O. Lowden Papers, Department of Special Collections, Joseph Regenstein Library, 1100 East 57th Street, The University of Chicago, Chicago, IL)

21. *Carbon copy of letter from Frank O. Lowden to J. Hutcheson, Director, Virginia Cooperative Extension, Blacksburg, Virginia, December 30, 1933.* (Archives of Farm Foundation, 1301 West 22nd Street, Suite 615, Oak Brook, IL). This text was used repeatedly to respond to general requests.

22. *Letter from Chris Christensen to Frank O. Lowden, December 14, 1933.* (Frank O. Lowden Papers, Department of Special Collections, Joseph Regenstein Library, 1100 East 57th Street, The University of Chicago, Chicago, IL)

23. *Memorandum from Wm. S. Elliott, Secretary, to All Trustees of the Farm Foundation, May 9, 1934.* (Archives of Farm Foundation, 1301 West 22nd Street, Suite 615, Oak Brook, IL).

24. *Minutes of Annual Meeting of Board of Trustees, June 22, 1934.* (Archives of Farm Foundation, 1301 West 22nd Street, Suite 615, Oak Brook, IL). p. 2.

25. Charles L. Burlingham. *Report Submitted to the Trustees of the Farm Foundation at the Annual Meeting, June 22, 1934.* It was copied 7/14/43 from a file loaned to the Farm Foundation by Frank E. Mullen, National Broadcasting Company, Rockefeller Center, New York, N.Y. (Archives of Farm Foundation, 1301 West 22nd Street, Suite 615, Oak Brook, IL)., p. 3

26. Burlingham, p. 10.

27. *Minutes of Annual Meeting of Board of Trustees, June 22, 1934.* p. 5-6.

28. William T. Hutcheson. *Lowden of Illinois: The Life of Frank O. Lowden.* Chicago: University of Chicago Press, 1957, p. 696.

29. *Letter from Dan A. Wallace, United States Department of Agriculture/Food Distribution Administration to Frank E. Mullen, National Broadcasting Company, April 27, 1943.* (Archives of Farm Foundation, 1301 West 22nd Street, Suite 615, Oak Brook, IL)

30. *Handwritten Letter from Henry C. Taylor to Frank Peck, June 11, 1952.* (Archives of Farm Foundation, 1301 West 22nd Street, Suite 615, Oak Brook, IL) It should be noted that Charles C. Teague did attend the 1934 board meeting. The fourth board member who Henry C. Taylor alludes to as not serving was probably Mary Harriman Rumsey. She provided a substitute for the 1933 meeting, missed the 1934 meeting, and was deceased by the 1935 meeting.

31. *Copy of letter from Chris Christensen, University of Wisconsin, to H.C. Taylor, Rome Italy, March 28, 1935.* (Frank O. Lowden Papers, Department of Special Collections, Joseph Regenstein Library, 1100 East 57th Street, The University of Chicago, Chicago, IL)

32. *Memorandum from F.A. Steuert, July 31, 1931.* (Cyrus H. McCormick, Jr. Papers, Archives of the State Historical Society of Wisconsin, 816 State St, Madison, WI)

33. *Memorandum from F.A. Steuert, April 14, 1933.* (Cyrus H. McCormick, Jr. Papers, Archives of the State Historical Society of Wisconsin, 816 State St, Madison, WI)

34. *Memorandum from F.A. Steuert, December 9, 1933.* (Cyrus H. McCormick, Jr. Papers, Archives of the State Historical Society of Wisconsin, 816 State St, Madison, WI)

35. "Contributions by Dr. Farrell lauded." *The Manhattan Mercury,* February 16, 1976.

36. *Letter from Dan A. Wallace, The Farmer to William Elliott, International Harvester Company, May 19, 1933.* (Archives of Farm Foundation, 1301 West 22nd Street, Suite 615, Oak Brook, IL)

37. "George MacDonald: Philanthropist; Papal Marquis; Director of Banks and Business Corporations; Servant of the Public." Undated two-page contemporary biographical document. (Archives of Farm Foundation, 1211 West 22nd Street, Suite 216, Oak Brook, IL)

38. "Albert R. Mann—Biographical Information." *Albert R. Mann Library, Cornell University.* http://www.mannlib.cornell.edu/about/albert.html

39. Arthur F. Marquette. *Brands, Trademarks and Good Will: The Story of The Quaker Oats Company.* New York, NY: McGraw-Hill Book Company, 1967, p. 98.

40. "Resources at the Herbert Hoover Presidential Library for National History Day Projects, 2001." *The Herbert Hoover Presidential Library-Museum Homepage.* http://www.nara.gov/education/historyday/frontier/nlh.html

41. "Young, Owen D." *Biography.* http://search.biography.com/print_record.pl id=21029.

42. *The Farm Foundation: 1933-1945.* Chicago, IL: Farm Foundation, 1945. (Archives of Farm Foundation, 1301 West 22nd Street, Suite 615, Oak Brook, IL)

42. "William L. Clayton Professorship In International Economics." *Named Professorships, Deanships, and Directorships - The Johns Hopkins University* http://webapps.jhu.edu/namedprofessorships/professorshipdetail.cfm?professorshipID=267

43. John A. Lupton. "October 15-21, 2001." *The Illinois Political Journal on WUIS.* http://www.wuis.org/IPJ-Archives/IPJ_10-15.html

44. "The Will of Alexander Legge." Quoted in *The People of the State of Illinois vs. The First National Bank of Chicago et al.* 364 Ill. (1936), p. 264.

Chapter 4

1. Kenneth H. Parsons. "Henry Charles Taylor, 1873-1969: Organizer and First Head of USDA's BAE." in *Choices,* Second Quarter 1991, pp 28.

2. *Letter from Charles L. Burlingham to Wm. S. Elliott, Chairman of the Farm Foundation Executive Committee, July 30, 1934.* (Archives of Farm Foundation, 1301 W. 22nd Street, Suite 615, Oak Brook, IL)

3. *Letter from Charles L. Burlingham.*
4. *Letter from Charles L. Burlingham.*
5. *Letter from Charles L. Burlingham.*
6. *Letter from Charles L. Burlingham.*
7. Charles L. Burlingham. *Community Cooperatives.* Report prepared by Farm Foundation, July 31, 1934. (Archives of Farm Foundation, 1301 W. 22nd Street, Suite 615, Oak Brook, IL), p. 5.
8. Charles L. Burlingham. *Soil Conservation: Grass, Erosion, Etc.* Report prepared for Farm Foundation, July 25, 1934. (Archives of Farm Foundation, 1301 W. 22nd Street, Suite 615, Oak Brook, IL), p. 3-4.
9. E.G. Nourse. *Memorandum by Dr. E.G. Nourse of Brookings Institute, June 27, 1935.* Memo prepared for the board of trustees and attached to the June 28, 1935 board of trustees minutes. (Archives of Farm Foundation, 1301 W. 22nd Street, Suite 615, Oak Brook, IL), p. 2.
10. Aldo Leopold. *Report to the Farm Foundation on the Role of Conservation in Farm Life.* Includes cover letter from Chris L. Christensen to the board of trustees dated August 20, 1935. (Archives of Farm Foundation, 1301 W. 22nd Street, Suite 615,Oak Brook, IL), p. 1.
11. Leopold, p. 16.
12. National Committee on Boys and Girls Club Work. *National 4-H Soil Saving Program: A Plan for Cooperation with the 4-H Clubs Submitted to the Farm Foundation.* Chicago, National Committee on Boys and Girls Club Work, March 1935.
13. *Letter from William S. Elliott, Chairman of the Executive Committee,* Farm Foundation, to G.L. Noble, Managing Director, 4-H Club, July 5, 1935. (Frank O. Lowden Papers, Department of Special Collections, Joseph Regenstein Library, 1100 East 57th Street, The University of Chicago, Chicago, IL)
14. *Minutes of the Annual Meeting of Board of Trustees, June 28, 1935.* (Archives of Farm Foundation, 1301 W. 22nd Street, Suite 615, Oak Brook, IL). p. 4.
15. This section is based on Parsons, pp 28-31, and Taylor's autobiography, *A Farm Economist in Washington.* Madison, WI: University of Wisconsin-Madison, Department of Agricultural Economics, posthumously published, 1992.
16. *Carbon Copy of Letter from Henry C. Taylor to Frank O. Lowden, dated May 4, 1935.* (Henry C. Taylor Papers, 1896-1968, Archives of the State Historical Society of Wisconsin, 816 State St, Madison, WI)
17. *Letter from Chris L. Christensen to Henry C. Taylor, June 29, 1935.* (Archives of Farm Foundation, 1301 W. 22nd Street, Suite 615, Oak Brook, IL)
18. William T. Hutchinson, *Lowden of Illinois* Chicago, IL: The University of Chicago Press, 1957, p. 698.
19. *Undated press release from E.S. Simpson announcing the hiring of Henry C. Taylor by Farm Foundation.* Includes a November 26, 1935, cover note from William S. Elliott, International Harvester to Cyrus H. McCormick, Jr. and Harold F. McCormick. (Cyrus H. McCormick, Jr. Papers. Archives of the State Historical Society of Wisconsin, 816 State St., Madison, WI).
20. Jim Phillips. "Edwin G. Nourse." in *Turning the Century 100: Agriculture's Most Influential Leaders of the 20th Century.* Birmingham, AL: Progressive Farmer, 2000
21. Earl Manning. "Aldo Leopold." in *Turning the Century 100: Agriculture's Most Influential Leaders of the 20th Century.* Birmingham, AL: Progressive Farmer, 2000

Chapter 5

1. Revised document on the activities of Farm Foundation developed by Henry C. Taylor in response to a March 18, 1938, letter from Robert Paige, assistant director of the Public Administration Clearing House of Chicago, IL, requesting information for their *Directory of Organizations in the Field of Public Administration.* (Archives of Farm Foundation, 1301 West 22nd Street, Suite 615, Oak Brook, IL).
2. Farm Foundation. *The Farm Foundation: 1933-1945.* Chicago, IL: Farm Foundation, 1945. (Archives of Farm Foundation, 1301 West 22nd Street, Suite 615, Oak Brook, IL). The 1945 publication drew on an earlier 10-year history *The Farm Foundation: 1933-1943.* Chicago, IL: Farm Foundation, 1943. (Archives of Farm Foundation, 1301 West 22nd Street, Suite 615, Oak Brook, IL).
3. Henry C. Taylor. *Recommendations of Henry C. Taylor, Director, for a Program of Activity.* Appended to the minutes of the annual meeting of the board of trustees, June 24, 1936. (Archives of Farm Foundation, 1301 West 22nd Street, Suite 615, Oak Brook, IL).
4. Farm Foundation. *Minutes of Annual Meeting of Board of Trustees, June 24, 1936.* (Archives of Farm Foundation, 1301 West 22nd Street, Suite 615, Oak Brook, IL), p. 4.

5. Henry C. Taylor. *The Director's Report to the Trustees of the Farm Foundation at the Annual Meeting on June 28th, 1937*. Appended to the minutes of the annual meeting of the Board of Trustees, June 28, 1937. (Archives of Farm Foundation, 1301 West 22nd Street, Suite 615, Oak Brook, IL).

6. Henry C. Taylor. *Preliminary Report to the Trustees of the Farm Foundation*. Appended to the minutes of the annual meeting of the board of trustees, June 13, 1938. (Archives of Farm Foundation, 1301 West 22nd Street, Suite 615, Oak Brook, IL) p. 1. The building referenced was the home of Farm Foundation until its move to 1211 West 22nd Street, Oak Brook, Illinois in 1976. The 15-story, 175,000 square-foot International Harvester building is currently the main campus building of Columbia College—Chicago's visual, performing, media communication arts college. In 2006, the Farm Foundation offices moved to 1301 W. 22nd Street, Suite 615, Oak Brook, Illinois.

7. *Preliminary Report to the Trustees of the Farm Foundation*, p. 2.

8. *Preliminary Report to the Trustees of the Farm Foundation*, p. 11.

9. Henry C. Taylor. *Recommendations of Henry C. Taylor, Director, for a Program of Activity*. Appended to the minutes of the annual meeting of the Board of Trustees, June 24, 1936. (Archives of Farm Foundation, 1301 West 22nd Street, Suite 615, Oak Brook, IL), p. 4.

10. The General Education Board was established by John D. Rockefeller to aid U.S. education at all levels.

11. *The Farm Foundation: 1933-1945*. p. 39.

12. L.B. Bacon and F.C. Schloemer. *World Trade in Agricultural Products: Its Growth; its Crisis; and the New Trade Policies*. Rome, Italy: International Institute of Agriculture, 1940. The plan of publication was conceived by Henry C. Taylor and carried out under his direction.

13. Henry C. Taylor and Anne Dewees Taylor. *World Trade in Agricultural Products*. New York, NY: The Macmillan Company, 1943.

14. Theodore Willliam (T.W.) Schultz (April 30, 1902-February 25, 1998) won the Nobel Price in Economics in 1979. He was a professor at the University of Chicago beginning in 1943.

15. Farm Foundation. *Farm Foundation Since 1933*. Oak Brook, IL: Farm Foundation, 1983, p. 2. (Archives of Farm Foundation, 1301 West 22nd Street, Suite 615, Oak Brook, IL)

16. *Report on Activities of the Executive Committee since the Annual Meeting, June 8, 1944*. Document appended to the Board minutes. (Archives of Farm Foundation, 1301 West 22nd Street, Suite 615, Oak Brook, IL) p. 7.

17. Roland L. Guyotte. "Hutchins of Chicago: The University President as Publicist." *Illinois Heritage* Vol. 1, No. 1, Fall 1997, p. 34.

18. Elin Lilja Anderson. *Rural Health and Social Policy*. Selections from her writings, collected and published in her memory by some of her friends; with excerpts of remarks made at a memorial meeting in Washington, June 11, 1951. (Archives of Farm Foundation, 1301 West 22nd Street, Suite 615, Oak Brook, IL).

Chapter 6

1. Farm Foundation. *Reaching the Grass Roots: An Investment in Enduring Values*, Farm Foundation, Chicago, IL, 1952, p. 21. (Archives of Farm Foundation, 1301 West 22nd Street, Suite 615, Oak Brook, IL).

2. *Telephone Interview with Rita Dohrmann MacMeekin, December 17, 2002*. (Archives of Farm Foundation, 1301 West 22nd Street, Suite 615, Oak Brook, IL).

3. *Letter from Rita D. MacMeekin to David P. Ernstes, January 24, 2003*. (Archives of Farm Foundation, 1301 West 22nd Street, Suite 615, Oak Brook, IL).

4. *Telephone Interview with Mae Ramclow Tappendorf, December 19, 2002*. (Archives of Farm Foundation, 1301 West 22nd Street, Suite 615, Oak Brook, IL).

5. *Letter from Rita D. MacMeekin*.

6. Robert Paarlberg and Don Paarlberg, "Agricultural Policy in the Twentieth Century" in *Agricultural History*, Volume 74, Number 2, Spring 2000 pp. 136-137.

7. Ernest A. Engelbert, "Agriculture and the Political Process." *Increasing Understanding of Public Problems and Policies*: 1953. Chicago, IL: Farm Foundation: 1953, pp. 140-150.

8. Committee on Corn Belt Land Tenure. *Report of the Corn Belt Conference on Land Tenure, Davenport, Iowa, June 2-3, 1939*. (Archives of Farm Foundation, 1301 West 22nd Street, Suite 615, Oak Brook, IL), p.2.

9. Farm Foundation. *Farm Foundation Since 1933*. Oak Brook, IL: Farm Foundation, 1983, p. 17.

10. Farm Foundation. *Human Relations in Agriculture and Rural Life*. Chicago, IL: Farm Foundation, 1950.

11. *Letter from J.C. Kennedy, Hotel Blackhawk, Davenport, Iowa, to Joseph Ackerman, Farm Foundation, April 19, 1939*. (Archives of Farm Foundation, 1301 West 22nd Street, Suite 615, Oak Brook, IL). The Hotel Blackhawk was built in 1915 and is listed on the National Register of Historic Places. It is still in business

as the President Casinos Blackhawk Hotel, 200 East Third Street, Davenport, Iowa.
12. *Carbon copy of letter from Joseph Ackerman, Farm Foundation to J.C. Kennedy, Hotel Blackhawk, Davenport, Iowa, May 2, 1939.* (Archives of Farm Foundation, 1301 West 22nd Street, Suite 615, Oak Brook, IL).

Chapter 7
1. United States Department of Agriculture, Extension Service. *Educational Work on Public Policy Problems and Their Relationship to Agriculture.* Report of a conference June 20-24, 1949 in Washington, D.C. Washington, D.C.: United States Department of Agriculture, p. 59-60.
2. The first two sections of this chapter benefit greatly from an uncredited mimeographed paper, *The Birth of an Institution: The Beginning of the National Public Policy Education Conference* which was prepared for the program of 25th Anniversary of the National Public Policy Education Conference dinner, September 10, 1975. (Archives of Farm Foundation, 1301 West 22nd Street, Suite 615, Oak Brook, IL).
3. United States Department of Agriculture, Extension Service. *Educational Work on Public Policy Problems and Their Relationship to Agriculture.* Report of a conference June 20-24, 1949 in Washington, D.C. Washington, D.C.: United States Department of Agriculture, p. 1.
4. *Minutes of July 26-27, 1949, Meeting on Public Policy in the Field of Agriculture,* Union League Club, Chicago, Illinois. (Archives of Farm Foundation, 1301 West 22nd Street, Suite 615, Oak Brook, IL), p. 2-3.
5. *Minutes of July 26-27, 1949, Meeting,* pp. 2-3.
6. *Minutes of July 26-27, 1949, Meeting,* pp. 2-3.
7. *Minutes of July 26-27, 1949, Meeting,* p. 6.
8. The proceedings of the conference are contained in National Committee on Agricultural Policy. *Educational Methods Conference in Public Policy.* Conference was January 19-21, 1949, in Chicago, Illinois. Chicago, IL: Farm Foundation, 1950.
9. F.W. Peck, "Where Do We Go From Here?" in: *Educational Methods Conference in Public Policy.* Conference was January 19-21, 1949, in Chicago, Illinois. Chicago, IL: Farm Foundation, 1950, p. 93.
10. Charles M. Hardin, professor of political science at the University of Chicago, John D, Black professor of economics at Harvard University, and T.W. Schultz, professor of economics at the University of Chicago, participated in the regional and national conferences. USDA economists and extension workers were also present.
11. Proceedings of the workshop are contained in National Education Committee on Public Policy. *Proceedings: Western Region Extension Conference on Public Policy.* Conference was September 6-8, 1950, Boise, Idaho. No publication information. Copy in Farm Foundation Archives, 1950.
12. Proceedings of the workshop are contained in National Education Committee on Public Policy. *Report of Work Conference on Public Policy Problems for Extension Workers Northeastern States.* Conference was September 11-15, 1950, Petersham, Massachusetts. Chicago, IL: Farm Foundation, 1950.
13. Proceedings of the workshop are contained in National Education Committee on Public Policy. *Discussing Public Policy: A Report of the North Central States Conference for Extension Workers.* Conference was September 18-21, 1950, Madison, Wisconsin. Madison, WI: University of Wisconsin Extension Service, January, 1951.
14. Proceedings of the workshop are contained in National Education Committee on Public Policy. *Report of the Work Conference on Public Policy Problems.* Conference was December 4-6, 1950, Atlanta, Georgia. Chicago, IL: Farm Foundation, 1951.
15. *Minutes of March 2, 1951, Meeting of the National Committee on Agricultural Policy,* Union League Club, Chicago, Illinois. (Archives of Farm Foundation, 1301 West 22nd Street, Suite 615, Oak Brook, IL), p. 13.
16. *Minutes of January 25, 1952, Meeting of the National Committee on Agricultural Policy,* Union League Club, Chicago, Illinois. (Archives of Farm Foundation, 1301 West 22nd Street, Suite 615, Oak Brook, IL), p.1.
17. Philip Favero and Mary K. Fitzgerald. *Participants' Reflections on the National Public Policy Education Conference.* College Park, MD: University of Maryland Institute for Governmental Service, August 1998, p. 9.
18. Farm Foundation. *Increasing Understanding of Public Problems and Policies.* Oak Brook, IL: Farm Foundation, 1951-1998.
19. *Minutes of 1989 National Public Policy Education Committee Meeting,* New Orleans, Louisiana, September 19, 1989. (Archives of Farm Foundation, 1301 West 22nd Street, Suite 615, Oak Brook, IL), p. 8.
20. Kathleen Ward, ed. *Increasing Understanding of Public Problems and Policies: Executive Summary.* Oak Brook, IL: Farm Foundation, 1996.

21. David P. Ernstes, ed. *Emerging Issues in Public Policy: Highlights of the 1999 National Public Policy Education Conference.* Oak Brook, IL: Farm Foundation, November 1999.
22. *Minutes of 1974 Meeting of the National Public Policy Education Committee,* Osage House, Lake of the Ozarks, Missouri, September 10-12, 1974. (Archives of Farm Foundation, 1301 West 22nd Street, Suite 615, Oak Brook, IL), p. 3.
23. *By-Laws of the National Public Policy Education Committee.* The by-laws were approved at a special meeting of all participants at the 1975 National Public Policy Education Conference at the Inn-at-the-Peak, Clymer, New York, September 9, 1975. (Archives of Farm Foundation, 1301 West 22nd Street, Suite 615, Oak Brook, IL), p. 1.
24. Farm Foundation. *Nomination Information for R.J. Hildreth Award for Career Achievement in Public Policy Education.* (Archives of Farm Foundation, 1301 West 22nd Street, Suite 615, Oak Brook, IL).
25. Farm Foundation. *Nomination Information for Outstanding Public Issues Education Program Award.* (Archives of Farm Foundation, 11301 West 22nd Street, Suite 615, Oak Brook, IL).
26. ECOP Task Force on Public Policy Education in Home Economics. *Public Policy in Extension Home Economics.* Ithaca, NY: Cornell University Media Services, June 1984, p. 6.
27. Alan J. Hahn, Jennifer C. Greene and Carla Waterman. *Educating About Public Issues: Lessons from Eleven Innovative Public Policy Education Programs.* Ithaca, NY: Cornell University Media Services, June 1994, p. 2.
28. D.D. Dale and A.J. Hahn, eds. *Public Issues Education: Increasing Competence in Resolving Public Issues.* Public Issues Education Materials Task Force of the National Public Policy Education Committee and PLC and PODC subcommittees of the Extension Committee on Organization and Policy. Madison, WI: University of Wisconsin-Extension, 1994.
29. *Minutes of September 3, 1952, Meeting of the National Committee on Agricultural Policy,* Allerton Park, Monticello, Illinois. (Archives of Farm Foundation, 1301 West 22nd Street, Suite 615, Oak Brook, IL), p.1.
30. They are presently known as the North Central, Northeast and Western Public Policy Committees and the Southern Public Affairs Committee.
31. *Minutes of September 13, 1983, Meeting of the National Public Policy Education Committee,* Illinois Beach Resort, Zion, Illinois. (Archives of Farm Foundation, 1301 West 22nd Street, Suite 615, Oak Brook, IL), p. 5.
32. *Minutes of September 13, 1988, Meeting of the National Public Policy Education Committee,* Cincinnati, Ohio. (Archives of Farm Foundation, 1301 West 22nd Street, Suite 615, Oak Brook, IL), p. 4.
33. The 2001 National Public Policy Education Conference was canceled due to the September 11, 2001 terrorist attacks.

Chapter 8

1. Farm Foundation. *Farm Foundation Annual Report 1968-69.* (Archives of Farm Foundation, 1301 West 22nd Street, Suite 615, Oak Brook, IL) pp. 2-3.
2. *Typewritten response by Howard W. Ottoson to Farm Foundation survey, December 24, 2002.* (Archives of Farm Foundation, 1301 West 22nd Street, Suite 615, Oak Brook, IL).
3. *E-mail response by Bernard F. Stanton to Farm Foundation survey, December 12, 2002.* (Archives of Farm Foundation, 1301 West 22nd Street, Suite 615, Oak Brook, IL).
4. *Typewritten response by Neil E. Harl to Farm Foundation survey, December 23, 2002.* (Archives of Farm Foundation, 1301 West 22nd Street, Suite 615, Oak Brook, IL).
5. *Handwritten response by Larry J. Connor to Farm Foundation survey, December 11, 2002.* (Archives of Farm Foundation, 1301 West 22nd Street, Suite 615, Oak Brook, IL).
6. *Handwritten response by Esther Olsen to Farm Foundation survey, January 24, 2003.* (Archives of Farm Foundation, 1301 West 22nd Street, Suite 615, Oak Brook, IL).
7. *Handwritten response by Howard Diesslin to Farm Foundation survey, February 24, 2003.* (Archives of Farm Foundation, 1301 West 22nd Street, Suite 615, Oak Brook, IL).
8. Economic Research Service. "Farmers and the Land" in *A History of American Agriculture.* http://www.usda.gov/history2/text3.htm. January 14, 2003.
9. Don Paarlberg and Philip Paarlberg. *The Agricultural Revolution of the 20th Century.* Ames, IA: Iowa State University Press, 2000.
10. National Advisory Commission on Rural Poverty. *The People Left Behind: A Report.* Washington, D.C.: U.S. Government Printing Office, 1967.

Chapter 9

1. *E-mail from Connie Greig to the authors, September 29, 1999.* (Archives of Farm Foundation, 1301 West 22nd Street, Suite 615, Oak Brook, IL).
2. *Draft letter to the Commissioner of Internal Revenue prepared by Kirkland & Ellis, January 24, 1974.* Letter was a request to the Internal Revenue Service for a ruling on the proposed merger of Farm Foundation with the Foundation for American Agriculture. (Archives of Farm Foundation, 1301 West 22nd Street, Suite 615, Oak Brook, IL).
3. *Report of Joint Committee on the Foundation for American Agriculture and The Farm Foundation, December 1, 1970.* (Archives of Farm Foundation, 1301 West 22nd Street, Suite 615, Oak Brook, IL), p. 3.
4. Charles Dana Bennett. *Making a Difference: Reflections of Charles Dana Bennett on the Formative Years of Farm Foundation's Bennett Agricultural Round Table.* (Archives of Farm Foundation, 1301 West 22nd Street, Suite 615, Oak Brook, IL), pp. 1-2.
5. *Typewritten response by Lorenzo N. Hoopes to Farm Foundation survey, December 30, 2002.* (Archives of Farm Foundation, 1301 West 22nd Street, Suite 615, Oak Brook, IL).
6. *Typewritten response by William Erwin to Farm Foundation survey, January 21, 2003.* (Archives of Farm Foundation, 1301 West 22nd Street, Suite 615, Oak Brook, IL).
7. *Typewritten response by Clayton Yeutter to Farm Foundation survey, January 20, 2003.* (Archives of Farm Foundation, 1301 West 22nd Street, Suite 615, Oak Brook, IL).
8. *Handwritten response by Don Lerch to Farm Foundation survey, December 31, 2002.* (Archives of Farm Foundation, 1301 West 22nd Street, Suite 615, Oak Brook, IL).
9. Jim Roe. *Charles Dana Bennett Tribute.* Prepared and presented at the June 11, 1987, dinner meeting of Farm Foundation's Bennett Agricultural Round Table, Rosemont, Illinois. (Archives of Farm Foundation, 1301 West 22nd Street, Suite 615, Oak Brook, IL).
10. *Handwritten response by Don Lerch to Farm Foundation survey, December 31, 2002.* (Archives of Farm Foundation, 1301 West 22nd Street, Suite 615, Oak Brook, IL).
11. *Typewritten response by Clayton Yeutter.*
12. *Report of the Long Range Planning Committee, transcribed from the minutes of the Board of Directors meeting of the Foundation for American Agriculture, June 23, 1970.* (Archives of Farm Foundation, 1301 West 22nd Street, Suite 615, Oak Brook, IL).
13. *Report of the Long Range Planning Committee, transcribed from the minutes of the Board of Directors meeting of the Foundation for American Agriculture, June 23, 1970.* (Archives of Farm Foundation, 1301 West 22nd Street, Suite 615, Oak Brook, IL).
14. *Report of Joint Committee on the Foundation for American Agriculture and The Farm Foundation, December 1, 1970.* (Archives of Farm Foundation, 1301 West 22nd Street, Suite 615, Oak Brook, IL), p. 2.
15. *Letter from R.J. Hildreth, Farm Foundation, to James W. Cook, Cook, Nelson and Tuthill, Inc., January 22, 1973.* (Archives of Farm Foundation, 1301 West 22nd Street, Suite 615, Oak Brook, IL).
16. *Letter from R.J. Hildreth.*
17. *Letter from R.J. Hildreth.*
18. *Letter from R.J. Hildreth.*
19. *Letter from Carry Ann Bechly, Kirkland & Ellis, to R.J. Hildreth, Farm Foundation, May 29, 1973.* (Archives of Farm Foundation, 1301 West 22nd Street, Suite 615, Oak Brook, IL).
20. Farm Foundation. *Minutes of the Annual Meeting of the Board of Trustees of the Farm Foundation, May 31, 1973, Washington, D.C.* (Archives of Farm Foundation, 1301 West 22nd Street, Suite 615, Oak Brook, IL), p. 9.
21. Bennett received a $25,000/year salary.
22. *Typewritten response by Clayton Yeutter.* Other Round Table members who served the George W. Bush Administration: Ann Veneman, Secretary of Agriculture; James R. Moseley, deputy secretary of agriculture; J.B. Penn, under secretary for farm and agricultural services; and Thomas C. Dorr, under secretary for rural development.
23. Jim Roe. *Charles Dana Bennett Tribute.* Prepared and presented at the June 11, 1987, dinner meeting of Farm Foundation's Bennett Agricultural Round Table, Rosemont, Illinois. (Archives of Farm Foundation, 1301 West 22nd Street, Suite 615, Oak Brook, IL).
24. *Typewritten response by Clayton Yeutter.*
25. *Typewritten response by William Erwin to Farm Foundation survey, January 21, 2003.* (Archives of Farm Foundation, 1301 West 22nd Street, Suite 615, Oak Brook, IL).

26. *Typewritten response by Clayton Yeutter.*
27. *Handwritten response by Gary H. Baise to Farm Foundation survey, January 7, 2003.* (Archives of Farm Foundation, 1301 West 22nd Street, Suite 615, Oak Brook, IL).

Chapter 10

1. Jim Hildreth was insistent that this chapter not reflect his personality or leadership at Farm Foundation. As I researched this chapter, I quickly discovered that you could not recount the Farm Foundation story of the 1970s and 1980s without focusing on Jim Hildreth. Jim was always hesitant to discuss his accomplishments with me, but I found that his many friends were always eager to relate the difference Jim made in their lives and careers.—David P. Ernstes
2. *E-mail response by Robert G.F. Spitze to Farm Foundation survey, December 17, 2002.* (Archives of Farm Foundation, 1301 West 22nd Street, Suite 615, Oak Brook, IL).
3. *Handwritten response by Joe Coffey to Farm Foundation survey, December 9, 2002.* (Archives of Farm Foundation, 1301 West 22nd Street, Suite 615, Oak Brook, IL).
4. *E-mail response by Bernard F. Stanton to Farm Foundation survey, December 12, 2002.* (Archives of Farm Foundation, 1301 West 22nd Street, Suite 615, Oak Brook, IL).
5. *Handwritten response by Larry Libby to Farm Foundation survey, December 16, 2002.* (Archives of Farm Foundation, 1301 West 22nd Street, Suite 615, Oak Brook, IL).
6. *Typewritten response by Howard W. Ottoson to Farm Foundation survey, December 24, 2002.* (Archives of Farm Foundation, 1301 West 22nd Street, Suite 615, Oak Brook, IL).
7. *E-mail response by Bernard F. Stanton.*
8. *Handwritten response by Lowell Hill to Farm Foundation survey, December 11, 2002.* (Archives of Farm Foundation, 1301 West 22nd Street, Suite 615, Oak Brook, IL).
9. *Handwritten response by Larry Libby to Farm Foundation survey, December 16, 2002.* (Archives of Farm Foundation, 1301 West 22nd Street, Suite 615, Oak Brook, IL).
10. *Typewritten response by Warren McCord to Farm Foundation survey, January 7, 2003.* (Archives of Farm Foundation, 1301 West 22nd Street, Suite 615, Oak Brook, IL).
11. *Handwritten response by Larry J. Connor to Farm Foundation survey, December 11, 2002.* (Archives of Farm Foundation, 1301 West 22nd Street, Suite 615, Oak Brook, IL).
12. *Typewritten response by Barry Flinchbaugh to Farm Foundation survey, December 12, 2002.* (Archives of Farm Foundation, 1301 West 22nd Street, Suite 615, Oak Brook, IL).
13. This section benefitted greatly from the work of Barry J. Barnett. "The U.S. Farm Financial Crisis of the 1980s." *Agricultural History*, Vol. No. 74, Issue no. 2, pages 366-380 and David P. Ernstes, Joe L. Outlaw, and Ronald D. Knutson. *Southern Representation in Congress and U.S. Agricultural Legislation.* AFPC Policy Issues Paper 97-3. College Station, TX: Agricultural and Food Policy Center, Department of Agricultural Economics, Texas A&M University, September 1997.
14. Economic Research Service. "Farmers and the Land" in *A History of American Agriculture.* http://www.usda.gov/history2/text3.htm. January 14, 2003.
15. Willard W. Cochrane and C. Ford Runge. *Reforming Farm Policy.* Ames, Iowa: Iowa State University Press, 1992.
16. Farm Foundation. *Farm Foundation Annual Report 1972-73.* Chicago, IL: Farm Foundation, 1973. p. 4.
17. This section benefitted from the comments of David Ruesink, retired faculty member in the Texas A&M University Department of Rural Sociology.
18. Farm Foundation. *Farm Foundation Since 1933.* Oak Brook, IL: Farm Foundation, 1983, p. 18.
19. R.J. "Jim" Hildreth. *Reflections on Farm Foundation Board Member Contributions.* Unpublished document dated May 9, 2001. (Archives of Farm Foundation, 1301 West 22nd Street, Suite 615, Oak Brook, IL).
20. Ibid.
21. Ibid.
22. Ibid.
23. Ibid.
24. Ibid.
25. Ibid.
26. Ibid.
27. Ibid.
28. Ibid.

Endnotes

29. *Typewritten response by W. Neill Schaller to Farm Foundation survey, February 15, 2003.* (Archives of Farm Foundation, 1301 West 22nd Street, Suite 615, Oak Brook, IL).

30. R.J. Hildreth. *Farm Foundation's Past 50 Years.* Address given at the Farm Foundation 50th Year Celebration, Kansas City Club, November 8, 1983. (Archives of Farm Foundation, 1301 West 22nd Street, Suite 615, Oak Brook, IL).

Chapter 11

1. Farm Foundation. *1993 Annual Report,* (Archives of Farm Foundation, 1301 West 22nd Street, Suite 615, Oak Brook, IL), p. 10.
2. Farm Foundation. *Minutes of Farm Foundation Board Meeting, June 26, 1992, Sacramento, California.* (Archives of Farm Foundation, 1301 West 22nd Street, Suite 615, Oak Brook, IL), p. 2.
3. Trustees are elected for five-year terms and may not serve more than two consecutive terms.
4. *"Food Safety News." Food Safety Monitor.* http://foodsafety.docspages.com/meat-recall-companies.html March 6, 2003.
5. Farm Foundation. *Minutes of Farm Foundation Board Meeting, January 3, 1992, Boca Raton, Florida.* (Archives of Farm Foundation, 1301 West 22nd Street, Suite 615, Oak Brook, IL), p. 12.
6. Farm Foundation. 1993 Annual Report, (Archives of Farm Foundation, 1301 West 22nd Street, Suite 615, Oak Brook, IL), pp. 8-10.
7. Farm Foundation. *1994 Annual Report.* (Archives of Farm Foundation, 1301 West 22nd Street, Suite 615, Oak Brook, IL), p. 4.
8. Farm Foundation. *Minutes of Farm Foundation Board Meeting, June 26, 1992, Sacramento, California.* (Archives of Farm Foundation, 1301 West 22nd Street, Suite 615, Oak Brook, IL), p. 7.
9. Farm Foundation. "Farm Foundation Strategic Plan, May 24, 1996 (Draft) Attachment F" in *Farm Foundation Trustees, June 7, 1996, Morrilton, Arkansas.* (Archives of Farm Foundation, 1301 West 22nd Street, Suite 615, Oak Brook, IL), p. 23.
10. Strategic Plan, May 24, 1996 (Draft), p. 22.
11 Strategic Plan, May 24, 1996 (Draft), p. 23.
12 Farm Foundation. *Minutes of Farm Foundation Trustees Meeting, June 20, 1997, Monterey, California.* (Archives of Farm Foundation, 1301 West 22nd Street, Suite 615, Oak Brook, IL), p. 5.
13 Farm Foundation. "Farm Foundation Operating Scenarios Attachment #2" in *Farm Foundation Trustees Minutes, April 29, 2004, Rosemont, Illinois.* (Archives of Farm Foundation, 1301 West 22nd Street, Suite 615, Oak Brook, IL), pp. 13-19.
14 Farm Foundation. "Farm Foundation Strategic Plan, Draft May 2004, Attachment #10" in *Farm Foundation Trustees Minutes, June 12, 2004, Fargo, North Dakota.* (Archives of Farm Foundation, 1301 West 22nd Street, Suite 615, Oak Brook, IL), p. 20.
15. Henry C. Taylor. "The Development of the American Farm Economic Association." *Journal of Farm Economics,* Volume IV, Number 2, April, 1922, p. 92-99.
16. J.R. Raeburn and J.O. Jones. *The History of the International Association of Agricultural Economists: Towards Rural Welfare World Wide.* Worcester, Great Britain: Billing & Sons Ltd., 1990.

Chapter 12

1. *Minutes of the Annual Meeting of the Board of Trustees of the Farm Foundation, May 21, 1953.* p. 4. (Archives of Farm Foundation, 1301 West 22nd Street, Suite 615, Oak Brook, IL).
2.. *Letter from Dan A. Wallace, United States Department of Agriculture/Food Distribution Administration to Frank E. Mullen, National Broadcasting Company, April 27, 1943.* (Archives of Farm Foundation, 1301 West 22nd Street, Suite 615, Oak Brook, IL).
3. These individuals were all executives at International Harvester.
4. *The People of the State of Illinois vs. The First National Bank of Chicago et al.* 364 Ill. (1936), p. 264.
5. *The People of the State of Illinois vs. The First National Bank of Chicago et al.* 364 Ill. (1936), p. 262.
6. *The People of the State of Illinois vs. The First National Bank of Chicago et al.* 364 Ill. (1936), p. 266.
7. *The People of the State of Illinois vs. The First National Bank of Chicago et al.* 364 Ill. (1936), p. 272.
8. "Articles of Incorporation of the Fairway Farms Company filed with the Secretary of State together with application for charter, March 21, 1924." *Minutes of the Fairway Farms Company, p. 2.* (Archives of Farm Foundation, 1301 West 22nd Street, Suite 615, Oak Brook, IL).

9. "Request for a Research Grant to The Research Foundation at Montana State College." enclosure in *Letter from Roy E. Huffman to Joseph Ackerman, February 2, 1955.* In the late-1950s, Farm Foundation provided a grant of $7,500 to Montana State University to study the Fairway Farms experiment. Apparently the study was never completed. (Archives of Farm Foundation, 1301 West 22nd Street, Suite 615, Oak Brook, IL).

10. Ronald Lee Kenney. *The Fairway Farms: An Experiment in a New Agricultural Age.* Master's Thesis, Montana State University, June 1969, p. 39.

11. "Minutes of the Eighth Annual Meeting of the Fairway Farms Corporation Held in the commercial National Bank Building, Bozeman, Montana, February 25, 1933." *Minutes of the Fairway Farms Company, p. 152.* (Archives of Farm Foundation, 1301 West 22nd Street, Suite 615, Oak Brook, IL).

12. *Last Will and Testament of Frank Orren Lowden, January 14, 1943.* (Archives of Farm Foundation, 1301 West 22nd Street, Suite 615, Oak Brook, IL).

13. *Letter from the Treasury Department to Farm Foundation, c/o First Union Trust and Savings Bank, Chicago, Illinois, June 1, 1933.* (Archives of Farm Foundation, 1301 West 22nd Street, Suite 615, Oak Brook, IL).

14. *Minutes of Annual Meeting of Board of Trustees, June 28, 1937.* p. 2. (Archives of Farm Foundation, 1301 West 22nd Street, Suite 615, Oak Brook, IL).

15. *Minutes of the Annual Meeting of the Board of Trustees of Farm Foundation, May 26, 1949.* p. 3. (Archives of Farm Foundation, 1301 West 22nd Street, Suite 615, Oak Brook, IL).

16. *Minutes of the Annual Meeting of the Board of Trustees of Farm Foundation, May 25, 1950.* p. 5. (Archives of Farm Foundation, 1301 West 22nd Street, Suite 615, Oak Brook, IL).

17. *Minutes of the Annual Meeting of tThe Board of Trustees of the Farm Foundation, June 3, 1957.* p. 7. (Archives of Farm Foundation, 1301 West 22nd Street, Suite 615, Oak Brook, IL).

18. Background information was derived from, Simon N. Whitney. *Inflation Since 1945: Facts and Theories.* New York: NY: Praeger Publishers, 1982; and "Inflation and Interest Rates (United States, 1961-2000)" *Bill Craighead's Web Page.* http://www.people.virginia.edu/~wdc4e/Real%20Interest%20Rates.pdf.

19. "Historical Data (updated weekly)." *Board of Governors of the Federal Reserve System Website.* http://www.federalreserve.gov/releases/h15/data/ww/fedfund.txt.

20. *Minutes of the Annual Meeting of the Board of Trustees of Farm Foundation, June 10, 1982.* p. 8. (Archives of Farm Foundation, 1301 West 22nd Street, Suite 615, Oak Brook, IL).

21. *Minutes of the Annual Meeting of the Board of Trustees of Farm Foundation, June 10, 1982.* p. 6. (Archives of Farm Foundation, 1301 West 22nd Street, Suite 615, Oak Brook, IL).

22. *Farm Foundation Board of Directors Meeting, January 26, 1984.* p. 7. (Archives of Farm Foundation, 1301 West 22nd Street, Suite 615, Oak Brook, IL).

23. *Minutes of the Annual Meeting of the Board of Trustees of Farm Foundation, January. 3, 1992.* p. 3. (Archives of Farm Foundation, 1301 West 22nd Street, Suite 615, Oak Brook, IL).

24 *Statement of R.G. Collins of the First National Bank of Chicago made at the Annual Meeting of the Board of Trustees of the Farm Foundation on June 10, 1942.* (Archives of Farm Foundation, 1301 West 22nd Street, Suite 615, Oak Brook, IL).

25. *What You Need to Know About Mutual Funds.* "Worst Stock Market Crashes: The 10 worst stock market crashes in U.S. History." http://mutualfunds.about.com/library/weekly/aa102802a.htm

26. Haskins & Sells. *Report on Examination for the Period from Inception of the Trust, February 10, 1933, to April 30, 1938.* Chicago, IL: Haskins & Sells, August 23, 1938, p. 3. (Archives of Farm Foundation, 1301 West 22nd Street, Suite 615, Oak Brook, IL).

27. *Minutes of the Annual Meeting of the Board of Trustees of Farm Foundation, June 6, 1946, p. 4.* (Archives of Farm Foundation, 1301 West 22nd Street, Suite 615, Oak Brook, IL) and subsequent board minutes.

Chapter 13

1. E-mail from Dan Smalley to Mary Thompson, October 2007. (Archives of Farm Foundation, 1301 West 22nd Street, Suite 615, Oak Brook, IL).

2. *Constitution of the Agricultural Service Foundation.* Printed 12-page 8" x 5" document developed by Alexander Legge. (Frank O. Lowden Papers, Department of Special Collections, Joseph Regenstein Library, 1100 East 57th Street, The University of Chicago, Chicago, IL).

3. *Minutes of the Annual Meeting of the Board of Trustees of the Farm Foundation, May 27, 1954.* p. 14. (Archives of Farm Foundation, 1301 W. 22nd Street, Suite 615, Oak Brook, IL).

4. *Letter from W.W. Waymack to Joseph Ackerman, February 9, 1957.* (Archives of Farm Foundation, 1301 W. 22nd Street, Suite 615, Oak Brook, IL).

5. *Minutes of the Annual Meeting of the Board of Trustees of the Farm Foundation, May 21, 1953.* p. 10. (Archives of Farm Foundation, 1301 W. 22nd Street, Suite 615, Oak Brook, IL).

6. *Minutes of the Annual Meeting of the Board of Trustees of the Farm Foundation, May 27, 1954.* p. 13. (Archives of Farm Foundation, 1301 W. 22nd Street, Suite 615, Oak Brook, IL).

7. *Letter from Owen D. Young to Henry C. Taylor, October 5, 1943.* (Archives of Farm Foundation, 1301 W. 22nd Street, Suite 615, Oak Brook, IL).

8. *Letter from Dan A. Wallace, United States Department of Agriculture/Food Distribution Administration to Frank E. Mullen, National Broadcasting Company, April 27, 1943.* (Archives of Farm Foundation, 1301 W. 22nd Street, Suite 615, Oak Brook, IL).

9. R.J. Hildreth. *Farm Foundation's Past 50 Years.* Address given at the Farm Foundation 50th Year Celebration, Kansas City Club, November 8, 1983. (Archives of Farm Foundation, 1301 W. 22nd Street, Suite 615, Oak Brook, IL).

10. Typewritten response to survey by Barry Flinchbaugh, December 12, 2002. (Archives of Farm Foundation, 1301 W. 22nd Street, Suite 615, Oak Brook, IL).

11. *Typewritten Response to Farm Foundation Survey by Howard W. Ottoson, December 24, 2002.* (Archives of Farm Foundation, 1301 W. 22nd Street, Suite 615, Oak Brook, IL).

12. *Typewritten Response to Farm Foundation Survey by Neil Harl, December 23, 2002.* (Archives of Farm Foundation, 1301 W. 22nd Street, Suite 615, Oak Brook, IL).

13. E-mail from Ann Veneman to Mary Thompson, October 2007. (Archives of Farm Foundation, 1301 West 22nd Street, Suite 615, Oak Brook, IL).

14. E-mail from Dan Smalley to Mary Thompson, October 2007. (Archives of Farm Foundation, 1301 West 22nd Street, Suite 615, Oak Brook, IL).

15. *Typewritten Response to Farm Foundation Survey by Lee R. Kolmer, January 15, 2003.* (Archives of Farm Foundation, 1301 West 22nd Street, Suite 615, Oak Brook, IL)

16. E-mail from Charles Stenholm to Mary Thompson, October 2007. (Archives of Farm Foundation, 1301 West 22nd Street, Suite 615, Oak Brook, IL).

17. E-mail from William Boehm to Mary Thompson, October 2007. (Archives of Farm Foundation, 1301 West 22nd Street, Suite 615, Oak Brook, IL).

18. Letter from Alex Legge to Frank O. Lowden, July 11, 1929. (Frank O. Lowden Papers, Department of Special Collections, Joseph Regenstein Library, 1100 East 57th Street, The University of Chicago, Chicago, IL).

19. Farm Foundation. *Farm Foundation Since 1933.* Oak Brook, IL: Farm Foundation, 1983, p. 20.

Appendix

Secretaries of Agriculture as Farm Foundation Trustees, 1953-2007

Besides **Ezra Taft Benson** (see Chapter 6, page 105) and **Earl Butz** (see Chapter 8, page 139), the following agriculture secretaries served on Farm Foundation's Board of Trustees prior to or after their government service:

- **Clifford M. Hardin** was Chancellor of the University of Nebraska from 1954 to 1969, when he was named Secretary of Agriculture in the Nixon administration. He left his post in 1971 for a position with the Ralston Purina Company. Hardin was a Farm Foundation Trustee from 1973 to 1983.
- **Bob Bergland** was a congressman from Minnesota before serving as Secretary of Agriculture in the Carter administration from 1977 to 1981. Bergland served on Farm Foundation's Board from 1983 to 1993.
- **John R. Block** served as Secretary of Agriculture in the Reagan administration from 1981 to 1986. Prior to that, he was Secretary of Agriculture of the State of Illinois. Block left his federal post to become president of the National-American Wholesale Grocers' Association. Block was a Farm Foundation Trustee from 1971 to 1981.
- **Richard E. Lyng's** career started in the family seed and bean business. After posts in California state government, service as president of the American Meat Institute, and executive service at USDA, Lyng served as Secretary of Agriculture from 1986 to 1989. Lyng was a Farm Foundation Trustee from 1985 to 1986.
- **Clayton Yeutter** was U.S. Secretary of Agriculture from 1989 to 1991. Yeutter was president of the Chicago Mercantile Exchange and later was named U.S. Trade Representative, and chairman of the Republican National Committee. Yeutter was a member of Farm Foundation's Board from 1980 to 1985.
- **Mike Espy** was elected to three terms in the U.S. House of Representatives from Mississippi. He was appointed Secretary of Agriculture in the Clinton Cabinet in 1993. Since leaving office, Espy has focused on agriculture and

agribusiness partnerships between entities in the United States and Africa. Espy was elected to Farm Foundation's Board of Trustees in 2002.

- **Daniel R. Glickman** served as Secretary of Agriculture from 1995 to 2001. Prior to that, he represented Kansas in the U.S. House of Representatives for 18 years. He currently heads the Motion Picture Association of America. Glickman served on Farm Foundation's Board of Trustees from 2001 to 2006.

- **Ann M. Veneman's** career included executive positions in USDA and service as California's agriculture secretary. Veneman served as Secretary of Agriculture in the George H.W. Bush administration from 2001 to 2005. She currently heads the United Nations UNICEF Program. She was a Farm Foundation Trustee from 1996 to 2001.

Farm Foundation Trustees, 1933 to 2007

Appendix

Meetings of Farm Foundation's Board of Trustees

Chairman	Date	Location
Frank O. Lowden	July 21, 1933	Palmer House, Chicago, Illinois
Frank O. Lowden	June 22, 1934	Chicago Club, Chicago, Illinois
Frank O. Lowden	June 28, 1935	Chicago Club
Frank O. Lowden	June 24, 1936	Chicago Club
Frank O. Lowden	June 28, 1937	Chicago Club
Chris L. Christensen[1]	June 13, 1938	Union League Club, Chicago, Illinois
Frank O. Lowden	June 12, 1939	Union League Club
Frank O. Lowden	June 10, 1940	Union League Club
Frank O. Lowden	June 9, 1941	Union League Club
William S. Elliott[2]	June 10, 1942	Union League Club
William S. Elliott[3]	June 9, 1943	Union League Club
Chris L. Christensen	June, 8, 1944	Union League Club
Thomas E. Wilson	June 7, 1945	Union League Club
Thomas E. Wilson	June 6, 1946	Union League Club
Thomas E. Wilson	February 20, 1947[4]	Union League Club
Thomas E. Wilson	June 5, 1947	Union League Club
Ralph Budd	May 2 1948	Union League Club
John Stuart[5]	May 26, 1949	Union League Club
John Stuart	May 25, 1950	Union League Club
John Stuart	May 24, 1951	Union League Club
John Stuart	May 22, 1952	Union League Club
John Stuart	May 21, 1953	Union League Club
Allan B. Kline	May 27, 1954	Union League Club
Allan B. Kline	May 26, 1955	Union League Club
Allan B. Kline	June 4, 1956	Union League Club
Allan B. Kline	June 3, 1957	Union League Club
Allan B. Kline	June 2, 1958	Union League Club
Allan B. Kline	June 1, 1959	Union League Club
Allan B. Kline	June 6, 1960	Union League Club
Allan B. Kline	June 5, 1961	Union League Club
Paul C. Johnson	June 11, 1962	Union League Club
Paul C. Johnson	May 28, 1963	Union League Club
Allan B. Kline	May 27, 1964	Union League Club
Allan B. Kline	June 2, 1965	Union League Club
Allan B. Kline	June 1, 1966	Union League Club
Allan B. Kline	June 1, 1967	Union League Club
Allan B. Kline	June 6, 1968	Mid-America Club, Chicago, Illinois
William F. McCurdy	June 5, 1969	Mid-America Club
William F. McCurdy	June 4, 1970	Mid-America Club
William F. McCurdy	June 3, 1971	Mid-America Club
Orville G. Bentley	June 1, 1972	Mid-America Club
Orville G. Bentley	May 31, 1973	Mid-America Club
Orville G. Bentley	May 29, 1974	First National Bank of Chicago, Chicago, Illinois

Chairman	Date	Location
Orville G. Bentley	May 28, 1975	Union League Club
Orville G. Bentley	May 19, 1976	Plaza Inn, Kansas City, Missouri
Orville G. Bentley	June 2, 1977	Oak Brook Hyatt House, Oak Brook, Illinois
Orville G. Bentley	June 1, 1978	Union League Club
W.R. Peirson	May 31, 1979	Oak Brook Hyatt House
W.R. Peirson	May 29, 1980	Oak Brook Hyatt House
W.R. Peirson	May 28, 1981	Hyatt Regency O'Hare, Rosemont, Illinois
Joseph P. Sullivan	June 10, 1982	Hyatt Oak Brook, Oak Brook, Illinois
Clayton Yeutter[6]	January, 26, 1984	Washington, D.C.
Joseph P. Sullivan	June 14, 1984	Fargo, North Dakota
Joseph P. Sullivan	January 10, 1985	Tucson, Arizona
Joseph P. Sullivan	June 13, 1985	Oak Brook, Illinois
Royce Ramsland	January 7, 1986	Phoenix, Arizona
Royce Ramsland	June 13, 1986	Rosemont, Illinois
Joseph P. Sullivan	January 5, 1987	Phoenix, Arizona
Joseph P. Sullivan	June 11, 1987	Rosemont, Illinois
Donald V. Fites[7]	January 7, 1988	Phoenix, Arizona
Joseph P. Sullivan	June 16, 1988	Rosemont, Illinois
Rollie M. Hendrickson[8]	January 7, 1989	Phoenix, Arizona
Joseph P. Sullivan	June 8, 1989	Rosemont, Illinois
Rollie M. Hendrickson	January 4, 1990	Phoenix, Arizona
Rollie M. Hendrickson	June 7, 1990	Rosemont, Illinois
John R. Block	January 4, 1991	Phoenix, Arizona
John R. Block	June 6, 1991	Washington, D.C.
Robert L. Thompson	January 3, 1992	Boca Raton, Florida
Robert L. Thompson	June 26, 1992	Sacramento, California
William R. Gordon	January 8, 1993	Phoenix, Arizona
William R. Gordon	June 11, 1993	Atlanta, Georgia
Art Fogerty	January 7, 1994	Phoenix, Arizona
Art Fogerty	June 10, 1994	Bettendorf, Iowa
Bud Porter	January 6, 1995	Palm Desert, California
Bud Porter	June 9, 1995	Burlington, Vermont
Paul Brower	January 5, 1996	Orlando, Florida
Paul Brower	June 7, 1996	Morrilton, Arkansas
Emmett Barker	January 10, 1997	Mexico City, Mexico
Emmett Barker	June 20, 1997	Monterey, California
Dan Smalley	January 9, 1998	Tucson, Arizonia
Dan Smalley	June 5, 1998	Omaha, Nebraska
Bill Kirk	January 7, 1999	Kona, Hawaii
Bill Kirk	June 11, 1999	Banff, Alberta, Canada
Gary Baise	January 7, 2000	Corpus Christi, Texas
Gary Baise	June 9, 2000	Kohler, Wisconsin
Alan Johnson	January 5, 2001	Jupiter, Florida
Alan Johnson	June 8, 2001	Sun Valley, Idaho

Appendix

Chairman	Date	Location
Ronald D. Knutson	January 9, 2002	Coral Gables, Florida
Ronald D. Knutson	June 14, 2002	Wilmington, Delaware
Roderick Stacey	January 10, 2003	Coronado, California
Roderick Stacey	June 6, 2003	Birmingham, Alabama
Donald Villwock	January 10, 2004	Tucson, Arizona
Donald Villwock	April 29, 2005	Rosemont, Illinois
Donald Villwock	June 12, 2005	Fargo, North Dakota
Nicholas Babson	January 8, 2005	Coral Gables, Florida
Nicholas Babson	June 18, 2005	Portland, Oregon
Daniel Dooley	January 7, 2006	Phoenix, Arizona
Daniel Dooley	June 17, 2006	Wichita, Kansas
Victor Lechtenberg	January 7, 2007	Ponce, Puerto Rico
Victor Lechtenberg	June 9, 2007	Chapel Hill, North Carolina

---

1. In the absence of Chairman Frank O. Lowden, Vice Chairman Christensen presided.
2. In the absence of Chairman Frank O. Lowden and Vice Chairman Ralph Budd, Elliott presided.
3. With the death of Chairman Frank O. Lowden and the absence of the Vice Chairman Ralph Budd, Elliott was elected chairman of the meeting by the board.
4. Special meeting to consider selling the Lowden Plantation.
5. In the absence of Chairman Ralph Budd, Vice Chairman John Stuart presided.
6. In the absence of Chairman Joseph P. Sullivan, Yeutter served as acting chair.
7. In the absence of Chairman Joseph P. Sullivan, Fites served as acting chair.
8. In the absence of Chairman Joseph P. Sullivan, Hendrickson served as acting chair.

Farm Foundation Staff

Employee	Position[1]	Began/End Service
Charles L. Burlingham	Assistant Secretary[2]	May 1, 1934 – June 30, 1934
Dr. Henry C. Taylor[3]	Managing Director	November 1, 1935 – 1949
Dr. Howard J. Stover	Assistant to the Director	November 1, 1936 – 1942
Robert V. Wilson	Secretary	November 1936 – August 1938[4]
Iman E. Schatzmann	Executive Secretary	September 1, 1938 – unknown
Mary K. Wheatley Armstrong[5]	Secretary to Director	October 1938 – unknown
Dr. Joseph Ackerman[6]	Managing Director	February 11, 1939 – December 31, 1969
Theordora Reimers	Secretary	October 1939 – February 1940
Elise Darling	Secretary	October 1939 – December 1939
Harriet R. Jeffries	Secretary for Rural Education	March 1940 – July 1940
Mary Evans Spencer[7]	Secretary to Director	March 1940 – October 1942
Elin L. Anderson	Project Director	April 26, 1940 – June 30, 1947
Constance Cavender	Secretary	June 1940 – unknown
Olive M. Biddison	Secretary	October 1940 – July 21, 1941
Mary Shaw	Secretary	February 1941 – July 22, 1941
Harriet Houwers	Secretary	June 26, 1941 – unknown
Effie Bathurst	Secretary	November 1941 – April 30, 1942
Sarah Jane Statham	Secretary	May 1942 – unknown
Elizabeth Ackerman	Secretary	May 1942 – unknown
Mary M. Stover	Secretary	July 1942 – unknown
Gladys Rogne	Secretary	November 1942 – unknown
Anne Dewees Taylor[8]	Research Assistant	unknown – unknown
Detta Schmidt	Secretary to Director	1941 – 1943
Rita Dohrmann MacMeekin	Secretary to Associate Director	August 1943 – 1944
Mae Ramclow Tappendorf	Secretary to Director	November 1943 – April 1949
Agnes Boyton Lorentzen	Research Assistant	February 1, 1944 – October 1949
Marguerite L. Ingram	Research Assistant	July 1, 1944 – unknown
Maudie Nakada Noma[9]	Research Assistant	August 1945 – April 30, 1976[10]
Dr. Leland B. Tate	Rural Sociologist	September 1, 1945 – August 31, 1946
Frank W. Peck[11]	Managing Director	October 1, 1945 – January 1, 1955
Madeline Simi	Typist	May 1946 – September 1948
Mildred Hoyt	Typist	September 20, 1948 – April 27, 1950
Alice Russell[12]	Research Assistant	October 1, 1949 – October 2, 1950
Lois Bell	Secretary to Director	October 10, 1949 – September 20, 1950
Lore Gerden	Typist	May 1, 1950 – June 30, 1955
Grace Bacon	Secretary to Associate Director	October 2, 1950 – October 22, 1953
Mary Lally	Secretary to Director	October 9, 1950 – September 18, 1952
Margaret J. Kuechler	Secretary to Director	September 17, 1952 – January 18, 1954
Geraldine Berg Locklin	Secretary to Associate Director	November 2, 1953 – October 14, 1955
Jeanne Grout	Secretary to Director	January 28, 1954 – August 27, 1954
Roberta Mott	Secretary to Director	September 7, 1954 – September 30, 1957
Dr. Howard G. Diesslin	Associate Managing Director	February 1, 1955 – July 1962
Marilyn Tobin	Typist	June 27, 1955 – September 30, 1955
Marlene Bress Kraemer	Typist	October 5, 1955 – April 30, 1976[13]
Irene M. Gardner Black	Secretary to Associate Director	October 17, 1955 – August 10, 1956

Appendix

Employee	Position[1]	Began/End Service
Elaine Martenson[14]	Secretary to Director	October 8, 1956 – April 4, 1958
Alice Matson	Secretary to Director	October 1, 1957 – November 29, 1957
Kay Kamfner	Secretary to Director	December 2, 1957 – February 28, 1958
Madelyn Naumes	Secretary to Director	April 11, 1958 – January 31, 1980
Esther Olson	Secretary to Associate Director	April 1, 1958 – January 31, 1970
Dr. R.J. "Jim" Hildreth[15]	Managing Director	July 1, 1962 – December 1, 1991
Dr. W. Neill Schaller	Associate Managing Director	October 1969 – July 1977
Carol Mandra	Secretary to Associate Director	February 22, 1970 – October 9, 1970
Mae Mattson	Secretary to Associate Director	October 12, 1970 – April 30, 1976[16]
C. Dana Bennett	Special Consultant	July 1, 1975 – 1984
Michelle Skivington	Secretary to Associate Director	April 1976 – May 1977
Janell Hull	Secretary to Associate Director	May 1976 – January 1978
Sandra Young	Administrative Assistant	September 12, 1977 – Present
Janice Alison	Secretary to Associate Director	January 1978 – September 1978
Dr. Walter J. Armbruster[17]	President	March 20, 1978 – Present
Lillian Lang	Secretary to Director	November 13, 1978 – September 14, 1979
Antoinette Purves Russin	Administrative Assistant	February 15, 1980 – February 2005
Teddee Grace	Editor	1984 – 1993
Dr. Steve A. Halbrook	Vice President	July 1, 1992 – Present
David P. Ernstes	Texas A&M Contract	October 27, 1997 – April 30, 2003
Mary M. Thompson	Communications Director	July 22, 2002 – Present
Laurie Marsh	Administrative Assistant	March 2005 – Present
Colleen Joy	Administrative Assistant	April 1, 2005 – October 2005
Vicki Liszewski	Administrative Assistant	November 2005 – Present
Julia Walski	Administrative Assistant	August 2006 – Present

1. Indicates last position held
2. Temporary position created by executive committee action.
3. After serving as managing director (November 1, 1935 - September 30, 1945), Taylor served as a consultant to Farm Foundation from 1945 to 1949 while working on *The Story of Agricultural Economics*.
4. Wilson died in an automobile accident.
5. Armstrong served as secretary to director from October 1938 to March 12, 1940, as secretary in 1941, and as secretary and research assistant on the medical care and health services project beginning in 1945.
6. Land tenure specialist, 1939-1942, associate managing director, 1942-1954, managing director, 1955-1969
7. Employed elsewhere January -May 1942
8. Anne Dewees Taylor, wife of Henry C. Taylor, served as both a unpaid and paid employee.
9. Was secretary to associate director until October 2, 1950.
10. Associated with the relocation of the office from downtown Chicago to suburban Oak Brook, Illinois.
11. Peck continued to serve as a consultant after his term as managing director.
12. Began in Chicago office September 5, 1949 as secretary to director (Peck). Formerly secretary to Henry C. Taylor in Washington, D.C.
13. Associated with the relocation of the office from downtown Chicago to suburban Oak Brook, Illinois.
14. Was secretary to associate director until March 3, 1958.
15. Associate managing director, 1962-1970, managing director, 1970-1991
16. Associated with the relocation of the office from downtown Chicago to suburban Oak Brook, Illinois.
17. Associate managing director, 1978-1991, managing director/president, 1991-present

About the Authors

The authors represent three different eras and perspectives at Farm Foundation. Combined, their experiences and expertise offer a rich assessment of Farm Foundation's history, programs and legacy.

David P. Ernstes is a research associate at the Agricultural and Food Policy Center at Texas A&M University. He worked on a contract basis for Farm Foundation from 1997 to 2003 and was involved with the implementation and outreach of many projects.

The late R.J. "Jim" Hildreth joined the staff of Farm Foundation as associate managing director in 1962. As managing director, he oversaw day-to-day operations of the Foundation from 1970 to 1991.

Ronald D. Knutson, professor emeritus at Texas A&M University, attended his first Farm Foundation program in 1966. As a Land Grant university professor, he was involved in numerous foundation projects and programs. He was a member of the Board of Trustees from 1995 to 2004 and served as chairman of the Board of Trustees in 2002-2003.